A Structuralist Theory of Economics

Economists have long grappled with the problem of how economic theories relate to empirical evidence: how can abstract mathematized theories be used to produce empirical claims? How are such theories applied to economic phenomena? What does it mean to "test" economic theories? This book introduces, explains, and develops a structural philosophy of economics which addresses these questions and provides a unifying philosophical/logical basis for a general methodology of economics.

The book begins by introducing a rigorous view of the logical foundations and structure of scientific theories based upon the work of Alfred Tarski, Patrick Suppes, Karl Marx, and others. Using and combining their methods, the book then goes on to reconstruct important economic theories – including utility theory, game theory, Marxian economics, Sraffian economic theory, and econometrics – proving all the main theorems and discussing the key claims and the empirical applicability of each theory. Through these discussions, this book presents, in a systematic fashion, a general philosophy of economics grounded in the structural view.

Offering rigorous formulations of important economic theories, *A Structuralist Theory of Economics* will be invaluable to all readers interested in the logic, philosophy, and methodology of economics. It will also appeal particularly to those interested in economic theory.

Adolfo García de la Sienra is research fellow at the Instituto de Filosofía, and professor of logic, philosophy, mathematics, and economic theory at the Universidad Veracruzana, Mexico.

Routledge INEM Advances in Economic Methodology

Series Editor: Esther-Mirjam Sent
University of Nijmegen, the Netherlands

The field of economic methodology has expanded rapidly during the last few decades. This expansion has occurred in part because of changes within the discipline of economics, in part because of changes in the prevailing philosophical conception of scientific knowledge, and also because of various transformations within the wider society. Research in economic methodology now reflects not only developments in contemporary economic theory, the history of economic thought, and the philosophy of science; but it also reflects developments in science studies, historical epistemology, and social theorizing more generally. The field of economic methodology still includes the search for rules for the proper conduct of economic science, but it also covers a vast array of other subjects and accommodates a variety of different approaches to those subjects.

The objective of this series is to provide a forum for the publication of significant works in the growing field of economic methodology. Since the series defines methodology quite broadly, it will publish books on a wide range of different methodological subjects. The series is also open to a variety of different types of works: original research monographs, edited collections, as well as republication of significant earlier contributions to the methodological literature. The International Network for Economic Methodology (INEM) is proud to sponsor this important series of contributions to the methodological literature.

The Individual and the Other in Economic Thought
An Introduction
Edited by Ragip Ege and Herrade Igersheim

Economics and Performativity
Exploring Limits, Theories and Cases
Nicolas Brisset

A Structuralist Theory of Economics
Adolfo García de la Sienra

For more information about this series, please visit: www.routledge.com/Routledge-INEM-Advances-in-Economic-Methodology/book-series/SE0630

A Structuralist Theory of Economics

Adolfo García de la Sienra

Routledge
Taylor & Francis Group
LONDON AND NEW YORK

First published 2019
by Routledge
2 Park Square, Milton Park, Abingdon, Oxon OX14 4RN

and by Routledge
52 Vanderbilt Avenue, New York, NY 10017

First issued in paperback 2020

Routledge is an imprint of the Taylor & Francis Group, an informa business

British Library Cataloguing-in-Publication Data
A catalogue record for this book is available from the British Library

Library of Congress Cataloging-in-Publication Data
Names: García de la Sienra, Adolfo, author.
Title: A structuralist theory of economics / Adolfo García de la Sienra.
Description: 1 Edition. | New York : Routledge, 2019. | Series: Routledge INEM advances in economic methodology | Includes bibliographical references and index.
Identifiers: LCCN 2018039630 (print) | LCCN 2018041087 (ebook) | ISBN 9781315100609 (Ebook) | ISBN 9781138295643 (hardback : alk. paper) | ISBN 9781315100609 (ebk)
Subjects: LCSH: Economics. | Econometric models. | Game theory.
Classification: LCC HB141 (ebook) | LCC HB141 .G367 2018 (print) | DDC 330.1–dc23
LC record available at https://lccn.loc.gov/2018039630

ISBN 13: 978-0-367-66318-6 (pbk)
ISBN 13: 978-1-138-29564-3 (hbk)

Typeset in Times New Roman
by Apex CoVantage, LLC

This book is dedicated to Luz María and to the memory of Elena Minerva and Adolfo

Contents

Preface

Before anything else, it must be kept in mind that this is not a book of economics but one of *philosophy*. It is true that it deals with economic theories and presents them in a rigorous form, but for the same reason it is a book on *metatheory*. It intends to present each economic theory as an intellectual realm, a systematic and integral unit, including a general explication of its application to empirical phenomena. We must recall, as Hegel used to say, that philosophy returns over the real (albeit in this case the 'real' are only economic theories) in order to reconstruct it as a an intellectual kingdom. It appears in the twilight painting its object in gray:

> Wenn die Philosophie ihr Grau in Grau malt, dann ist eine Gestalt des Lebens alt geworden, und mit Grau in läßt sie sich nicht verjüngen, sonder nur erkennen: die Eule der Minerva beginnt erst mit der einbrechenden Dämmerung ihren Flug (*Grundlinien der Philosophie des Rechts*: 28).

Coatepec, Veracruz, Mexico, July 2018

Acknowledgments

Research leading to this book was made possible by the Consejo Nacional de Ciencia y Tecnología (CONACYT) of Mexico, through the project *Filosofía de la Economía* 127380.

Section 5 of Chapter 2 is a modified translation of A. García de la Sienra "Teoría general de las clases", originally published in A. García de la Sienra (ed.) *Reflexiones sobre la paradoja de Orayen*. Mexico: Universidad Nacional Autónoma de México/Instituto de Investigaciones Filosóficas, 2010, pp. 119–36.

Chapter 4 is a modified version of A. García de la Sienra, "Idealization in Economics: A Structuralist View", originally published in G. Borbone and K. Brzechczyn (eds.) *Idealization XIV: Models in Science*. Leiden and Boston: Brill/Rodopi, 2016, pp. 113–29.

Chapter 7 is a modified version of A. García de la Sienra, "Continuously Differentiable Preferences". *Contaduría y Administración* 61(2) (2016), pp. 334–52.

Chapter 8 is a modified translation of A. García de la Sienra, "La estructura lógica de la teoría de los juegos". *Crítica* 41(122) (2009), pp. 3–27.

Figure 1.1 was taken from F. A. Muller, "Reflections on the Revolution at Stanford". *Synthese* 183 (2011), pp. 87–114. It is reproduced here with permission of Springer.

Figure 2.1 was taken from P. Suppes, *Introduction to Logic*. New York: Dover, 1999, p. 223. It is reproduced here with permission of Dover Publications.

1 Introduction

The project of this book is to provide structuralist rational reconstructions of some economic theories in order to show their logical structure and address their methodological issues. By 'structuralism' I understand here a family of meta-theories of the sciences originated in what Muller (2011) has described as the model revolution at Stanford. Muller attributes the paternity of this revolution to Patrick Suppes, but there were prophets that anticipated it.

Actually, just after World War II, the theoretical activity of several economists and logicians at Stanford departed from the standard positivist conception of theories as sets of sentences (typically conceived as sentences of a formalized theory in first-order logic), a conception that can be conveniently labeled the '$\mathcal{L}$-View'. The motive of the departure was not of an abstract philosophical character, but rather the urgency of formulating with precision mathematized theories relevant to the demands of military intelligence. As Mirowski (2002) reports, Kenneth Joseph Arrow, Samuel Karlin, and Charles Chenoweth ("Chen") McKinsey, just to mention some of the best-known names, were associated with the work of the Rand Corporation in Santa Monica, California. As a matter of fact, Stanford's relationship with Rand was so tight that when the latter tried to part with the Douglas Aircraft Company, in 1948, Stanford's Department of Economics made a bid to absorb Rand (Collins and Kusch 1998: 294 n.; quoted by Mirowski 2002: 299, n. 74). Actually, Mirowski (2002: 299) refers to the Stanford of that epoch as the "major West Coast outpost of military-academic research".[1] What is of utmost importance for this story is that the standard logical methodology of the Stanfordite theoreticians working in military projects was Alfred Tarski's, as almost all of them were his disciples.

To begin with, Arrow took a course on the calculus of relations with Tarski during the year in which the great Polish logician taught at the City College in New York (1940). Olaf Helmer, who came later to be in charge of recruiting formal logicians in order to do operations research at Rand, translated Tarski's textbook, while Arrow was in charge of reading the proofs of the translation. There is no doubt (by his class notes) that his way of approaching the preference relation comes from there (cf. Mirowski 2002: 297).

In the autumn of 1950, the young Patrick ("Pat") Suppes, who had just finished a PhD in philosophy at Columbia University, began to teach at Stanford. Shortly thereafter he met Chen McKinsey, who became his postdoctoral tutor. McKinsey taught Suppes the set-theoretical methods that would eventually make him justly famous but, reports Suppes:

> It was not, however, just set-theoretical methods as such that McKinsey taught me but also a passion for clarity that was unparalleled and had no precedent in my own prior education.
>
> (Suppes 1979: 8)

McKinsey told Suppes (with some exaggeration) that "he had learned everything he knew from Tarski", and encouraged him to attend the seminar that Tarski was giving at Berkeley. Suppes described Tarski as a "ruthless taskmaster" but, above all,

> as one of the great examples of the Polish school of logic, [...] unwilling to go forward on a single point unless everything covered thus far was completely clear – in particular, unless it was apparent to him that the set-theoretical framework within which the discourse was operating could be made totally explicit. It was from McKinsey and Tarski that I learned about the axiomatic method and what it means to give a set-theoretical analysis of a subject.
>
> (Ibid.)

It was with McKinsey and A. C. Sugar that he wrote his classical paper "Axiomatic Foundations of Classical Particle Mechanics", which was presented in a rather patronizing way by Clifford Truesdell – a distinguished physicist, above all by his great modesty – who had no qualms in referring to Newton's crowning achievement as the "degenerate and conceptually insignificant special case of particle mechanics," with the hope that the "publication of this paper may arouse the interest of students of mechanics and logic alike, thus perhaps leading eventually to a proper solution of this outstanding but neglected problem [an axiomatization of general mechanics that clarifies the concept of force]" (McKinsey, Sugar, and Suppes 1953: 253; communicator's note). Indeed, this paper, owing to the beauty and simplicity with which it treats a 'flesh and bone' theory, historically important and sufficient for a host of applications in engineering, is a wonderful introduction to the use of set-theoretical methods in the axiomatization of empirical theories.[2]

The view of the axiomatic method that was emerging out of the work of all these logicians was exposed to the world for the first time in an international symposium that took place in Berkeley between December 26, 1957, and January 4, 1958. The president of the organizing committee was Tarski and the symposium was focused on the foundations of geometry and physics, as well as on general problems of the axiomatic method.[3] In 1960 a great congress on logic, methodology, and philosophy of science was celebrated at Stanford, after overcoming the obstacles accumulated by the National Research Council and the National Science Foundation, who insisted that the organizers (led by Suppes) should join the historians of science in order to organize the congress of *the latter*. But Tarski's opposition was able to overcome the obstacles and the congress finally took place as it had originally been planned.[4]

Other important influences in Suppes' thought were those of David Blackwell and M. A. Girschik, while they were writing their influential book *Theory of Games and Statistical Decisions* (1954), but above all that of R. Duncan Luce, with whom afterwards (together with Amos Tverski and David Krantz) he would publish the famous trilogy on the foundations of measurement (KLST 1971, 1989, 1990). Actually, Suppes produced perhaps more on social sciences than on physics. From 1952 to 1992 he was chairman of the Institute for Mathematical Studies in the Social Sciences at Stanford, and he was Arrow's close friend and partner until his death on November 17, 2014. Another important fellow at Stanford working on the foundations of economics along the lines of the new methodology was Peter J. Hammond, a brilliant mathematical economist who incorporated to Arrow and Suppes' circle in 1979.

1.1 A new view of scientific theories

In the introduction to his *Representation and Invariance of Scientific Structures* (Suppes 2002), Suppes addresses the question about the nature of a scientific theory. Neverthless, in contradistinction to questions for which we can expect a clear and definite answer, like *What is a rational number?* or *What is a nectarine?*, Suppes warns that this question

> fits neither one of these patterns. Scientific theories are not like rational numbers or nectarines. Certainly they are not like nectarines, for they are not physical objects. They are like rational numbers in not being physical objects, but they are totally unlike rational numbers in that scientific theories cannot be defined simply or directly in terms of other nonphysical, abstract objects.
>
> (Suppes 2002: 2)

Since the question we are considering cannot be answered directly in simple terms, philosophers have intended to address it from different angles. One approach has been what Suppes calls the traditional sketch (also known as the 'statement view', 'Carnap's approach', or '$\mathcal{L}$-View'), according to which

> a scientific theory consists of two parts. One part is an abstract logical calculus, which includes the vocabulary of logic and the primitive symbols of the theory. The logical structure of the theory is fixed by stating the axioms or postulates of the theory in terms of its primitive symbols. For many theories the primitive symbols will be thought of as theoretical terms like 'electron' or 'particle', which cannot be related in any simple way to observable phenomena.
>
> The second part of the theory is a set of rules that assign an empirical content to the logical calculus by providing what are usually called 'co-

> ordinating definitions' or 'empirical interpretations' for at least some of the primitive and defined symbols of the calculus. It is always emphasized that the first part alone is not sufficient to define a scientific theory; for without a systematic specification of the intended empirical interpretation of the theory, it is not possible in any sense to evaluate the theory as a part of science, although it can be studied simply as a piece of pure mathematics.
>
> (Ibid.: 2, 3)

Notice here Suppes' use of the term 'science': it is not pure mathematics, "but we mean by *science*, as opposed to *mathematics*, the development of theory and the confronting of theory with quantitative data" (Suppes 1968: 651).

In order to explain in some detail Suppes' view of theories, it will be useful to resort to Muller's precise description of the $\mathcal{L}$-View. Even though the question *What is a scientific theory?* cannot be answered in a straightforward way, a very common practice has been to think that any particular theory can be identified through a set of sentences formulated in a formal language. More precisely, a representation of a scientific theory **T**, according to the $\mathcal{L}$-View, is mounted upon a first-order logical language $\mathcal{L}_{\mathbf{T}}$ and contains the following eight components:

$$\text{LEX}(\mathcal{L}_{\mathbf{T}}), \text{SENT}(\mathcal{L}_{\mathbf{T}}), \text{AX}(\mathcal{L}_{\mathbf{T}}), \text{OBS}(\mathcal{L}_{\mathbf{T}}), \text{TH}(\mathcal{L}_{\mathbf{T}}), \vdash, \mathsf{T}, \mathcal{O}_t(\mathbf{T})$$

where:

(1) $\text{LEX}(\mathcal{L}_{\mathbf{T}})$ is the lexicon of $\mathcal{L}_{\mathbf{T}}$. It contains a finite number of predicates, interpreted to express the fundamental concepts of **T**.

(2) $\text{SENT}(\mathcal{L}_{\mathbf{T}})$ is the set of sentences of the language, defined recursively in the usual way.

(3) $\text{AX}(\mathcal{L}_{\mathbf{T}})$ is a subset of $\text{SENT}(\mathcal{L}_{\mathbf{T}})$, whose members are taken as axioms for **T**. They should be "formalisations of the postulates, principles and laws that characterise **T** and are considered not to be deducible from other postulates, principles and laws in *T*" (Muller 2011: 89).

(4) $\text{OBS}(\mathcal{L}_{\mathbf{T}})$ is the set of 'observational' predicates, which refer to observable objects or events.

(5) $\text{TH}(\mathcal{L}_{\mathbf{T}})$ is the set of theoretical predicates, where 'theoretical' means that it refers to putative entities inaccesible to observation.

(6) $\vdash$ is the derivation relation: if Γ is a set of formulas of $\mathcal{L}_{\mathbf{T}}$, and φ is any formula of this language, $\mathcal{L}_{\mathbf{T}} \vdash \varphi$ means that φ is derivable from formulas in Γ by means of the rules of inference of $\mathcal{L}_{\mathbf{T}}$.

(7) T is the deductive closure of $\text{AX}(\mathcal{L}_{\mathbf{T}})$; i.e.

$$\mathsf{T} = \{\varphi \in \text{SENT}(\mathcal{L}_{\mathbf{T}}) | \text{AX}(\mathcal{L}_{\mathbf{T}}) \vdash \varphi\}.$$

(8) $\mathcal{O}_t(\mathbf{T})$, a subset of $\text{SENT}(\mathcal{L}_{\mathbf{T}})$, is "the set of observation sentences verified by scientists until historical time that are relevant for **T**" (Muller 2011: 90).

The deductive system $\mathbf{F}_{\mathrm{T}}$ built over $\mathcal{L}_{\mathrm{T}}$; i.e.

$$\mathbf{F}_{\mathrm{T}} = \langle \text{LEX}(\mathcal{L}_{\mathrm{T}}), \text{SENT}(\mathcal{L}_{\mathrm{T}}), \text{AX}(\mathcal{L}_{\mathrm{T}}), \vdash, \mathsf{T}, \rangle$$

is *observationally adequate* at *t* iff

> **T** is (consistent and) every established empirical truth relevant for **T** – i.e. every verified observation sentence in $\mathcal{O}_t(\mathbf{T})$ – is a member of T; in other words, iff
>
> $$\mathcal{O}_t(\mathbf{T}) \subset \mathsf{T} \subset \text{SENT}(\mathcal{L}_{\mathrm{T}}). \quad \text{(Ibid.)}$$

It seems that the scientists working at Rand saw that the formulation of real-life scientific theories within the framework of the $\mathcal{L}$-View was utterly impractical, particularly when the theory under analysis presupposed more than first-order logic (for in such a case it becomes necessary, in order to formulate the theory, to include first-order formulations of all those presupposed theories: set theory, real analysis, and so on). Since complex scientific theories are similar to the theories studied in pure mathematics in their degree of complexity,

> in such contexts it is very much simpler to assert things about the models of the theory rather than to talk directly and explicitly about the sentences of the theory, perhaps the main reason for this being that the notion of sentence of the theory is not well defined when the theory is not given in standard formalization.
>
> (Suppes 1967: 58)

Here the relevant notion of model is precisely the one that Bourbaki (1968) defined under the label 'mathematical structure'. These structures are introduced by Suppes through the definition of a set-theoretical predicate, like '$\mathfrak{A}$ *is a topological space*' or '$\mathfrak{A}$ *is a game*'.

Suppes proposed to characterize or identify any scientific theory through a certain class of structures since, even if it appears formulated intrinsically – by means of a certain set of statements (not necessarily capable of being formulated as sentences of first-order logic) – the question of whether such a formulation is adequate, or whether a formulation in first-order logic is feasible, can only be answered after an extrinsic characterization of the same is given. Even though Suppes thought that it is not important to provide precise definitions of the concept of scientific theory in terms of necessary and sufficient conditions, of the form "*X* is a scientific theory if and only if so-and-so", and had a certain tendency to shy away from grand schemes about scientific theories and their relations, he recognized that an essential ingredient of any sophisticated scientific discipline is a hierarchy of theories, starting with models of data and culminating with what he calls a fundamental theory.

Muller formulates Suppes' view of theories – which he calls the *Informal-Structural View* or $\mathfrak{S}$-View – in a way that facilitates comparison with the $\mathcal{L}$-

View. Instead of the eight components of the $\mathcal{L}$-View, the $\mathfrak{S}$-View contains merely two, namely:

$$\mathbf{T}, \mathcal{D}_t(\mathbf{T}),$$

where **T** is the class of all set-theoretical structures that satisfy a specified set-theoretical predicate, and $\mathcal{D}_t(\mathbf{T})$ is the class of all data-structures obtained until historical time t "from the measurement-results of experiments or observations relevant for **T**, which are extracted from 'the phenomena' that **T** is supposed to save" (Muller 2011: 92).

Muller characterizes the $\mathfrak{S}$-View on observational adequacy as follows: **T** is *observationally adequate* at t iff

> for every data-structure $\mathfrak{D} \in \mathcal{D}_t(\mathbf{T})$, there is some structure (model) $\mathfrak{S} \in \boldsymbol{T}$ such that $\mathfrak{D}$ is imbeddable in $\mathfrak{S}$, where 'imbeddability' is broadly constructed as some morphism from $\mathfrak{D}$ into (some part of) $\mathfrak{S}$.
>
> (Muller 2011: 92)

According to Muller's rendering of the $\mathfrak{S}$-View, any theory **T** has attached to it a family of phenomena that it is supposed to describe. As this family grows more varied,

> whilst **T** remains observationally adequate, **T** becomes *better confirmed*. If a number of repeatedly obtained data-structures in $\mathcal{D}_t(\mathbf{T})$ are not imbeddable into any structure in **T**, then **T** is no longer observationally adequate ...; then **T** has been *falsified*.
>
> (Muller 2011: 93)

In order to further clarify the $\mathfrak{S}$-View, it will prove useful to compare it with the eight points that characterize the $\mathfrak{L}$-View.

Concerning point (1), the language used is plain English (or some vernacular language) with the usual mathematical symbols in the informal language of standard mathematics, even though it has at its disposition the language of first-order logic if it wants to formulate some theory (like set-theory) in a formal way. Thus, the theories are formulated in an informal way, as mathematical theories are usually formulated.

Concerning (2), certainly the set of sentences is not defined in a precise way, but the articulation of sentences follows the grammatical rules of the vernacular language and the conventions regarding the use of mathematical symbols.

In order to formulate the axioms (3), the terms of the theory are divided into primitive and those that can be defined by means of the former. In their scientific use, these terms have a definite meaning, but the $\mathfrak{S}$-View abstracts the set-theoretical form of their extensions, which in any event are *sets*. Depending upon the meaning of the term, the set can be a 'bare' set, a relation, or a function defined over appropriate sets. The definition of the models of the theory requires a specification of the set-theoretical nature of the extensions of the primitive terms (set, relation, function). Since the theory is scientific (i.e. empirical), specific axioms expressing the laws and/or other theoretical systematizations are also required.

The 𝔖-View does not have a clear-cut distinction between 'observational' and 'theoretical' terms (4, 5), a distinction which is rather positivist. At any rate, it distinguishes among the terms those that define the 'empirical structures' representing the phenomena the theory deals with, that the theory is supposed to explain, from those terms used to explain the phenomena. A clear example of this is the distinction in classical mechanics between kinematic and dynamic terms. Position and time are kinematic; mass and force are dynamic. I shall discuss later how this distinction can be made precise in general.

Regarding (6), the derivation rules are those of informal mathematics, with occasional appeal to formalized logic, but the deductive closure of the axioms (7) can be clearly defined if the axioms are written in the formal language of set theory. Nevertheless, the concept is not very useful for the analysis of empirical theories.

Finally, an analogue of the 'observation' sentences (6) can be defined, namely those sentences that use only 'kinematic' terms. These can be used to characterize empirical structures representing the phenomena to be explained by the theory. It will be useful, in order to fix ideas, to illustrate the 𝔖-View by means of a simple example taken from economics.

1.2 The 𝔖-view in action: an example

In order to illustrate the 𝔖-View, let us consider a rather general theory: individual choice theory. Just as classical dynamics proposed to explain the motion of bodies by means of the concept of force, individual choice theory proposes to explain the behavior of the agent by means of the concept of preference. The description of the behavior of the agent is the 'kinematics' of the theory, while the preference relation constitutes the 'dynamics' by means of which the former is explained.

The 'kinematics' intends to describe all the circumstances in which the agent is bound to make a choice of a certain type, as well as the choices that the agent would make under such circumstances, by means of unspecified but invariant decision rules. The choice circumstances are represented by subsets of a fixed set of options X, called 'opportunity sets'. The opportunity sets B are collected in a family $\mathcal{B}$ which represents the collection of all the possible choice circumstances. The choices that the agent would actually make at the circumstances are described by means of a function η: $\eta(B)$ is the choice (or set of choices) the agent would make, according to his decision rule, if he found himself in circumstance B.

This conceptual apparatus can be formulated by means of the definition of a set-theoretical predicate. The predicate is defined through a set of necessary and sufficient conditions divided into two classes: characterizations, which are so called because they just characterize the set-theoretical nature of the terms, as well as additional ones specific to the object to be represented. Sometimes the predicate adopts the name of the object represented, if care is taken to make it clear that nobody is confusing reality with its representation. Let us call 'choice structure' this one.

1.2.1 Definition

$\mathfrak{C}$ is a *choice structure* iff there exist X, $\mathcal{B}$, and η such that

(0) $\mathfrak{C} = \langle X, \mathcal{B}, \eta \rangle$;
(1) X is a nonempty set;
(2) $\mathcal{B}$ is a family of subsets of X;
(3) $\eta: \mathcal{B} \rightarrow X$ is a correspondence;
(4) $\eta(B) \subset B$, for each $B \in \mathcal{B}$.

'$\mathfrak{C}$ is a *choice structure*' is the set-theoretical predicate with letter '$\mathfrak{C}$' performing as a variable: Any thing that satisfies the conditions is a choice structure, and any choice structure has to satisfy the conditions. Condition (0) just exhibits the similarity type of the structures satisfying the predicate, (1)–(3) are the characterizations, and condition (4) is not a characterization, but states the obvious truth that options are to be chosen among those that are available.

The 'dynamic' part of the theory is provided by a concept of preference defined over the set X of options, as characterized by the following definition.

1.2.2 Definition

$\mathfrak{P}$ is a *regular preference structure* iff there exist X and $\succsim$ such that

(0) $\mathfrak{P} = \langle X, \succsim \rangle$;
(1) X is a nonempty set;
(2) $\succsim$ is a binary relation over X;
(3) $\succsim$ is connected over X;
(4) $\succsim$ is transitive over X.

Given a family of opportunity sets $\mathcal{B}$, we say that the preference relation $\succsim$ over X *rationalizes* the choice function η iff $\succsim$ satisfies the Condorcet condition, namely: for every opportunity set $B \in \mathcal{B}$, $\eta(B)$ is the set of maximally preferred elements of B modulo $\succsim$; i.e. $x \in \eta(B)$ implies $x \succsim x'$ for every $x' \in B$. If $\succsim$ rationalizes η, we also say that the choice structure $\langle X, \mathcal{B}, \eta \rangle$ is *generated by* the preference structure $\langle X, \succsim \rangle$. Using the concepts previously defined we are in position to define the basic theory-element of individual choice theory.

1.2.3 Definition

$\mathfrak{I}$ is an *individual choice structure* iff there exist X, $\mathcal{B}$, η, and $\succsim$ such that

(0) $\langle X, \mathcal{B}, \eta, \succsim \rangle$;
(1) $\langle X, \mathcal{B}, \eta \rangle$ is a choice structure;
(2) $\langle X, \succsim \rangle$ is a regular preference structure;
(3) $\succsim$ rationalizes η.

Axioms (1) and (2) are a compact way of writing down the characterizations, but (3) is properly an axiom. It says that the agent is actually maximizing a preference relation when he makes his choices.

A data-structure for an individual choice structure $\mathfrak{C}$ is a system of the same similarity type as that of $\mathfrak{C}$ that recodes observations about a single agent during some specified interval of time. Out of the observation of the behavior of the agent, the data-structure

$$\mathfrak{D} = \langle X, \hat{\mathcal{B}}, \hat{\eta} \rangle$$

is obtained, where $\hat{\eta}$ is a function defined over the finite set $\hat{\mathcal{B}}$ of actually observed choice circumstances presented to the agent during the time interval. $\hat{\eta}$ is a recording of the choices that the agent was observed making. Since the size of $\hat{\mathcal{B}} \subset \mathcal{B}$ is manageable, the observations can be recorded in a table (see Table 1.1). The data are explained if $\mathfrak{D}$ can be isomorphically imbedded in the choice structure $\mathfrak{C}$ generated by some preference structure.

1.3 Problems of the $\mathfrak{S}$-view

Muller (2011) points out three problems for the $\mathfrak{S}$-View. These he describes as the *Problem of Lost Beings*, the *Problem of the Unavailable Stories*, and the *Problem of the Lost Content.* I will discuss in this section these problems as a preparation for the presentation of my own version of the structuralist theory.

Let us start with the Problem of Lost Beings. This problem arises out of the definition of a scientific theory as a class of structures in the universe of set

Table 1.1 A data-structure

Argument	*Value of* $\hat{\eta}$
B_1	$\hat{\eta}(B_1)$
B_2	$\hat{\eta}(B_2)$
$\vdots$	$\vdots$
B_i	$\hat{\eta}(B_i)$
$\vdots$	$\vdots$
B_n	$\hat{\eta}(B_n)$

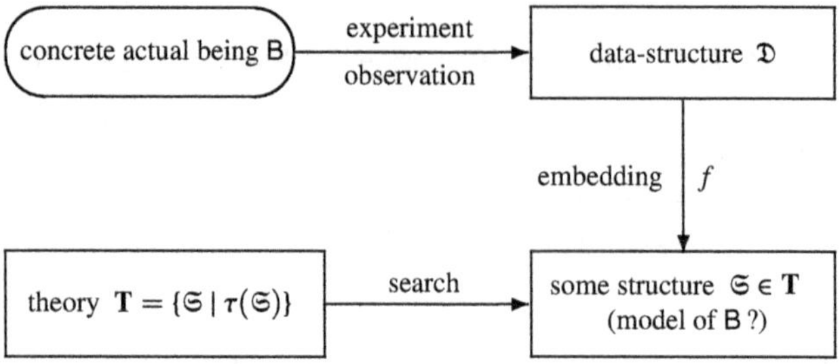

Figure 1.1 The informal 𝔖-view

theory. Asks Muller: "How can any scientific theory **T** thus reconstructed be about any concrete being in the world, say B (of 'Being')?". He believes that the 𝔖-View ignores (passes over in silence) the fact that a scientific theory must be about "a specific set of *actual beings* (objects, processes, events, entities, persons, organisms, periods, structures…), frequently called its *domain or scope*" (Muller 2011: 95, 97). After drawing a picture to illustrate the informal 𝔖-View (ibid.: 98; Figure 1.1 here), Muller claims that

> as soon as the data-structure 𝔇 is obtained, we can forget all about the concrete actual beings at hand, or so it seems. The 𝔖-View says next to nothing about how the models 𝔖 (the theory **T**) are related to the concrete beings B they are supposed to provide knowledge of.

Thus, the problem seems to be that of the lack of a doctrine explaining how the set-theoretical structures relate to the elements within the scope of the theory.

The Problem of the Unavailable Stories arises when someone missing the relevant information is presented with a data-structure without any further explanations. According to Muller (2011: 101)

> When we arrive with our data-structure in the realm of theories, by telling some story, we know for which scientific theory or theories the data-structure is relevant. But when we only have rigorous construals of all scientific theories in accordance with the 𝔖-View, to which of the sets or set-structures should we go in order to find a structure that imbeds an obtained data-structure? The 𝔖-View lacks the resources to tell the necessary stories: language.

Hence, again, the problem seems to be that of the information available to someone facing a given set-theoretical structure.

Since the aim of modern science is to provide knowledge of concrete actual beings,

> A necessary condition any model 𝔖 must pass in order to be considered as a piece of theoretical scientific knowledge about a particular kind of concrete actual being B is that 𝔖 should imbed all the relevant actual data-structures obtained by observing B or performing experiments with B, or both. But what does set-structure 𝔖, or a theory for that matter (**T** ∋ 𝔖) say about B? Where has the conceptual and propositional content of the scientific theory T, as used by scientists, gone to when reconstructed as **T**? Call this the Problem of the Lost Content.
>
> (Muller 2011: 101)

Muller also finds difficult to see where and how does truth fit in the 𝔖-View. He says:

> If there are 'truth-makers' of propositions that are somehow determined by means of 𝔖 (or of **T**), then surely they are, or somehow reside in, the concrete actual being B that 𝔖 (or **T**) is supposed to be about. For if B is neither the truth-maker nor involved in the truth-making of sentences about B, then the concept of truth gets dissociated from the actual concrete beings, and such a concept of truth does not seem to be the concept of truth that is used and understood in science. Surely in science truths and falsehoods are truths and falsehoods about the world. What else could they be about? Well, how does this precisely work, then, according to the 𝔖-View?
>
> (Muller 2011: 101–2)

In forthcoming chapters I will provide a version of the structuralist view that responds to all these questions and solves the three problems posed by Muller, but also additional problems faced by any structuralist theory of science, like the distinction between theoretical and non-theoretical terms, the place of representational measurement within a scientific theory, the problem posed by the Ramsey sentence, and objections specific to the application of the structuralist theory to economics raised by Wade Hands (1985).

In Chapter 2 I will define in a rigorous and complete way the relevant concept of set-theoretical structure, presenting the concept of a model of a first-order language as a special case of the former. SVT will be presented in detail in Chapter 3.

In Chapter 5 I will expose the doctrine of representational, in particular fundamental measurement, in order to discuss the role it plays in the structuralist view of scientific theories (SVT). I will try to respond to the objections and criticisms raised against the doctrine of representational measurement by Michell (2007) and, above all, by Boumans (2007, 2008, 2012, 2016).

In Chapter 4 I will provide my own version of Marx's method of political economy in order to discuss the notions of abstraction, idealization, and concretization. A clear distinction will be introduced between the concept of model as an imagined real system and that of a model as set-theoretical structure, but also a doctrine explaining the way the are related. This doctrine should solve the three problems formulated by Muller and prepare the way to a full-fledged structuralist theory of economics.

The terrain will be ready, then, to discuss specific economic theories and their methodology in the remaining chapters. Game theory, Marxian economics, Sraffian economics, and econometrics will be treated in corresponding chapters.

Notes

1 See Lowen (1997) for an assessment of the military background underlying the rise of Stanford's reputation.

2 Other papers on the foundations of physics written with McKinsey are McKinsey and Suppes (1953, 1955). With Rubin (Rubin and Suppes 1954) he wrote a paper on transformations of systems of relativistic particle mechanics, of which he said in 1979 that it was a "a long and very complicated piece of work that has not been read, I suspect, by very many people" (Suppes 1979: 10).

3 The proceedings of this symposium were published by Henkin, Suppes, and Tarski (1959). See the review of this event in Feferman and Feferman (2004: 232–237).

4 The proceedings of this second symposium were published by Nagel, Suppes, and Tarski (1962). For a review of this symposium see Feferman and Feferman (2004: 253–256).

2 Models and structures

2.1 The rise of the concept of structure

Mathematical logic is introduced in textbooks in such a way that they induce the beginners to imagine that the formalized languages descend from heaven seeking to incarnate in some earthly interpretation. The problems of lost beings, unavailable stories, and lost content, pointed out by Muller for the 𝔖-View, appear in such textbooks in a dramatic form. As in the case of the 𝔖-View, there is a (lost and long) story behind the rise of such languages. Formalized languages were created originally in order to express propositions about certain mathematical domains, mainly the domain of arithmetic. Frege's *Begriffsschrift* (1879), which introduced through a graphic language the first system of elementary logic, was written with the intention of determining the logical theory out of which, and by means of which, the foundations of arithmetic had to be established. With severe logical deficiencies,[1] Peano (1889) characterized arithmetic by means of axioms that have prevailed thus far. The primitive terms of his system are *numerus* (the set of positive integers, denoted by N), *unitas* (the number 1), and *sequens* (the successor function, S) "*sive n plus 1*" (ibid.: 1). These terms were introduced with their usual meaning, in order to refer to the familiar positive integers and to the operation of taking the successor of any of these numbers, starting with 1.

On the other hand, the development of algebra since the middle of the nineteenth century gave rise to the concept of algebraic structure. Bartel Leendert van der Waerden's text *Moderne Algebra* (1949), published originally in two volumes in 1930 and 1931, makes systematic use of the concept of algebraic structure in order to organize what is now known as universal or modern algebra. This important work, in addition to that of the logicians Leopold Löwenheim, Thoralf Skolem, and mainly Alfred Tarski, set the stage for the definition of the general concept of relational structure, or model. If it were possible to pinpoint the year in which the concept of model reached its maturity, it would be 1930, or perhaps 1931, when Tarski introduced his concept of truth for formalized languages (cf. Tarski 1930–1931, 1956: 152–278). We shall revise this concept in the next section, giving some examples of its use in the formulation of theories relevant for economics.

Even though this concept of a model is useful and important for the sciences, it is well-known that it is not sufficient. The Nicolas Bourbaki group provided, in 1957, a concept of structure that gave the pattern for the formulation of a more general concept (cf. Bourbaki 1968: chapter 4). Unfortunately, the syntactic terms in which it was defined made impossible its application in the practice of mathematics. It is probably due to it that, as Corry (1992) points out, Bourbaki made no use at all of the concept for the rest of its work. This means that, even though the concept of structure had been used successfully in an informal way in the formulation of non-first-order theories (like topology), in mathematics as well in the empirical sciences, until 1987 nobody had given a satisfactory definition of the notion. In set-theoretic, non-syntactic terms, Balzer, Moulines, and Sneed (1987) reformulated Bourbaki's concept of structure in order to clarify Suppes' dictum that to axiomatize a theory is to define a set-theoretical predicate. Along the same lines, one year later there appeared a paper published by Newton da Costa and Rolando Chuaqui (1988), in which they proposed a similar but more detailed definition. It was given within the framework of ZFC, but it is possible to give it in a more general setting which is even useful to define categories and functors (the collection of all structures of a given type is not a set, but a proper class). I will do this in the fifth section of this chapter.[2]

2.2 Models for first-order logic

It will be useful, in order to motivate the definition of a more general concept of structure, to start with the historically important one of model for a first-order language.

A structure or relational system (or just a *system*) is a sequence

$$\mathfrak{A} = \langle A, R_\xi, G_\zeta, a_\varsigma \rangle_{\xi \in \mathfrak{a}, \zeta \in \mathfrak{b}, \varsigma \in \mathfrak{c}},$$

where $\mathfrak{a}$, $\mathfrak{b}$ and $\mathfrak{c}$ are order-types, pairwise disjoint and isomorphic to respective cardinal numbers α, β, γ; A is a nonempty set; for each $\xi \in \mathfrak{a}$, R_ξ is a relation over A; for each $\zeta \in \mathfrak{b}$, G_ζ is a function over A; and, for each $\varsigma \in \mathfrak{c}$, a_ς is an element of A. Any of the sets $\mathfrak{a}$, $\mathfrak{b}$, $\mathfrak{c}$ can be empty, but $\mathfrak{a}$ y $\mathfrak{b}$ cannot be so simultaneously. If $\mathfrak{a} = \varnothing$, $\mathfrak{A}$ must involve, at least, a function (i.e. $\mathfrak{b}$ must be nonempty); in this case, $\mathfrak{A}$ is called an *algebraic structure*. The *order* κ of the structure is the cardinal number of the sum $\mathfrak{a} + \mathfrak{b} + \mathfrak{c}$ of the order-types $\mathfrak{a}$, $\mathfrak{b}$ and $\mathfrak{c}$.[3] It is easy to see that there is an order isomorphism between κ and $\mathfrak{a} + \mathfrak{b} + \mathfrak{c}$. Clearly, since each of the orders $\mathfrak{a}$, $\mathfrak{b}$, $\mathfrak{c}$ have a first element, we can map the first element of $\mathfrak{b}$ in $\alpha + 1$ and get an isomorphism between $\mathfrak{b}$ and $\mathfrak{b}' = \{\zeta \in \alpha + \beta | \alpha + 1 \leq \zeta < \alpha + \beta\}$. Analogously, we can get an isomorphism between $\mathfrak{c}$ and $\mathfrak{c}' = \{\varsigma \in \alpha + \beta + \gamma | \alpha + \beta + 1 \leq \varsigma < \alpha + \beta + \gamma\}$. That is why, from now on, we shall identify the set $\mathfrak{a}$ with α, $\mathfrak{b}$ with $\mathfrak{b}'$, and $\mathfrak{c}$ with $\mathfrak{c}'$. Indeed, $\kappa = \mathfrak{a} \cup \mathfrak{b} \cup \mathfrak{c}$.

The *similarity type* of structure $\mathfrak{A}$ is the function $\mu \in \omega^{\kappa}$ such that

$$\mu(\imath) = \begin{cases} n & \text{if } \imath \in \mathfrak{a} \text{ and } R_\imath \subset A^n. \\ m & \text{if } \imath \in \mathfrak{b} \text{ and } G_\imath \text{ is a function from } A^m \text{ into } A. \\ 0 & \text{if } \imath \in \mathfrak{c}. \end{cases}$$

If $\imath \in \mathfrak{a}$, the number $\mu(\imath)$ is called the *arity* of relation $R_\imath$. If $\imath \in \mathfrak{b}$, the function $G_\imath$ is a function with $\mu(\imath)$ arguments. A is the *domain* of structure $\mathfrak{A}$ and the R_ξ are the *fundamental relations* of the same. The elements of A are also called *elements* of $\mathfrak{A}$. Two relational systems are *similar* if they are of the same similarity type. The class of structures of similarity type μ is called the *similarity type* of μ.

Let $\mathfrak{A} = \langle A, R_\xi, G_\zeta, a_\varsigma \rangle$ and $\mathfrak{B} = \langle B, S_\xi, H_\zeta, b_\varsigma \rangle$ be two similar structures. $\mathfrak{A}$ is a *substructure* or *subsystem* of $\mathfrak{B}$ ($\mathfrak{A} \subset \mathfrak{B}$) iff (1) $A \subset B$; (2) for each ξ, $R_\xi = S_\xi \cap A^n$, where $n = \mu(\xi)$; (3) G_ζ is the restriction of H_ζ to A; (4) $a_\varsigma = b_\varsigma$. $\mathfrak{B}$ is also called an *extension* (or *enlargement*) of $\mathfrak{A}$.

A *homomorphism* from $\mathfrak{A}$ into $\mathfrak{B}$ is a function $f: A \to B$ that preserves the relations and functions, in the following sense:

(1) $(x_1, \ldots, x_{\mu(\xi)}) \in R_\xi$ implies $(f(x_1), \ldots, f(x_{\mu(\xi)})) \in S_\xi$.
(2) $f(G_\zeta(x_1, \ldots, x_{\mu(\zeta)})) = H_\zeta(f(x_1), \ldots, f(x_\zeta))$.
(3) $f(a_\varsigma) = b_\varsigma$.

If the function is one to one, it is said that the homomorphism is a *monomorphism*; if it is onto, an *epimorphism*; if it is one to one an onto, an *isomorphism*. We say that $\mathfrak{B}$ is a *homomorphic image* of $\mathfrak{A}$ if there exists an epimorphism from A into B. The structure $\mathfrak{A}$ is said to be *imbedded* in system $\mathfrak{B}$ if $\mathfrak{A}$ is isomorphic to a subsystem of $\mathfrak{B}$; this isomorphic image of $\mathfrak{A}$ in $\mathfrak{B}$ is called the *imbedding* of $\mathfrak{A}$ into $\mathfrak{B}$. An isomorphism from a structure into itself is called an *automorphism*. If $\mathfrak{A}$ is isomorphic to $\mathfrak{B}$ we write $\mathfrak{A} \simeq \mathfrak{B}$. Notice that if f is an isomorphism, the biconditional

$$(x_1, \cdots, x_{\mu(\xi)}) \in R_\xi \quad \text{iff} \quad (f(x_1), \cdots, f(x_{\mu(\xi)})) \in S_\xi$$

actually holds.

In order to formulate sentences about the elements of a structure, language is required. Thus, for each similarity type μ, a language is introduced, *the language of similarity type* μ, $\mathcal{L}(\mu)$ or just $\mathcal{L}$ if no confusion can arise. Any structure of type μ is called a *model* of language $\mathcal{L}$. One important sense of the term 'model' is precisely this one: model is a semantic notion stressing a connection between some language and a class of structures. This concept should not be confused with other concepts of model, especially those consisting of idealized images (what is called below 'model system'). When the relationship between the structures and their language is not the focus of the discussion, it is better to call them 'structures'.

The logical constants of any language $\mathcal{L}(\mu)$ are a countable set of individual variables x, typically the connectives conditional ($\rightarrow$) and negation ($\neg$), parentheses, and the identity symbol = (which is optional except for algebraic structures). Beside these, $\mathcal{L}(\mu)$ consists of parameters, namely:

(1) The universal quantifier $\forall$.
(2) For each $\xi \in \mathfrak{a}$ a predicate symbol P_ξ, with arity $\mu(\xi)$.
(3) For each $\zeta \in \mathfrak{b}$ a function symbol F_ζ for $\mu(\zeta)$ arguments.
(4) For each $\varsigma \in \mathfrak{c}$ a constant symbol c_ς.

The cardinality $\| \mathcal{L} \|$ of language $\mathcal{L}$ is the cardinality of the set of its parameters.

Both individual variables x and constants c are the basic terms of the language. Other, more complex terms are built out the basic terms by means of the function symbols F: if F is a function symbol for n arguments, and $\tau_1,\ldots, \tau_n$ are terms, then $F\tau_1\ldots\tau_n$ is a term. Beside these and the basic terms, there are no other terms. The basic or atomic formulas of the language are of the form $P\tau_1\ldots\tau_n$, where n is the arity of predicate P, and of the form $\tau_1 = \tau_2$ if it contains the identity symbol. Complex formulas are built out of the basic ones in the standard way: if φ and ψ are formulas, $\neg\varphi$, $\varphi \rightarrow \psi$, and $\forall x\varphi$ are formulas, and there is no other way of building formulas. It is said that variable x occurs *free* in formula φ if it occurs in φ and φ is atomic; or φ is of the form $\neg\psi$, and x occurs free in ψ; or φ is of the form $\psi \rightarrow \theta$ and x occurs free in ψ or θ; or φ is of the form $\forall x'\psi$, x occurs free in ψ, and x is not variable x'. A formula in which no free variables occur is called a *sentence*.

It is important for the purposes of this book to distinguish between several acceptations of the word 'model'. I already defined the concept of a model of *language* $\mathcal{L}(\mu)$. Another concept is that of a model of a *sentence* of language $\mathcal{L}(\mu)$. When a reference to Tarski's concept of model is made, the reference is to this last concept. I will define in what follows this important concept.

The presence of free variables in the formulas introduces some complications in the definition of Tarski's concept of model. These complications were overcome by means of his notion of a sequence. Consider a model $\mathfrak{A}$ of language $\mathcal{L}(\mu)$. This means, in the first place, that quantifier $\forall$ ranges over the universe A of $\mathfrak{A}$: '$\forall x$' means "for all elements x of A". As we already saw, from a different point of view, $\mathfrak{A}$ assigns to predicate P_ξ relation R_ξ of $\mathfrak{A}$, to F_ζ function G_ζ of $\mathfrak{A}$, and to constant c_ς element a_ς of the universe A of $\mathfrak{A}$. A *sequence* for model $\mathfrak{A}$ is a function $\hat{s}$ that maps all the variables of $\mathcal{L}(\mu)$ into the universe A of $\mathfrak{A}$. A sequence can be expanded in a unique fashion to a function s over all terms of $\mathcal{L}(\mu)$ by means of the classical recursive definition, namely

$$s(\tau) = \begin{cases} \hat{s}(x) & \text{if } \tau \text{ is variable } x. \\ a_\varsigma & \text{if } \tau \text{ is constant symbol } c_\varsigma. \\ G_\zeta(s(\tau_1), \cdots, s(\tau_{\mu(\zeta)})) & \text{if } \tau \text{ is } F_\zeta\tau_1 \cdots \tau_{\mu(\zeta)}. \end{cases}$$

Now we are in position to define the famous notions of truth, satisfaction and model, also recursively, by means of sequences s. Notation: '$\mathfrak{A} \models \varphi\ [s]$' means that formula φ is satisfied by $\mathfrak{A}$ with s; $[s(x|a)]$ denotes a function identical to s, except that it assigns to variable x element $a \in A$. Hence, for any formulas φ, ψ and variable x:

(1) If τ_1 and τ_2 are terms,

$$\mathfrak{A} \models \tau_1 = \tau_2\ [s] \quad \text{iff} \quad s(\tau_1) = s(\tau_2).$$

(2) If P_ξ is a predicate symbol,

$$\mathfrak{A} \models P_\xi \tau_1 \cdots \tau_{\mu(\xi)}\ [s] \quad \text{iff} \quad (s(\tau_1), \cdots, s(\tau_{\mu(\xi)})) \in R_\xi.$$

(3) $\mathfrak{A} \models \neg\varphi\ [s]$ iff $\mathfrak{A} \not\models \varphi\ [s]$.
(4) $\mathfrak{A} \models (\varphi \rightarrow \psi)\ [s]$ iff $\mathfrak{A} \not\models \varphi\ [s]$, or $\mathfrak{A} \models \psi\ [s]$, or both.
(5) $\mathfrak{A} \models \forall x\varphi\ [s]$ iff $\mathfrak{A} \models \varphi\ [s(x|a)]$ with every $a \in A$.

A formula φ is *satisfiable* iff there is a structure $\mathfrak{A}$, together with a sequence s, such that $\mathfrak{A} \models \varphi\ [s]$. The set of formulas Γ is *satisfiable* iff there is a structure $\mathfrak{A}$ and a sequence s such that $\mathfrak{A}$ satisfies every element of Γ with s. The crucial concept of logical consequence can be defined as follows. Let Γ be a set of formulas and φ any formula. Say that Γ *logically implies* φ, or that φ is a *logical consequence* of Γ ($\Gamma \models \varphi$) iff, for every structure $\mathfrak{A}$ of type μ and every sequence s for $\mathfrak{A}$: if $\mathfrak{A}$ satisfies every formula in Γ with s, then $\mathfrak{A}$ also satisfies φ with s. Say that φ is *valid* in $\mathfrak{A}$ if φ is satisfied by $\mathfrak{A}$ with any s. φ is *logically valid* iff φ is satisfied by every $\mathfrak{A}$ with every s. A set Γ of formulas is *valid* in $\mathfrak{A}$ if every element of Γ is valid in $\mathfrak{A}$; in this case we say that $\mathfrak{A}$ is a *model* of Γ. It can be shown that if φ is a sentence, and $\mathfrak{A}$ a model for the language, then either φ is satisfied by $\mathfrak{A}$ with *every* s, or it is not satisfied by *any* s at all. If it is so satisfied, we say that φ is *true* in $\mathfrak{A}$, and it can be seen that $\mathfrak{A}$ is a model of φ. Thus, in particular, if φ is a sentence and Γ is a set of sentences, then φ is a logical consequence of Γ iff every model of Γ is a model of φ.

Given a structure $\mathfrak{A}$ define the *theory* of $\mathfrak{A}$, Th($\mathfrak{A}$), as the set of all sentences of $\mathcal{L}(\mu)$ that are true in $\mathfrak{A}$. Analogously, if $\mathcal{M}$ is a family of structures of type μ, the *theory* of $\mathcal{M}$, Th($\mathcal{M}$) is the set of all sentences that are true in every element of $\mathcal{M}$. A *theory* T of $\mathcal{L}$ is defined as a set of sentences of $\mathcal{L}$. T is a *closed* iff

$$T \models \varphi \quad \Rightarrow \quad \varphi \in T.$$

A set of sentences Γ is *consistent* iff there is no formula φ such $\Sigma \vdash \varphi \wedge \neg\varphi$, where the derivation relation, $\vdash$, is defined modulo some appropriate set of derivation rules (as those pointed out below). Let Σ be a consistent set of sentences, and Mod Σ the set of all models of Σ. The set of the *consequences* of Σ (Cn Σ) is defined as Th(Mod Σ). It is obvious that T is a closed theory iff $T = \text{Cn } T$. The class of all the models of a finite consistent set of sentences Γ is called an *elementary* or *arithmetical class*. Modern algebra provides a good deal of examples of elementary classes: monoids, semi-groups, groups, rings, fields, partial orderings, simple or linear orderings, weak orders, dense simple orderings, and many others. Actually, we shall see below that the most important single structures in economic theory, the preference structures, constitute elementary classes.

A set Σ of formulas is *decidable* if there is an algorithm that can compute, in a finite number of steps, whether a given sentence is, or is not, an element of Σ.[4] A theory T is *axiomatizable* iff there exists a decidable set of sentences Σ such that $T = \text{Cn}\ (\Sigma)$. In particular, if Σ is finite, it is said that T is *finitely axiomatizable.*

The logical axioms are usually comprised by all tautologies, axioms concerning the quantifier, including universal specification and generalization rules, and, if the identity symbol is included, axioms concerning identity. The inference rules are usually *modus ponens* (from $\varphi \to \psi$ and φ infer ψ) and generalization (from φ infer $\forall x\varphi$).[5]

Model theory is an interesting chapter in logic dealing with the relationships between formal languages and the relational systems in which theories are realized. The entrance gate to the garden of model theory is Gödel's completeness theorem (1930). Starting with this theorem, I will provide in what follows (without proof) a list of theorems that are interesting in their own right, but also useful in economic methodology. Some definitions are required in order to do this.

We say that two models $\mathfrak{A}$ and $\mathfrak{B}$ of language $\mathcal{L}$ are *elementary equivalent,* written $\mathfrak{A} \equiv \mathfrak{B}$, iff both models satisfy the same sentences of $\mathcal{L}$. $\mathfrak{B}$ is an *elementary extension* of $\mathfrak{A}$ (or $\mathfrak{A}$ is an *elementary subsystem* of $\mathfrak{B}$), written $\mathfrak{A} \prec \mathfrak{B}$, iff $\mathfrak{A}$ is a subsystem of $\mathfrak{B}$ and, for every formula φ of $\mathcal{L}$ and sequence s, $\mathfrak{A}$ satisfies φ with s iff $\mathfrak{B}$ satisfies φ with s. A theory T is *complete* iff all its models are elementarily equivalent. T is an *α-categorical theory* iff all its models of power α are isomorphic. T is a *model complete theory* iff, for any two models $\mathfrak{A}$, $\mathfrak{B}$ of T such that $\mathfrak{A} \subset \mathfrak{B}$, $\mathfrak{A} \prec \mathfrak{B}$. $\mathfrak{A}$ is a *prime model* of T iff every model of T contains a subsystem isomorphic to $\mathfrak{A}$. T admits *quantifier elimination* iff, for each formula φ of L, there exists a formula ψ without quantifiers such that $T \vdash \varphi \leftrightarrow \psi$. A class $\mathcal{M}$ of models is *closed under isomorphism* iff $\mathfrak{A} \in \mathcal{M}$ and $\mathfrak{B} \simeq \mathfrak{A}$ implies $\mathfrak{B} \in \mathcal{M}$.

An interesting and useful list of model-theoretic results which are relevant for economic theory is the following (the proofs are omitted).

2.2.1 Theorem

If $\mathfrak{A} \simeq \mathfrak{B}$ then $\mathfrak{A} \equiv \mathfrak{B}$. The converse is also true if the models are finite.

2.2.2 Theorem

If $\mathfrak{A} \prec \mathfrak{B}$ then $\mathfrak{A} \equiv \mathfrak{B}$.

2.2.3 Theorem (Gödel completeness theorem (1930))

For every sentence φ and every model of $\mathcal{L}$, $\Sigma \vdash \varphi$ iff $\Sigma \models \phi$.

2.2.4 Theorem (Compactness theorem (Maltsev 1936))

A set of sentences Σ has a model iff every finite subset of Σ has a model.

2.2.5 Theorem (Extended completeness theorem)

Any set of sentences Σ is consistent iff Σ has a model.

2.2.6 Theorem (Löwenheim-Skolem-Tarski (LST) theorem)

Every consistent theory T in $\mathcal{L}$ has a model of power at most $\| \mathcal{L} \|$. If T is finite and it has an infinite model, then it has models of every infinite cardinality. If T is infinite and it has a model of power α, then it has a model of any power $\geqq \alpha$.

2.2.7 Theorem

Σ is complete iff, for every sentence φ of $\mathcal{L}$, either $\Sigma \vdash \varphi$ or $\Sigma \vdash \neg \varphi$.

2.2.8 Theorem (Lindenbaum)

Every theory T has a complete consistent extension.

2.2.9 Theorem (Robinson's model completeness test)

A theory T is model complete iff, whenever $\mathfrak{A} \subseteq \mathfrak{B} \in \text{Mod } T$, it is the case that if $\mathfrak{B} \models \varphi[s]$ then $\mathfrak{A} \models \varphi[s]$ for any wff φ and any sequence s.

2.2.10 Theorem (Quantifier elimination)

If a theory T admits quantifier elimination then it is model complete.

2.2.11 Theorem (Prime model test)

If a complete theory has a prime model then it is complete.

2.3 Elementary classes in economics

The most important relational systems occurring in economic and decision theory are those representing preference relations or, more generally, systems representing some sort of ordering.[6] These are structures

$$\mathfrak{A} = \langle A, R_\xi, G_\zeta, a_\varsigma \rangle_{\xi \in \mathfrak{a}, \zeta \in \mathfrak{b}, \varsigma \in \mathfrak{c}},$$

where $\mathfrak{b} = \mathfrak{c} = \varnothing$ and $\mathfrak{a}$ is finite. That is to say, classes of structures having the following aspect:

$$\mathfrak{A} = \langle A, R_\xi \rangle$$

where α is a finite sequence of positive integers such that $\mu(\xi)$ is the arity of relation R_ξ. The structure is called *numerical* if the domain A is a numerical set (like the set of real numbers). Of particular interest are structures of the form $\langle A, R\rangle$, where R is a binary relation over A; i.e. R is a subset of $A \times A$. Varied properties may be attributed to relation R, giving rise to different types of representations (usually called 'utility functions'). A rather complete list of such properties is found in Suppes (1957: 213–17). They can be defined as follows (xRy means $(x, y) \in R$).

2.3.1 *Definition*

Let R be a binary relation over (nonempty) set A.

(1) R is *reflexive* in A iff

$$\forall x(x \in A \rightarrow xRx).$$

(2) R is *irreflexive* in A iff

$$\forall x(x \in A \rightarrow \neg xRx).$$

(3) R is *symmetric* in A iff

$$\forall x \forall y((x \in A \wedge y \in A \wedge xRy) \rightarrow yRx).$$

(4) R is *asymmetric* in A iff

$$\forall x \forall y((x \in A \wedge y \in A \wedge xRy) \rightarrow \neg yRx).$$

(5) R is *antisymmetric* in A iff

$$\forall x \forall y((x \in A \wedge y \in A \wedge xRy \wedge yRx) \rightarrow x = y).$$

(6) R is *transitive* in A iff

$$\forall x \forall y \forall z((x \in A \wedge y \in A \wedge z \in A \wedge xRy \wedge yRz) \rightarrow xRz).$$

(7) R is *intransitive* in A iff

$$\forall x \forall y \forall z((x \in A \wedge y \in A \wedge z \in A \wedge xRy \wedge yRz) \rightarrow \neg xRz).$$

(8) R is *connected* in A iff

$$\forall x \forall y((x \in A \wedge y \in A \wedge x \neq y) \rightarrow (xRy \vee yRx)).$$

(9) R is *strongly connected* in A iff

$$\forall x \forall y((x \in A \wedge y \in A) \rightarrow (xRy \vee yRx)).$$

Almost every ordering found in economics is nothing but a combination of some of these properties. The most common of them are the quasi-orderings,

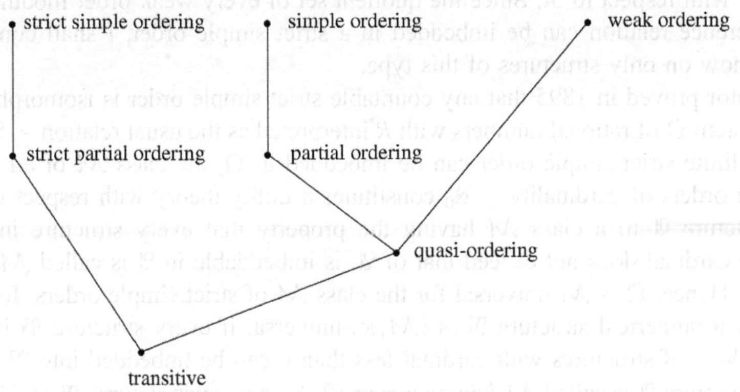

Figure 2.1 Net of main orderings

the partial, simple, strict partial, strict simple, and weak orderings. These are easily defined as follows. R is a *quasi-ordering* of set A iff R is reflexive and transitive in A. R is a *partial* ordering of set A iff R is reflexive, antisymmetric, and transitive in A. R is a *simple ordering* of set A iff R is antisymmetric, transitive, and connected in A. R is a *strict partial ordering of set A* iff R is asymmetric and transitive in A. R is a *strict simple ordering of set A* iff R is asymmetric, transitive, and connected in A. R is a *weak ordering* of set A iff R is transitive and strongly connected in A. Figure 2.1 (taken from Suppes 1957: 223) displays the relationships between all these orderings. The structures consisting of the set A together with R bear the name of the ordering, but are called 'orders'; for instance, the structure $\langle A, R\rangle$ is called a strict partial order if R is a strict partial ordering of A, and so on for the others.

Perhaps the single most important ordering in economic theory is what is called a regular or 'rational' preference ordering, which is just a weak ordering. Notice that a weak order is precisely a model of the set T_{wo} consisting of the following axioms:

$$\forall x \forall y (Rxy \vee Ryx)$$

$$\forall x \forall y \forall z (Rxy \wedge Ryz) \rightarrow Rxz)$$

where R (more correctly written as R_1) is now a predicate symbol of arity $\mu(1) = 2$. Hence, the class of weak orders is an elementary or arithmetical class. Since T_{wo} is consistent, finite, and has an infinite model, it follows (by the LST theorem) that it has models of any infinite cardinality.

Scott and Suppes (1958: 115) defined a *theory of measurement* as a class $\mathcal{M}$ of relational systems of type α closed under isomorphism for which there exists a numerical structure $\mathfrak{N}$, also of type α, such that all structures in $\mathcal{M}$ are imbeddable in $\mathfrak{N}$. For the case of preference structures the theory of measurement may be called a *utility theory*, as it is done by Skala (1975: 10). If all structures in class $\mathcal{M}$ are imbeddable in the numerical system $\mathfrak{N}$, we say that $\mathcal{M}$ is a utility theory with respect to $\mathfrak{N}$. Since the quotient set of every weak order modulo the indifference relation can be imbedded in a strict simple order, I shall consider from now on only structures of this type.

Cantor proved in 1895 that any countable strict simple order is isomorphic to the system $\mathfrak{Q}$ of rational numbers with R interpreted as the usual relation >. Since every finite strict simple order can be imbedded in $\mathfrak{Q}$, the class $\mathcal{M}$ of all strict simple orders of cardinality $\leq \aleph_0$ constitutes a utility theory with respect to $\mathfrak{Q}$. A structure $\mathfrak{A}$ in a class $\mathcal{M}$ having the property that every structure in $\mathcal{M}$, whose cardinal does not exceed that of $\mathfrak{A}$, is imbeddable in $\mathfrak{A}$ is called $\mathcal{M}$-universal. Hence, $\mathfrak{Q}$ is $\mathcal{M}$-universal for the class $\mathcal{M}$ of strict simple orders. In particular, a numerical structure $\mathfrak{N}$ is $(\mathcal{M}, \kappa)$-universal if every structure $\mathfrak{B}$ in the class $\mathcal{M}_{<\kappa}$ of structures with cardinal less than κ can be imbedded into $\mathfrak{N}$.

A structure $\mathfrak{A}$ is called $\mathcal{M}$*-homogeneous* iff, for any substructures $\mathfrak{B}$ and $\mathfrak{B}'$ of $\mathfrak{A}$, and isomorphism f of $\mathfrak{B}$ into $\mathfrak{B}'$, there is an automorphism g of $\mathfrak{A}$ which is an extension of f, as represented in the commutative diagram of Figure 2.2. Clearly, since any two finite strict orders $\mathfrak{B}$ and $\mathfrak{B}'$ of the same cardinal are isomorphic, with imbeddings $h(\mathfrak{B})$ and $h'(\mathfrak{B}')$ into $\mathfrak{Q}$, there must be an automorphism g of $\mathfrak{Q}$ such that g: $h(\mathfrak{B}) \simeq h(\mathfrak{B}')$. Therefore, $\mathfrak{Q}$ is also $\mathcal{M}$-homogeneous. Any infinite universal relational system $\langle A, R\rangle$ with $\|A\| \leq \aleph_0$ which is homogenous is unique, in the sense that it is isomorphic to $\mathfrak{Q}$.

The question that naturally arises now is whether the structure $\mathfrak{R}$ of the real numbers ordered by > is also $\mathcal{M}$-homogeneous and universal. Indeed, traditionally, since the time of the marginalists, it has been taken for granted that the suitable numerical structure to represent any preference structure of cardinal not exceeding $\mathfrak{c} = 2^{\aleph_0}$, the cardinal of the continuum, is $\mathfrak{R}$, as it provides the established framework for the use of calculus. Nobody can deny the enormous power of Newton's methods in the sciences, and of course Hölder's pioneer work on the foundations of measurement is guided by the interest of finding representations of magnitudes in the real number system. Yet, it is well known that there are lexicographic orderings that cannot be imbedded in $\mathfrak{R}$. A necessary and sufficient condition for a simple strict order A to be imbedded in $\mathfrak{R}$ is that it contains a countable subset B such that, for every $x, z \in A$, if xPz then there exists $y \in B$ with $xPyPz$.

In order to represent lexicographic preferences, the use of sequences of real numbers has been suggested, with each sequence of some fixed ordinal length.

> Nevertheless, this approach is not without its own difficulties: (i) It has been shown that, even for linearly ordered sets of power no greater than the continuum, ordinal sequences of countable length do not always suffice. (ii) The

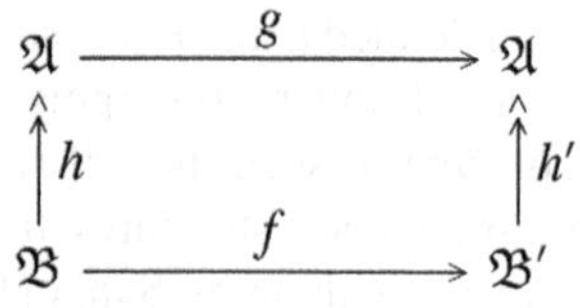

Figure 2.2 Automorphism extension

> techniques of classical analysis have not been extended in convenient fashion to sets of lexicographically ordered ordinal sequences.
>
> (Richter 1971: 40)

This is not surprising, as Scott and Suppes (1958: 117) had pointed out that

> among the morass of all possible numerical relational systems only a very few are of any computational value, indeed only those definable in terms of the ordinary arithmetical notions.

Hence, the problem of choosing an appropriate numerical system must be solved adopting only 'natural' systems, like the real number system, that have the desirable computational properties. Marcel K. Richter (1971) solved this problem for preference structures of the same power as $\mathfrak{c}$ by means of the introduction of nonstandard models of Th($\mathfrak{R}$). A nonstandard model of Th($\mathfrak{R}$) is an elementary extension $^*\mathfrak{R}$ of $\mathfrak{R}$ that contains infinitesimal, nonzero numbers, as well as numbers larger than any positive real number. Actually, $^*\mathfrak{R}$ has more desirable computational properties than $\mathfrak{R}$ and it is a utility theory for the class $\mathcal{M}$ of all simple strict orders of cardinal not exceeding $\mathfrak{c}$.

It might be thought that this result is sufficient for economic theory, but it is sometimes necessary to consider preference relations over sets of cardinal greater than $\mathfrak{c}$. Actually, there are useful games in which the cardinal of the set of strategies is greater than $\mathfrak{c}$. For instance, McKinsey (1952: 356) describes a two-person game in which the common set F of pure strategies is a function space, the class of integrable functions defined over the closed interval $[0, 1] \subset \mathbb{R}$. The problem with which McKinsey was concerned was that of defining the appropriate set of events for a probability space having F as sample space, in order to define the mixed strategies of the game. Our problem is to determine if there is a universal numerical system for the class $\mathcal{M}$ of simple strict orders containing spaces of cardinal greater than $\mathfrak{c}$. The solution of this problem is provided by the following theorem.

2.3.2 Theorem

The class $\mathcal{M}$ of all simple strict orderings contains a $\mathcal{M}$-universal and $\mathcal{M}$-homogeneous relational system of power κ for every transfinite cardinal κ. This system is unique up to isomorphism.

PROOF: We beginning by observing that the class $\mathcal{M}$ of simple strictly ordered sets is an elementary class, since it is precisely the class of models of sentence σ_0:

$$\begin{aligned}&\forall x \forall y (xPy \rightarrow \neg yPx) \wedge \\ &\quad \wedge \forall x \forall y \forall z ((xPy \wedge yPz) \rightarrow xPz)) \wedge \\ &\qquad \wedge \forall x \forall y ((x \neq y) \rightarrow (xPy \vee yPx)).\end{aligned}$$

A particular subclass of $\mathcal{M}$ is the class $\mathcal{D}$ of all dense strictly ordered sets without endpoints, which are those structures that, in addition to σ_0, also satisfy σ_1:

$$\begin{aligned} &\forall x \forall y(xPy \rightarrow \exists z(xPz \wedge zPy))\wedge \\ &\quad \wedge \forall x \exists y\, xPy \wedge \\ &\qquad \wedge \forall x \exists y\, yPx. \end{aligned}$$

$\mathcal{D}$ is an elementary class that has no finite models and therefore, by the LST theorem, it contains relational systems of arbitrarily large power. This establishes that $\mathcal{M}$ contains relational systems of arbitrarily large power.

Clearly, if $\mathfrak{A} \in \mathcal{M}$ and $\mathfrak{B} \simeq \mathfrak{A}$, then $\mathfrak{B} \equiv \mathfrak{A}$ and so $\mathfrak{B} \models \sigma$, which implies that $\mathfrak{B} \in \mathcal{M}$.

An atomic formula of the theory of simple strictly ordered sets is of the form Pxy or $x = y$. Clearly, if any of these formulas, or their negations, are satisfied by a structure $\mathfrak{B}$ with elements of a set $A \subset B$, then they are satisfied by the structure $\mathfrak{A}$ having A as domain, and its order relation being the restriction of that of $\mathfrak{B}$ to A. In other words, the models of the theory satisfy Robinson's model completeness test.[7] Hence, if $\langle \mathfrak{A}_\zeta : \zeta < \xi \rangle$ is any chain of relational systems such that, for every $\mathfrak{A}_\zeta \in \mathcal{M}$, $\mathfrak{A}_\zeta \subset \mathfrak{A}_\varsigma$, we have that $\mathfrak{A}_\zeta \prec \mathfrak{A}_\varsigma$. Thus, the union $\mathfrak{A} = \bigcup_{\zeta<\xi} \mathfrak{A}_\zeta$ is an elementary extension of each $\mathfrak{A}_\zeta$ and so it is in $\mathcal{M}$.

Let $\mathfrak{A} \in \mathcal{M}$ and let $\mathfrak{C}$ be a subsystem of $\mathfrak{A}$ of cardinal $< \kappa$. Since every relational system $\mathfrak{A} \in \mathcal{M}$ has only one relation (namely P), theorem 3.1 in Bell and Slomson (1969: 80) implies that there is a structure $\mathfrak{B} \in \mathcal{M}$ of cardinal $< \kappa$ such that $\mathfrak{C} \subset \mathfrak{B} \subset \mathfrak{A}$.

Finally, let $\mathfrak{A}, \mathfrak{B}, \mathfrak{C} \in \mathcal{M}$, f_0 and imbedding of $\mathfrak{A}$ into $\mathfrak{B}$, and f_1 an imbedding of $\mathfrak{A}$ into $\mathfrak{C}$. Since $f_0(\mathfrak{A}) \simeq f_1(\mathfrak{A})$, the diagram $(\mathfrak{B}, a)_{a \in B \cap C}$ of $\mathfrak{B}$ restricted to $B \cap C$ is elementarily equivalent to the diagram $(\mathfrak{C}, a)_{a \in B \cap C}$ of $\mathfrak{C}$ restricted to $B \cap C$. This implies the existence of a model $\mathfrak{D} \in \mathcal{M}$ and imbeddings g_0 of $\mathfrak{B}$ into $\mathfrak{D}$ and g_1 of $\mathfrak{B}$ into $\mathfrak{D}$ such that

$$g_0 \restriction B \cap C = g_1 \restriction B \cap C.$$

This establishes that $\mathcal{M}$ is a κ-class and so, by Jónsson's theorem,[8] $\mathcal{M}$ contains a $\mathcal{M}$-homogeneous, $\mathcal{M}$-universal structure of cardinal κ which is unique up to isomorphism. □

Actually, it is easy to see that the $\mathcal{M}$-universal and $\mathcal{M}$-homogeneous orderings of power $\aleph_\alpha$ must be Hausdorff's η_α-sets;[9] that is to say, simple strict orderings $\mathfrak{A} = \langle A, P \rangle$ having these two characteristics:

(1) For any two subsets A_1 and A_2 such that **card**$(A_1) < \aleph_\alpha$, **card**$(A_2) < \aleph_\alpha$ and $A_1 < A_2$ (i.e. $a_1 < a_2$ for every $a_1 \in A_1$ and $a_2 \in A_2$), there exists an element $a \in A$ with $a_1 < a < a_2$;

(2) A is neither cofinal nor coinitial with any set of power less than $\aleph_\alpha$. Thus, A has neither a first nor a last element.

The remaining preference structures may receive analogous treatment. Yet, many properties of preferences, like continuity or nonsatiation, cannot be expressed by means of first-order formulas. Even less can most of the economic theories be expressed in first-order languages. That is why it is necessary to introduce a more general notion of structure, which is the purpose of the next two sections.

2.4 Theory of classes

Following Ackerman (1956), Frederick A. Muller (2001) has proposed a theory of classes that seems to be an adequate conceptual framework for contemporary mathematics, including category theory. In this section I provide a modification of this theory fit for the methodology of empirical disciplines, since, in contradistinction to Muller's version, it makes room for urelements. The variables of the language of Muller's theory – labeled ARC because it is a generalization of that of Ackerman (1956) which includes a choice axiom – take as values only classes, where these objects are implicitly defined by the axioms. What this means is that the domain of discourse of this language is a philosophical category that cannot be conceived as a class itself, let alone a set. Hence, the objects the theory deals with are entities that satisfy the English predicate '*X is a class*', which expresses an intuitive notion with plenty of applications. Its meaning is further clarified by means of the given axioms.

The methodology of any empirical science requires a theory of classes with variables taking as values also urelements. Roughly speaking, urelements are entities which are not classes, and so the English predicate '*X is an urelement*' is roughly coextensive with what the Latin tradition called *ens* (being). Nevertheless, it is problematic to identify '*X is an urelement*' with '*X* is a being' since for the Latin this last predicate excluded abstract entities (*ens rationis*). Thus, in order to avoid complications, the set of urelements must be specified in each application of the theory.

Hence, in the modified theory – which I shall call ARCU – individual variables can take as values classes or urelements. ARCU is exactly identical to ARC, but for a modification of the axiom of completeness and the addition of a couple of axioms that characterize the urelements and distinguish them from classes. The original version of the completeness axiom expressed that every element of a set is a set; my version expresses that every element of a set is a set or an urelement. Thus the parameters or non-logical symbols of ARCU are $\in$, V, and U, where V is the class of all sets and U the set of all urelements.

A central notion of ARCU is that of a pure or safe predicate. Roughly speaking, $\varphi(x_1,\ldots, x_n)$ is a pure or safe predicate iff φ contains only terms for sets or urelements but V does not occur in φ. In order to be more precise, let us define a *set term* as the name of a set whose existence is derivable from the axioms. An urelement term is obviously a designator of an urelement, introduced as an individual constant. A *pure* or *safe* predicate is one in which all the terms occurring in it are set or urelement terms.

The first axiom of ARCU is more a general version of the axiom of extensionality.

2.4.1 Axiom (EXT)

Classes having the same elements are identical:

$$\forall x \forall y\,((x \notin U \wedge y \notin U) \rightarrow (\forall z(z \in x \leftrightarrow z \in y) \rightarrow x = y)).$$

Notice that this axiom asserts a sufficient condition for the identity of individuals other than urelements. Nonetheless, it does not guarantee the existence of any class. Actually, since the theory deals both with classes and urelements, it is necessary to stipulate some axiom guaranteeing in an explicit manner that both U and V are classes and not urelements. The following two axioms serve this purpose.

2.4.2 Axiom (CLEX)

Both U and V have elements but none in common. As a matter of fact, no urelement is a set, and no set is an urelement:

$$\exists x\, x \in V \wedge \exists y\, y \in U \wedge \neg \exists z(z \in V \wedge z \in U).$$

The next axiom provides a necessary condition to be an urelement: to lack elements. The only class that lacks elements is the empty class, but then elements are characterized as individuals other than the empty class that have no elements.

2.4.3 Axiom (U)

Anything having elements is not an urelement:

$$\forall x(\exists y\, y \in x \rightarrow x \notin U).$$

The next axiom, the axiom of class separation, provides a powerful method to prove the existence of classes.

2.4.4 Axiom (CLSEP)

For any wff $\varphi(x)$ and every class y there exists a class z containing exactly those elements of y that satisfy $\varphi(x)$:

$$\forall y(y \notin U \rightarrow \exists z(z \notin U \wedge \forall x(x \in z \leftrightarrow (x \in y \wedge \phi(x))))).$$

Class z is designated by the term '$\{x \in y | \phi(x)\}$', which is read thus: "the class of all x in y such that $\varphi(x)$".

By virtue of axioms CLEX and U, we know that V is a class. Out of the existence of this class we can prove the existence of a very important one: the empty class.

2.4.5 *Theorem*

There is a class that has no elements

PROOF: Since V is a class and '$x \neq x$' is a wff, a universally specified instance of CLSEP implies the following:

$$\exists z(z \notin U \wedge \forall x(x \in z \leftrightarrow (x \in V \wedge x \neq x))).$$

But this sentence asserts the existence of a class that has no elements. □

2.4.6 *Definition*

We say that z is an *empty class* iff z is not an urelement and has no elements:

$$\textbf{empty}\, z \equiv_d z \notin U \wedge \forall x(x \in z \leftrightarrow (x \in V \wedge x \neq x)).$$

2.4.7 *Theorem*

There is only one empty class.

PROOF: Suppose that both x and y are empty classes. If $x \neq y$, EXT implies

$$\neg\forall z\,(z \in x \leftrightarrow z \in y),$$

from which it follows

$$\exists z\,(\neg(z \in x \rightarrow z \in y) \vee \neg(z \in y \rightarrow z \in x))$$

or

$$\exists z\,((z \in x \wedge z \notin y) \vee (z \in y \wedge z \notin x)).$$

Hence, either x has an element or y has it. Since both x and y were by hypothesis empty, this shows that there can be no more than one empty class. □

As usual, the empty class is designated by the symbol $\varnothing$.

2.4.8 *Definition*

If y is a class, we say that x is a *subclass* of y, in symbols $x \subset y$, iff x is not an urelement and every element of x an element of y:

$$x \subset y \equiv_d x \notin U \wedge \forall z(z \in x \rightarrow z \in y).$$

2.4.9 *Theorem*

The empty class is a subclass of every class:

$$\forall x\, \varnothing \subset x.$$

PROOF: For any individual y it is the case that $y \notin \varnothing$. From here it tautologically follows that

$$y \notin \varnothing \vee y \in x$$

or, which is equivalent,

$$y \in \varnothing \rightarrow y \in x. \square$$

The completeness axiom asserts that subsets of sets are sets, and elements of sets other than urelements are also sets.

2.4.10 Axiom (COMPL)

The class V of all sets is complete; that is to say, every element of a set which is not an urelement is a set and every subclass of a set is a set:

$$\forall x \forall y((x \in V \wedge ((y \in x \wedge y \notin U) \vee y \subset x)) \rightarrow y \in V).$$

2.4.11 Theorem

The empty class is a set:

$$\varnothing \in V.$$

PROOF: $\varnothing$ is a subclass of every class, in particular of the classes that are sets. Hence, by COMPL, it is a set. $\square$

The following is the axiom schema of set existence. It allows the proof of the existence of sets by means of pure predicates.

2.4.12 Axiom (ACKSET)

For any pure predicate $\varphi(x)$, if the only individuals that satisfy $\varphi(x)$ are sets or urelements, then these individuals are grouped as a set:

$$\forall x(\phi(x) \rightarrow (x \in V \vee x \in U)) \rightarrow \exists y(y \in V \wedge \forall z(z \in y \leftrightarrow \phi(z))).$$

Set y thus formed can be denoted by '$\{x|\phi(x)\}$'.

2.4.13 Theorem

For any sets or urelements x and y, there exists the set that contains precisely x and y:

$$\forall x \forall y(((x \in V \vee x \in U) \wedge (y \in V \vee y \in U)) \rightarrow \exists z(z \in V \wedge \forall u(u \in z \leftrightarrow (u = x \vee u = y)))).$$

PROOF: Let x and y be arbitrary sets or urelements, and $\varphi(u)$ the condition '$u = x \vee u = y$'. Clearly, $\varphi(u)$ is a pure condition and the elements that satisfy it must be sets or urelements, so that (by ACKSET), the same form a set z. □

Set z is known as "the disordered pair x and y" and is also denoted as '$\{x, y\}$' or '$\{y, x\}$'. If $x = y$, the set is written as $\{x\}$ and is called *the singleton of* x.

2.4.14 Definition

For any set x we define the *intersection* of the elements of x, $\cap x$, as the class that contains as elements those individuals belonging to all the elements of x:

$$\bigcap x \equiv_d \{y | \forall z(z \in x \rightarrow y \in z)\}.$$

2.4.15 Theorem

For any set x, $\cap$x exists and, moreover, it is a set.

PROOF: Let x be a set and let $\varphi(y)$ be the condition '$\forall z(z \in x \rightarrow y \in z)$'. Clearly, any individual y that satisfies it is element of a class that in turns belongs to a set. Hence, y has to be a set or an urelement and ACKSET is applicable. It follows that

$$\exists u(u \in V \wedge \forall y(y \in u \leftrightarrow \phi(y))).$$

But set u is none other than $\cap x$. □

The next one is the axiom of regularity.

2.4.16 Axiom (REG)

Every nonempty set has an element that has no elements in common with itself:

$$\forall x((x \in V \wedge x \neq \varnothing) \rightarrow \exists y(y \in x \wedge \neg\exists z(z \in y \wedge z \in x))).$$

An immediate consequence of this axiom is the following:

2.4.17 Theorem

For every set x: $x \notin x$.

PROOF If x is a set, then the singleton $\{x\}$ is also a set, by virtue of theorem 2.4.13. Therefore, since $\{x\}$ is nonempty, there is a y such that $y \in \{x\}$ and $\{x\} \cap y = \{x\} \cap x = \varnothing$. But this implies that $x \notin x$. □

2.4.18 Definition

Set x is a *disjointed set*, **disy** x, iff x is nonempty, the elements of x are sets, $\varnothing \notin x$, and its elements are pairwise disjoint:

$$\forall y(y \in x \rightarrow y \in V) \wedge \varnothing \notin x \wedge \forall y \forall z((y \in x \wedge z \in x) \rightarrow y \cap z = \varnothing).$$

This definition provides the tools for the introduction of the last axiom of ARCU.

2.4.19 Axiom (c)

For every disjointed set x, there exists a nonempty choice set; i.e. a set containing exactly one element of each of the sets belonging to x:

$$\forall x(\mathbf{disy}x \rightarrow (\exists y y \in V \land \forall u \forall z(u \in z \land z \in x \rightarrow (u \in y \land \forall v(v \in y \cap z \rightarrow v = u))))).$$

As it has been shown in García de la Sienra (2008), ARCU, the theory of classes comprising axioms EXT, CLEX, U, CLSEP, COMPL, ACKSET, REG, and C, implies ZFC, Zermelo-Fraenkel's set theory with the axiom of choice. It is also shown thereby that it can be used to formulate the axioms of category theory, and so it proves to be an appropriate framework to formulate a general concept of structure, an endeavor to which we now turn.

2.5 The general concept of structure

Models of first-order logic quickly become insufficient and inadequate for mathematics and the empirical sciences. For instance, probability spaces cannot be seen as such models, since the universe of the structure must be the sample space, in order for the language to be able to talk about elementary events. But then the field of definition of any relation must be a subset of some Cartesian product of the set of elementary events. This precludes the set of events, which is a family of subsets of the sample space, and the probability measure, which is a function from the set of events into a numerical set (the interval [0, 1]), from being components of the structure.

Hence, we need a more general and powerful concept of structure. One such concept was inspired by the Bourbaki group with its concept of structure, but was developed by Balzer, Moulines, and Sneed (1987), and Da Costa and Chuaqui (1988). I shall freely borrow from both sources, as I deem convenient.

Roughly speaking, a structure is a list of sets together with relations built over such sets. Hence, from an ontological point of view, a structure is just a point in the class V of all sets. For instance, a probability space is a list $\langle S, \mathcal{F}, P \rangle$, where S is a nonempty set called sample space, $\mathcal{F}$ is a ring of sets over S, and P is a function from $\mathcal{F}$ into [0, 1]. In some sense, S is the principal set of the structure, but P cannot be characterized without the interval [0, 1] of real numbers. It is usual to call numerical sets used in the characterization of the principal sets 'auxiliary sets'. They are distinguished from principal sets in that they are invariant under the canonical transformations (isomorphisms) of the structures. For instance, even though sample spaces can be wildly diverse, all probability measures of the (standard) probability spaces must have their values in [0, 1].

Sometimes, in the empirical sciences, the distinction between principal and auxiliary sets becomes intuitive: principal sets contain empirical objects or name the objects the theory deals with (even though these objects may be idealized), whereas auxiliary sets are invariant sets of numbers or other mathematical objects used to represent magnitudes of objects pertaining to the principal sets.

In order to specify the precise set-theoretical nature of the components of a structure, and to define precisely what a structure is, we need the rather abstract notion of a type of n species or n-type. This is defined recursively as follows.

2.5.1 Definition

Let the sequence 1,..., n of positive integers be given. The set of *types of n species* or *n-types* is given as follows.

(1) For each positive integer $i \leq n$, i is a n-type.
(2) If σ is a n-type then $(\sigma, 0)$ is a n-type.
(3) If σ and τ are n-types then (σ, τ) is a n-type.

Notice that if (σ, τ) is a type, then $\sigma \neq 0$. A type of the form $(\sigma, 0)$ is intended to represent the power set of objects of type σ, whereas one of the form (σ, τ) the Cartesian product of objects of types σ and τ. More precisely, we have the following definition.

2.5.2 Definition

Let $\mathbf{D} = (D_1, \ldots, D_n)$ be a sequence of sets and σ a type of n species. Define the set $T_\sigma(\mathbf{D})$ of *objects of type* σ over $X_1,\ldots, X_n$ by means of the following conditions:

(1) If $\sigma = i$ with $1 \leq i \leq n$ then $T_\sigma(\mathbf{D}) = X_i$.
(2) If $\sigma = (\tau, 0)$ then $T_\sigma(\mathbf{D}) = \mathbf{power}\,(T_\tau(\mathbf{D}))$.
(3) If $\sigma = (\tau, \rho)$ with $\rho \neq 0$ then

$$T_\sigma(\mathbf{D}) = T_\tau(\mathbf{D}) \times T_\rho(\mathbf{D}).$$

(4) An object R *is of type* σ *over* $\mathbf{D}$ if $R \in T_\sigma(\mathbf{D})$.

Hence a n-type is one of the sets D_i ($i \leq n$) or some set-theoretical object built out of the sets D_i, namely some power set or some Cartesian product. In the example of the probability space, there is only one principal set, the sample space $S = D_1$, and only one auxiliary set, the interval $D_2 = [0, 1]$ of real numbers. Since $\mathcal{F}$ is a family of subsets of X_1, it is an element of $\mathbf{power}\,(\mathbf{power}\,(D_1)) = T_{((1,0),0)}(\mathbf{D})$. On the other hand, notice that P is the set of all pairs of the form (F, r), where F is an event in $\mathcal{F}$ and r is a number in $D_2 = [0, 1]$. Hence, $(F, r) \in \mathbf{power}(D_1) \times D_2$ and so $P \subset \mathbf{power}(D_1) \times D_2$ or

$$P \in \mathbf{power}(\mathbf{power}(D_1) \times D_2) = \mathbf{power}(T_{(1,0)}(\boldsymbol{D}) \times T_2(\boldsymbol{D}))$$
$$= \mathbf{power}(T_{((1,0),2)}(\boldsymbol{D}))$$
$$= T_{(((1,0),2),0)}(\boldsymbol{D}).$$

Thus, by means of the concept of type of n species we are in position to define one of the central notions of this work.

2.5.3 Definition

$\mathfrak{A}$ is a *system* or *structure* iff there exist $\boldsymbol{D}$, $\boldsymbol{R}$, $\boldsymbol{\sigma}$, and nonnegative integers p, n, and m, such that

(0) $\mathfrak{A} = \langle \boldsymbol{D}, \boldsymbol{R} \rangle$;
(1) $\boldsymbol{D}$ is a finite sequence of nonempty sets $D_1, \ldots, D_p, D_{p+1}, \ldots, D_n$, with $1 \leq p \leq n$;
(2) $\boldsymbol{\sigma}$ is a sequence $\sigma_1, \ldots, \sigma_m$ of types of n species;
(3) $\boldsymbol{R}$ is a finite sequence $R_1, \ldots, R_m$ of sets such that $R_i \in T_{\sigma_i}(\boldsymbol{D})$ for every i $(1 \leq i \leq m)$.

Some of the sets D_i, those labeled $D_{p+1}, \ldots, D_n$ are auxiliary, but there may be no auxiliary sets at all (in which case $p = n$). Clearly, a type of structure is completely determined by the length of the sequence $\boldsymbol{D}$, the distinction between principal and auxiliary sets, and the types $\boldsymbol{\sigma}$. Hence, and we are entitled to define the type of a structure as the triple $(n, p, \boldsymbol{\sigma})$. Two structures $\mathfrak{A}$ and $\mathfrak{B}$ are *similar* iff they are of the same type and have the same number of auxiliary sets.

It is possible to point out a minimum set to which all species belong. This can be done by means of the notion of universe of rank k over X. Let $D = D_1 \cup \cdots \cup D_n$ and define

$$V_0(X) = D$$
$$V_{k+1}(D) = V_k(D) \cup \mathbf{power}(V_k(D)).$$

$V_k(D)$ is the *universe of sets of rank k over D*. It is easy to see that $T_\sigma(D) \in V_k(D)$ from a certain $k < \omega$ on. Given a sequence $\boldsymbol{\sigma} = (\sigma_1 \ldots, \sigma_m)$ of types of n species, it can be seen that there is a k such that $T_{\sigma_i}(D) \in V_k(D)$ for every $i = 1, \ldots, m$, but $T_{\sigma_i}(D) \notin V_k(D)$ for some i. For instance, in order to define a certain probability space $\mathfrak{A} = \langle S, \mathcal{F}, P \rangle$, we must take D as the union $D_1 \cup D_2$, with $D_1 = S$ and $D_2 = [0, 1]$. Besides the points in $V_0(D)$, $V_1(D)$ contains all events F and $[0, 1]$ itself. Besides $V_1(D)$, $V_2(D)$ contains all pairs (F, r) and so $V_3(D)$ contains all subsets of such pairs, namely all subsets of $\mathcal{F} \times [0,1]$. Thus, S, $\mathcal{F}$ and P belong to $V_4(D)$ and the triple $\langle S, \mathcal{F}, P\rangle$ belongs to $V_5(D)$. This means that $\mathfrak{A}$ is a point in $V_5(D)$ and that the 'constants' S, $\mathcal{F}$, P are elements of the universe $B = V_5(D)$ of the first-order structure $\mathfrak{B} = \langle B, \in, S, \mathcal{F}, P\rangle$.

Nevertheless, it is more convenient and profitable to define the required type of structure as a point of V, in the language of ARCU, by means of characterizations; i.e. sentences of ARCU in informal language that specify the exact characteristics of the primitive terms. For instance, instead of merely saying that the probability measure P is of type $T_{(((1,0),2),0)}(\boldsymbol{D})$, we may stipulate that P is function from $\mathcal{F}$ into [0, 1]. Obviously, such a characterization implies the corresponding typification but it has the advantage of being more specific and easy to read than the clumsier and more general typification. A characterization, as its name indicates, is just a declaration that specifies the nature of some set-theoretical object. Since the concept of characterization is so important, it is convenient to define it in a precise way.

2.5.4 Definition

Let $\mathfrak{A} = \langle D_1, \ldots, D_n, R_1, \ldots, R_m\rangle$ be a structure of type $(n, p, \boldsymbol{\sigma})$. A *characterization* is a formula φ in the language of ARCU that contains, besides set-theoretical symbols and symbols for base sets, only symbols for precisely one of the relations $R_1, \ldots, R_m$.

A *set-theoretical predicate* is a formula of the form '$\mathfrak{A}$ is a $\mathcal{P}$', of the language of ARCU, asserting "$\mathfrak{A}$ is a system of similarity type $(n, p, \boldsymbol{\sigma})$ that satisfies Γ", where Γ is a set of sentences of ARCU. If $\mathfrak{A}$ satisfies $\mathcal{P}$, then $\mathfrak{A}$ is called a $\mathcal{P}$-structure. Every class $\mathcal{M}$ of $\mathcal{P}$-structures has associated with it a certain class of structures which we shall call 'potential models with respect to $\mathcal{M}$'. This is the class of all systems that satisfy all the characterization in Γ. Those formulas in Γ that are not characterizations will be called 'theoretical systematizations'. Clearly, some of these will be properly nomological statements or laws.

In the case of our example, a *probability space* is a triple $\langle S, \mathcal{F}, P\rangle$ (the auxiliary set [0, 1] is omitted) that satisfies the formulas in the set Γ consisting of the following sentences of ARCU:

(1) S is a nonempty set;
(2) $\mathcal{F}$ is a σ-algebra over S;
(3) P is a function from $\mathcal{F}$ into [0, 1];
(4) For every $A, B \in \mathcal{F}$: if $A \cap B = \varnothing$ then $P(A \cup B) = P(A) + P(B)$.

Sentences (1)–(3) are characterizations, while (4) is the fundamental law of probability theory. The class of all systems satisfying sentences (1)–(3) is the class of potential models of probability theory. Hence, probability spaces are those potential models that satisfy law (4): these are the models of probability theory.

Notes

1 The deficiencies of Peano's logic were discussed by Van Heijenoort (1967: 83–5).
2 I take for granted here ARCU, the theory of classes presented in García de la Sienra (2008). Since ARCU implies ZFC, as it is shown thereby, I will quote texts of authors exposing some aspect of the latter when that is convenient.
3 Cf. the definition of order-type and sum of order-types in Kamke (1950: 55–61).
4 Cf. Boolos, Burgess, and Jeffrey (2002: 71).
5 For a thorough exposition of these axioms and rules the reader is referred to Enderton (2001: 109–31).
6 Cf. Skala (1975: 2).
7 Cf. theorem 2.2.9 above, or Bell and Slomson (1969: 191–3).
8 Bell and Slomson (1969: 213).
9 Cf. Hausdorff (1914).

3 The structuralist view of theories

3.1 Origins

The structuralist view of theories (SVT) is a systematic development of Suppes' view of theories, grounded in his representation of them by means of axiomatizations via the definition of a set-theoretical predicate. This representation – which is called extrinsic – is also necessary for the task of providing an intrinsic characterization of the models of a first-order theory by means of axioms belonging to a strictly formalized language. An extrinsic characterization of the models of a scientific theory consists of describing its models in a precise and complete way, within the informal language of set theory. This is tantamount to an informal characterization of its logical structure as a previous step to the formulation of axioms within a formalized language.[1]

The development, started by Joseph D. Sneed (1971), is architectonic and systematic. It provides a map of scientific theories and their interrelationships, history, and applications. Outstanding is its conception of theoretical terms, as relative to a given theory *T* (*T*-theoretical). The present book makes use of SVT in order to provide systematic reconstructions of economic theories. After discussing the basic, intuitive ideas of SVT through a clear, simple, and realistic example drawn from physics, in dialogue with the prevalent (statement) view, this chapter motivates the introduction of the concepts of SVT in an intuitive way. The discussion of the objections raised against it by noted methodologists of economics will have to wait until the doctrine of idealization is introduced.

3.2 The concept and relevance of a metatheory

Every theory is the product of a process of theoretical practice. I shall follow Althusser's (2005: 166–7) beautiful elucidation of the notion of practice:

> By practice in general I shall mean any process of *transformation* of a determinate given raw material into a determinate *product*, a transformation effected by a determinate human labour, using determinate means (of 'production'). In any practice thus conceived, the *determinant* moment (or element) is neither the raw material nor the product, but the practice in the

> narrow sense: the moment of the *labour of transformation* itself, which sets to work, in a specific structure, men, means and a technical method of utilizing the means.

Thus, theoretical practice is a special kind of practice:

> It works on a raw material (representations, concepts, facts) which it is given by other practices, whether 'empirical', 'technical' or 'ideological'. In its most general form theoretical practice does not only include *scientific* theoretical practice, but also pre-scientific theoretical practice, that is, 'ideological' theoretical practice (the forms of 'knowledge' that make up the prehistory of a science, and their 'philosophies').
>
> (Ibid.: 167)

Althusser calls the raw material upon which scientific theoretical practice works 'Generality I', while the product of the process is called 'Generality III'. The means of production in the theoretical practice of science are called 'Generality II', which is "constituted by the corpus of concepts whose more or less contradictory unity constitutes the 'theory' of the science at the (historical) moment under consideration, the 'theory' that defines the field in which all the problems of the science must necessarily be posed" (ibid.: 185). Generality I can be constituted by pre-theoretical ideas and beliefs ("*Vorstellungen*"), or by already scientifically elaborated constructs "which belong nevertheless to an earlier phase of the science (an ex-Generality III). So it is by transforming this Generality I into a Generality III (knowledge) that the science works and produces" (ibid.: 184).

It is important for the philosophy of science that the unity of what Althusser calls 'theory'

> rarely exists in a science in the reflected form of a unified theoretical system. …The explicitly theoretical part proper is very rarely unified in a non-contradictory form. Usually it is made up of regions locally unified in regional theories that coexist in a complex and contradictory whole with a theoretically unreflected unity. This is the extremely complex and contradictory unity which is in action, in each case according to a specific mode, in the labour of theoretical production of each science. For example, in the experimental sciences, this is what constitutes the 'phenomena' into 'facts', this is what poses an existing difficulty in the form of problem, and 'resolves' this problem by locating the theoretico-technical disposition which makes up the real corpus of what an idealist tradition calls 'hypotheses', etc. etc.
>
> (Ibid.: 185, n. 21)

To make explicit the theoretical part and unify it in a non-contradictory form is the task and *raison d'être* of the theoretical practice that consists of the rational reconstruction of scientific theories. The means of production required for this task are clustered in a metatheory, and the result is a unified theoretical system together with explanations as to how this system operates as the main tool of the methodology of the discipline.

Althusser's main purpose in the text I have been quoting is to show that Marx's dialectics is essentially different from Hegel's, and to introduce the idea of a Theory (that he writes with capital T) as the foundation of a general method to transform 'ideological' Generalities I into scientific Generalities III. Hence, Theory would be something like an *ars inveniendi* that can be applied to any discipline in its pre-scientific stage in order to transform it into a scientific one.

Nevertheless, there is in the same text an apparently distinct idea of Theory (also with capital T, something which induces confusion), namely a theory of practices in general, which (Althusser claims) was obtained from Hegel's dialectics by means of an application of the other Theory, the theory of theoretical practices. For he says:

> I shall call Theory (with a capital T), general theory, that is, the Theory of practice in general, itself elaborated on the basis of the Theory of existing theoretical practices (of the sciences), which transforms into 'knowledges' (scientific truths) the ideological product of existing 'empirical' practices (the concrete activity of men). This Theory is the materialist dialectic which is none other than dialectical materialism.
>
> (Ibid.: 168)

Here I am interested in the Theory of theoretical practices, which clearly should be prior to dialectical materialism if it was indeed used by Marx in order to create the latter as a new Generality III. For it is impossible to use *T* as a tool in order to create *T*: the tool must be prior to the product obtained by means of its use in a labor process.

The version that Althusser provides of dialectical materialism (I do not dispute here whether this is an accurate reconstruction of Marx's intentions) is at any rate a substantial ontological theory that many (me included) find less than appealing. Moreover, it looks extremely unsuitable as a theory of science or a theory of the history of science. Clearly, trying to describe in terms of dialectical materialism, say the rise of the new physics as it is done by Cohen (1992), would turn out to be an extravagant *tour de force*. It does not seem natural to explain the rationality of the scientific changes that took place from Copernicus' introduction of the new astronomic system to Newton's dynamic in terms of concepts like "unity of opposites", "principal contradiction", "uneven development", or "overdetermination". Nevertheless, I think that something important and relevant to nowadays philosophy of science, specifically economic methodology, can be obtained from what Marx calls "method of political economy" in the *Grundrisse*. But, if this is the method by means of which Marx was able to overcome Hegel's dialectic and give rise to a radically new theory (as Althusser claimed), then it should be possible to describe the method without resorting to this theory. This I do in Chapter 4.

3.3 The ways of theoretical practice

Althusser's idea of a theoretical practice is one of his perennial accomplishments, but he never developed the theory of such a practice. This theory cannot be but a *philosophy of science*, a *Wissenschaftstheorie*. After clarifying the role of the theory of a discipline in its own theoretical practice, he says that "we must rest content with these schematic gestures and not enter into the dialectic of this theoretical labour. They will suffice for an understanding of the fact that theoretical practice produces Generalities III by the work of Generality II on Generality I" (ibid.: 185). This may have been sufficient for his purpose of showing the novelty of Marx's dialectics vis-à-vis that of Hegel, but it is certainly far from providing a complete, nay, even a sketch of a philosophy of science. Yet, Althusser's insight is important to solve the problems posed in Chapter 1 for the 𝔖-View, namely the *problem of lost beings, the problem of the unavailable stories, and the problem of the lost content.* I think that these problems appear precisely because the *process of production* of the theories is forgotten. A proper rational reconstruction of a scientific process must take into account the problems and motivations that led to the conceptual apparatus of the theory. This implies a description of the phenomena the theory intends to represent and explain.

3.4 A dialogue between the $\mathcal{L}$-view and the 𝔖-view

The Generality II required to rationally reconstruct a scientific theory (taken as a Generality I) is a metatheory of science, a view of what scientific theories are, and a method to represent its variegated aspects and component parts. The standard doctrine of science nowadays, mainly in the field of economic methodology, is what we have called the $\mathcal{L}$-View in Chapter 1. The view that I shall adopt here is known as the structuralist view of theories, which is a rather developed form of the 𝔖-View.

One of the best and most complete presentations of the $\mathcal{L}$-View is due to the distinguished philosopher Mario Bunge. According to Bunge, the specific trait of scientific hypothetical deductive systems is that their sentences contain factual predicates (Bunge 1974a: 61). A factual predicate refers to real beings like physical bodies or spatial regions. For instance, the predicate 'x is a particle', belonging to the context of classical particle mechanics CPM, is factual: it refers to a certain class of physical bodies (or their centers of mass). That is why CPM is a scientific theory, in contradistinction to a purely mathematical or 'formal' one like, say, algebraic topology. Another trait of scientific theories is that they must be subjected to empirical testing, and so they require empirical observation and the collecting of empirical data.

Using the example of CPM I will try to explain why there are reasons to move toward SVT. The first problem the $\mathcal{L}$-View has to face is that not all the sentences of a scientific theory have the same degree of generality. For instance, while Newton's second law '$F = ma$' holds in every system of CPM, there are other laws of CPM, like '$F = -\nabla V$', that are true only in some of them (this last law holds only in systems of particles with conservative forces). Hence, CPM cannot be defined just as the set of all mechanical laws in general.

Bunge tackles this problem postulating a distinction between a general and a special theory. Thus, CPM would comprise a general theory whose constitutive sentences hold in every particle mechanical system, together with other, more specialized theories that include sentences holding only in some such systems. Therefore, a scientific theory is not exactly a set of statements, but rather a family of such sets, connected in certain ways.

This represents a blow to the metamathematical concept of a scientific theory as a mere set of sentences. At any rate, it would seem more appropriate – if we insist in maintaining a statement view of theories – to think of theories as collections of systems of sentences, since the 'general' theory as much as its 'special theories' are integral parts of one and the same theory. For instance, the theory of systems with conservative forces is more special than the theory of mechanical systems with distance-dependent forces, which is in turn more general than the theory of systems of freely falling particles. But all these special theories are specializations of CPM, since they share its conceptual apparatus and '$F = ma$' holds in all of them.

Clearly, if theory T' is more special than theory T, then $T \subseteq T'$. But mere set-theoretical inclusion among families of sentences is not enough to define the specialization relation: according to Bunge, the special sentences introduced in the specializations must be semantically relevant to the assumptions of the more general theory. Roughly speaking, sentence ψ is *semantically relevant* for sentence φ if φ and ψ refer to the same entities and ψ determines, at least in part, the meaning of φ (cf. Bunge 1974a: 76).

If Γ, Γ' are sets of sentences, we say that Γ is *more general* than Γ' (written $\Gamma \rhd \Gamma'$) iff $\Gamma \subseteq \Gamma'$ and, for every $\psi \in \Gamma' \backslash \Gamma$, there exists $\varphi \in \Gamma$ such that ψ is semantically relevant for φ. If $\Gamma \rhd \Gamma'$, we say that Γ' is more special than Γ. The special theories may be called regional.

Being more general is a partial ordering. If Γ_0 is a set of sentences and $\mathcal{G} = \{\Gamma_0, \Gamma_1, \ldots, \Gamma_n\}$ is a family of sets of sentences more special than Γ_0, then $\langle \mathcal{G}, \rhd \rangle$ is a sup-semilattice. Returning to our example, it turns out that there is a set of sentences Γ_0 which are true in every mechanical system, or, more precisely, *define* what a system of classical particle mechanics is, and other sets $\Gamma_1, \ldots, \Gamma_n$ which are more special than Γ_0. From now on we shall think of a scientific theory T, in a first approach, as a sup-semilattice $\langle \mathcal{G}, \rhd \rangle$. The supremum Γ_0 of the lattice will be called the *basic theory-element of theory T*. We shall see, indeed, that every scientific theory has this structure.

If the former disquisitions are correct, it follows that the logical reconstruction of a scientific theory cannot consist merely of the axiomatization of a set of sentences, except in the limiting case in which it does not contain regional theories. Rather, what is required is the axiomatization of a family of sets of sentences. But there are different ways of axiomatizing systems of sentences.[2] Bunge proposes that scientific theories should be axiomatized within a language of first-order logic, pointing out that

> this theory [first-order logic] is necessary and sufficient in order to analyze the concepts, formulas and reasonings that appear in mathematics and science – or rather, to analyze their form. Actually, every mathematical or scientific sentence is, as far as its form is concerned, a formula of that calculus; and every valid reasoning is a particular case of an inferential pattern consecrated by the same theory.
>
> (Bunge 1978: 165; my translation)

We have seen that this position can be defended if we take the language of ARCU as our first-order language and relax it in order to use a more informal language. For the idea of axiomatizing scientific theories, translating them into a formalized language of any order is not convenient:

> The practical folly of such formalization is testified to by the fact that the branches of mathematics needed for physics have not been formalized, and the philosopher intent on formalizing mechanics, for instance, would first have to formalize not only the differential and integral calculus, but also the theory of matrices, the theory of ordinary and partial differential equations, and a good portion of the theory of functions of a real variable.
>
> (Suppes 1954: 244)

The axiomatization of a scientific theory within the language of informal class theory consists of the definition of a set-theoretical predicate $\mathcal{P}$ by means of a list of conditions formulated in that language, whose fulfillment by a structure $\mathfrak{A}$ is both necessary and sufficient to make true the clause '$\mathfrak{A}$ is a $\mathcal{P}$'. Returning to our didactical example, the basic theory-element of CPM can be be axiomatized as follows.

3.4.1 Definition

$\mathfrak{A}$ is a *system of classical particle mechanics* iff there exist P, T, s, m, f_i, such that, for every $p \in P$ and $t \in T$:

(0) $\mathfrak{A} = \langle P, T, s, m, f_1, \ldots, f_n \rangle$.
(1) P is a nonempty set.
(2) T is a closed interval of real numbers.
(3) $s\colon P \times T \to \mathbb{R}^3$ is a vector-valued function such that $d^2s(p, t)/dt^2$ exists.
(4) $m\colon P \times T \to \mathbb{R}^+$ is a real valued function taking as values only positive numbers.
(5) f_i is a functional of i_m arguments with values in $\mathbb{R}^3$.

(6) For every i there exist (scalar and vector) functions $g_{i_1},\ldots, g_{i_m}$ of p and/or t, and/or additional particles, and/or additional instants, such that

$$F = \sum_{i\in\mathbb{N}} f_i(g_{i_1}(p,t\cdots),\cdots,g_{i_m}(p,t,\cdots))$$

is absolutely convergent and

$$F = m(p)\cdot\frac{d^2s}{dt^2}.$$

A quick glance at this system of axioms reveals two well-defined sets of sentences. Axioms (1)–(5) are characterizations of the primitive terms, while (6) is a law properly speaking. This provides the mathematical structure of the basic theory-element, but not its empirical interpretation. This interpretation is not given through axioms, but rather by means of an informal narrative. In the case in point, the empirical intuitive meaning of term P is specified by saying that P must be interpreted as a set of point masses, or macroscopic bodies. Typically, an extensional list of entities is usually supplied in textbooks, but also an intensional description (like "macroscopic bodies not in collision, and not moving at very high speeds with respect to an inertial reference frame"). T is interpreted as an interval of time during which the motion is to be studied. Function s intends to represent the position of the particle in (some subspace of) $\mathbb{R}^3$ with respect to a given reference frame that should not be rotating with respect to the fixed stars. Function m represents the mass of the bodies along time T, and each f_i is a function measuring the force exerted upon each particle in each instant. Notice that endowing with empirical meaning the terms of a theory requires a rather complex narrative that presupposes a lot of information about the entities the theory deals with. This narrative solves the problems of lost beings, unavailable stories, and lost content. A proper logical reconstruction of a scientific theory must be accompanied by a narrative that makes explicit the empirical meaning of the terms. Each kind of application must specify the kind of beings to which the theory is being applied, the specific story behind the application, and in this form the content is made entirely explicit. It is not enough to provide the mathematical structure of the theory, and the physical, economic, biological, or other type of meaning cannot be reduced to mathematical or logical meaning.

In spite of the convenience of using set-theoretical predicates in order to provide axiomatizations of theories, Bunge rejects explicitly the usefulness of the concept of model or structure in the empirical sciences (Bunge 1978: 150–1, 1974b: 9–12). The reason he adduces is, essentially, that empirical theories are not "completely true", since they involve simplifications. But, he adds, the concept of a model would be useful only if the formulas of the theory were satisfied in an exact way by their referents (Bunge 1972: 49).

Let us discuss this notion, in connection with our particular example, and consider the conditions under which Newton's second law (NL) would be exactly satisfied by its referents. According to Bunge (1974a: 52), "the reference class of a quantified formula equals the reference class of the predicate occurring in the formula". According to this rule, the reference class of NL is the reference class of the binary predicate '=', namely the specific set over which the identity relation is defined, which in this case is the vector space $\mathbb{R}^3$ over the field of real numbers. Thus, NL is exactly satisfied by its referents iff, for every particle $p \in P$ and every instant $t \in T$, vector ds^2/dt^2 multiplied by scalar $m(p, t)$ is strictly identical to vector $F = \sum_{i \in N} f_i(g_{i_1}(p, t \ldots), \ldots, g_{i_m}(p, t, \ldots))$, where $m(p, t)$ is the *exact and true* measure of the mass of particle p at instant t, $s(p, t)$ is the *exact and true* position of particle p at t, and F is the sum of the *exact and true* values of all the forces acting upon p at t.

One problem that the former approach has is that the idea of an exact and true value of a magnitude does not have a clear meaning, given the continuous random fluctuations of the magnitudes.[3] But Bunge takes these variations into account pointing out that the magnitudes of the concrete systems have an exact and true value *in each instant* with respect to a system of measurement units (Bunge 1969: 773–80). That is why, for Bunge, "all theoretical sentences are, in the best cases, good approximations – and we expect we may improve upon them" (Bunge 1974b: 105). What all this boils down to is that a theoretical sentence is only approximately satisfied by the true and exact values of their corresponding magnitudes. This implies that a relational structure whose functions assign to the given entities the true and exact values of the relevant magnitudes could not be a model of the theory.

Representing theories by means of relational structures does not preclude seeing theoretical sentences as approximations to unknown truths about the world. It is only a way of representing how the practice of the sciences is actually carried out, at least in some of its aspects. Actually, just as many people speak in prose without knowing it, scientists build models unaware of the fact that they are doing so. Let us take a simple example to illustrate this claim.

Consider a typical textbook problem in classical mechanics, the problem of explaining the motion of a brick sliding on an inclined plane; that is to say, the problem of obtaining, by means of Newton's laws, a quantitative description of the motion of brick p along the inclined plane. Now, suppose that the plane has a length of 60 cm and forms an angle α with respect to the horizontal. The brick weighs $W = 1$ kilopond and slides from position A to B (see Figure 3.1).

In order to solve the problem, a reference frame is fixed with rectangular coordinates xyz, assuming that the motion takes place in the plane yz (see Figure 3.2). The time that it takes for p to pass from $A(0, 0, z)$ to $B(0, y, 0)$ is represented by means of an interval $T = [0, t^*]$ of real numbers, where t^* is a magnitude, to be determined numerically, that indicates the number of seconds that the motion lasts.

The problem is solved once we get a vector function $s(p, t)$ that gives the position of p, on segment AB, for each second $t \in T$. The assumption that is practically

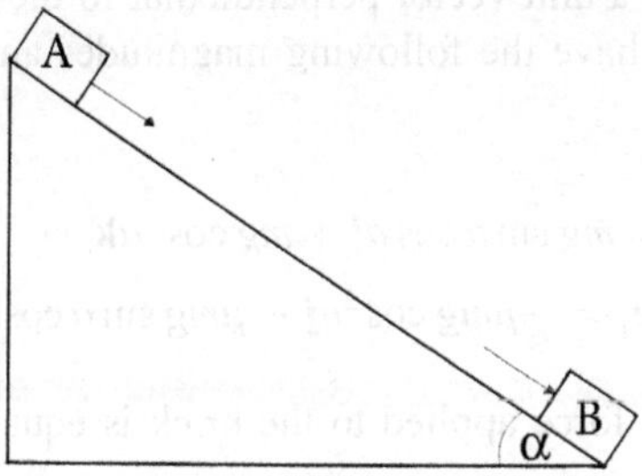

Figure 3.1 Brick sliding on an inclined plane

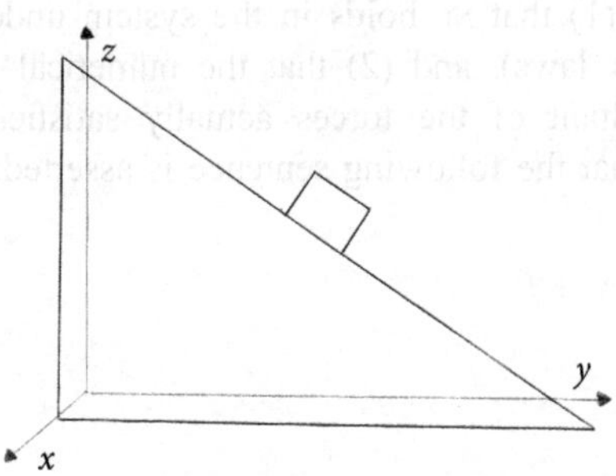

Figure 3.2 Reference system for the plane

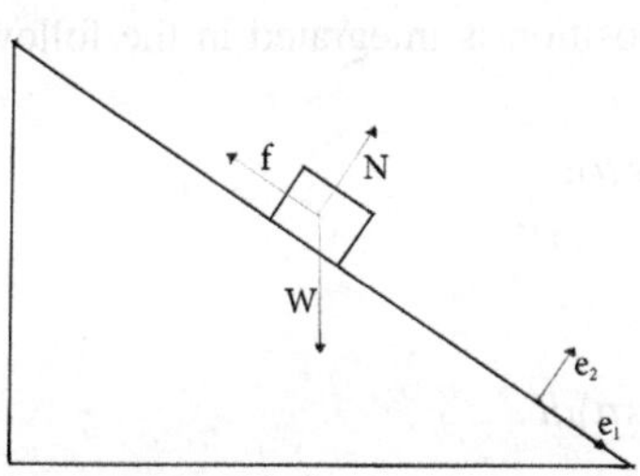

Figure 3.3 Forces operating on the brick

made by the physicists[4] is that there are only three forces acting upon p: force W (the weight of the brick) directed to the center of the earth and orthogonal to plane xy; force N, normal to the inclined plane, which is the force that the plane exerts upon the brick; and the force of friction f, opposed to the motion (Figure 3.3). Clearly, this assumption is an idealization, since it is neglecting the many other forces acting upon the brick. Now, if μ is the friction coefficient, $\mathbf{e}_1 = (0, \cos\alpha, \sin\alpha)$ is a unit vector parallel to the inclined plane, and

$\mathbf{e}_2 = (0, \sin\alpha, \cos\alpha)$ is a unit vector perpendicular to the same, by trigonometry we find that the forces have the following magnitudes and directions:

$$\begin{aligned} W &= -mg\mathbf{k} \\ N &= mg\cos\alpha\mathbf{e}_2 = mg\sin\alpha\cos\alpha\mathbf{j} + mg\cos^2\alpha\mathbf{k} \\ f &= -\mu mg\cos\alpha\mathbf{e}_1 = -\mu mg\cos^2\alpha\mathbf{j} + \mu mg\sin\alpha\cos\alpha\mathbf{k}. \end{aligned}$$

Therefore, the resultant force applied to the brick is equal to

$$W + N + f = mg(\sin\alpha - \mu\cos\alpha)\mathbf{e}_1.$$

We have reached now the crucial point of our example. This point is the following: once a specific formula for the forces is obtained, the physicist makes two assumptions; namely (1) that NL holds in the system under consideration (and eventually some other laws), and (2) that the numerical value of the specific formula for the resultant of the forces actually satisfies these laws. In the example this means that the following sentence is asserted:

$$m\frac{d^2}{dt^2}s\mathbf{e}_1 = W + N + f$$

or

$$\begin{aligned} \frac{d^2}{d^t}s\mathbf{e}_1 &= g\sin\alpha\mathbf{e}_1 - \mu g\cos\alpha\mathbf{e}_1 \\ &= g(\sin\alpha - \mu\cos\alpha)\mathbf{e}_1. \end{aligned}$$

From this last formula position is integrated in the following way:

$$\frac{dv}{dt} = g(\sin\alpha - \mu\cos\alpha);$$

thus,

$$dv = g(\sin\alpha - \mu\cos\alpha)dt$$

and so (since $v = 0$ and $a = 0$ at $t = 0$, I omit the integration constants)

$$\begin{aligned} v &= \int dv \\ &= \int g(\sin\alpha - \mu\cos\alpha)dt \\ &= g(\sin\alpha - \mu\cos\alpha)t; \end{aligned}$$

that is to say,

$$\frac{ds}{dt} = g(\sin\alpha - \mu\cos\alpha)t.$$

Therefore,

$$ds = g(\sin\alpha - \mu\cos\alpha)t\,dt$$

and so,

$$\begin{aligned} s &= \int ds \\ &= \int g(\sin\alpha - \mu\cos\alpha)t\,dt \\ &= \frac{1}{2}g(\sin\alpha - \mu\cos\alpha)t^2; \end{aligned}$$

from where it is finally obtained,

$$s\mathbf{e}_1 = \frac{1}{2}g(\sin\alpha - \mu\cos\alpha)t^2\mathbf{e}_1$$

The last formula provides the vector function of the position we were looking for. It is possible to obtain experimentally, out of it, a numerical value of the friction coefficient μ. The brick is left to slide several times, and we observe the distance from A to the brick at a given instant, say $t = 1$. If this distance is (say) 10 cm, then we take the value of constant g (981.4 cm/s^2) and, substituting and solving for μ, we get $\mu = 0.553$.

Once the value of μ is obtained, it is possible to compute the total duration of the motion of the brick by means of the position function. Solving for t we get

$$t = \left[\frac{2s}{(\sin\alpha - \mu\cos\alpha)}\right]^{1/2}$$

But, since the total distance traversed by the brick is a known datum (50 cm), the whole duration of the motion is found to be 2.198 s.[5] The available empirical data allow us also to compute the acting forces upon the brick. Since the weight of the brick is 1 kilopond = 981,400 dynes, its mass is equal to 1,000 grams, and so we can express the forces acting upon the brick as follows:

$$\begin{aligned} W &= \langle 0, 0, -mg\rangle \\ &= \langle 0, 0, -981.4 \cdot 10^3\rangle \end{aligned}$$

$$\begin{aligned} N &= \langle 0, mg\sin\alpha\cos\alpha, mg\cos^2\alpha\rangle \\ &= \langle 0, 490.7\sqrt{0.75}\cdot 10^3, 736.05\cdot 10^3\rangle \end{aligned}$$

$$\begin{aligned} f &= \langle 0, -\mu mg\cos^2\alpha, \mu mg\sin\alpha\cos\alpha\rangle \\ &= \langle 0, -407.03565\cdot 10^3, 271.3571\cdot\sqrt{0.75}\cdot 10^3\rangle. \end{aligned}$$

In this way we have obtained the structure $\mathfrak{A} = \langle P, T, s, m, f \rangle$, where p is the brick and

$$P = \{p\}$$
$$T = [0, 2.198]$$
$$s(p,t) = \tfrac{1}{2} g(\sin \alpha \mu \cos \alpha) t^2 \mathbf{e}_1$$
$$m(p) = 1000\,\text{gms.}$$
$$f(p, t, 1) = \langle 0, 0, -981.4 \cdot 10^3 \rangle$$
$$f(p,t,2) = \langle 0, 490.7 \cdot \sqrt{0.75} \cdot 10^3, 736.05 \cdot 10^3 \rangle$$
$$f(p,t,3) = \langle 0, -407.03565 \cdot 10^3, 271.3571 \cdot \sqrt{0.75} \cdot 10^3 \rangle$$
$$f(p, t, i) = \langle 0, 0, 0 \rangle \text{ for } i > 3.$$

It is easy to see that $\mathfrak{A}$ is a model of CPM. Actually, the resultant force (approximating up to ten millionths) is

$$\begin{aligned} \textstyle\sum_{i \in N} f(p,t,i) &= W + N + f \\ &= \langle 0, 17.9230156 \cdot 10^3, 10.3478579 \cdot 10^3 \rangle; \end{aligned}$$

while a simple calculations shows that

$$\begin{aligned} m \frac{d^2}{dt^2} s\mathbf{e}_1 &= mg \sin \alpha \mathbf{e}_1 - \mu mg \cos \alpha \mathbf{e}_l \\ &= \langle 0, 17.9230156 \cdot 10^3, 10.3478579 \cdot 10^3 \rangle. \end{aligned}$$

Thus, NL is exactly satisfied by its referents, precisely because it is assumed to be so, in order to integrate the motion out of the forces. Quite a different thing is the description of the motion obtained by means other than Newton's laws. It is clear that in classical mechanics forces are taken as the (efficient) causes of motion. Typically, a kinematical concept 'merely' provides a description of some phenomenon, whereas the dynamical one provides an explanation of the phenomenon in terms of certain relevant causes. In the example considered above, a kinematical representation of the inclined plane is just a description of the motion, obtained from a series of observations, of the brick sliding along the plane. The dynamical representation, on the other hand, is obtained by integrating the forces acting on the brick. This example suggests a general distinction within any theory *T*, to wit, between its kinematical part, which is normally elaborated independently of its dynamical part, and the dynamical conceptual apparatus, which allows the generation of representations of the phenomenon originally described by the kinematical part. In order to avoid mechanical language, let us call the 'dynamical' part of theory *T* the *T*-theoretical part, and the 'kinematical' one the non-*T*-theoretical part. Clearly, what counts as theoretical depends of the particular theory that is being considered. The notion of non-*T*-theoretical should not be assimilated to the concept of observational, although the development of non-*T*-theoretical representations always involves empirical observation.

An example in economics of the distinction just introduced is the distinction between the 'observed behavior' of an agent and the attempt to explain that behavior in terms of the concept of preference. The observed behavior is recoded in a certain structure $\hat{\mathfrak{C}}$ and the explanatory apparatus is a series of assumptions defining a structure $\mathfrak{P}$ that represents the preferences of the agent. Out of $\mathfrak{P}$ a representation $\mathfrak{C}$ of the behavior is generated and the explanation is considered successful if $\mathfrak{C}$ approximates $\hat{\mathfrak{C}}$ to an acceptable degree.

The former example illustrates the way in which particular models of a theory *T* are built. In the case of theories containing mainly metric concepts, a model is built when particular numerical values of the concepts are determined for the particular concrete system to which the theory is being applied (in this case the particular physical system consisting of the inclined plane and the brick sliding on it). That is to say, the corresponding magnitudes of the objects are measured (like the mass of the brick). This remark will be relevant when we discuss measurement below. But notice that measurement is a special case of a more general activity, which is that of determining relations for a particular concrete target system. In the case of theories not having metric concepts, models are built by means of the determination of the relations constituting its conceptual apparatus; i.e. by a specification of the particular ordered tuples belonging to the relations.

We shall see that the specification of relations and metric concepts sometimes requires essentially the use of the laws of the theory, so that they cannot be determined without presupposing that such laws are true of their intended objects. If concept *R* cannot be determined in any application without presupposing the validity at least of the fundamental law of theory *T*, we say that *R* is *T*-theoretical. In such a case we also say that *R* is determined in a *T*-dependent way. For instance, it is apparent that it is impossible to measure a particular mechanical force without presupposing NL, while the position function – at least in some applications – can be found independently of the dynamical laws. This will have consequences for the idea of a general theory of measurement.

Returning to our example, it is clear that the motion of the brick along the inclined plane can be represented by a structure whose construction does not require at all the use of mechanical laws. There are observation methods that allow the determination of the motion of the brick with certain precision. Let $\hat{\mathfrak{B}} = \langle P, \hat{T}, \hat{s} \rangle$ be a structure thus obtained, with

$$P = \{p\};$$
$$\hat{T} = [0, \hat{t}];$$
$$\hat{s}: P \times \hat{T} \rightarrow \mathbb{R}^3,$$

where t^* is the number of seconds during which the motion is observed to take place, and $\hat{s}$ is a curve obtained from the observation of the motion of the brick. It is clear that $\hat{\mathfrak{B}}$ satisfies axioms (1)–(3) of definition 3.4.1.

Notice that the type of $\hat{\mathfrak{B}}$ is different from that of $\mathfrak{A}$. The question is, then, How can they be compared? 'Kinematical', i.e. non-*T*-theoretical structures, will form part of larger structures comprising them together with the 'Dynamical', i.e. *T*-theoretical part. SVT calls the non-*T*-theoretical parts "partial potential models". The comparison is made between a partial potential model obtained out of the *T*-theoretical concepts, by means of the laws of *T*, with a previously given partial potential model that recodes observations obtained independently of *T*. Hence, using CPM and the relevant empirical data, we obtained the partial potential model

$$\mathfrak{B} = \langle \{p\}, [0, 2.198], (1/2) \cdot g(\sin \alpha \mu \cos \alpha) t^2 \mathbf{e}_1 \rangle.$$

The comparison that has to be made is between this structure and structure $\hat{\mathfrak{B}}$. $\mathfrak{A}$ will be deemed a successful application of *T* to the phenomenon of the inclined plane if it is the case that function s approximates function $\hat{s}$ to a reasonable degree; i.e. if $|t - \hat{t}| < \delta$ and $|s(p, t) - \hat{s}(p, t)| < \varepsilon$ for certain ε, $\delta > 0$ and for every t in the interval $[0, \min(2.198, \hat{t})]$. Clearly, theory *T* may fail to approximate a kinematical structure $\hat{\mathfrak{B}}$, but this does not mean that the theory has been refuted, since it may be successful in the explanation of other phenomena.

3.5 The structuralist view of theories

Perhaps the most notorious trait of SVT is its famous distinction between terms theoretical with respect to a theory *T*, *T*-theoretical, and those terms that are non-theoretical. It is important to stress that this distinction has nothing to do with the old positivist distinction between theoretical ('non-observational') terms and observational ones. The SVT criterion to make the distinction is between those relations that can be determined independently of the laws of the theory, at least in some cases, and those that presuppose that some application of theory *T* is successful. According to Sneed (1971: 32–3),

> An example of a *T*-dependent function is the mass function in an application of classical particle mechanics to a projectile problem. In this case we typically determine the mass of the projectile by "comparing" it to some standard body with a device like an analytical balance or an Atwood's machine. What we are doing, albeit indirectly, is determining the ratio of the mass of the projectile and the mass of an arbitrarily chosen standard. But, the only reason we believe that these comparison procedures yield mass-ratios, and not just numbers, completely unrelated to classical particle mechanics, is that we believe classical particle mechanics applies (at least approximately) to the physical systems used to make the comparisons. If someone asks why the number $(a/g - 1/a/g + 1)$, calculated from the acceleration observed in an Atwood's machine experiment, is the mass-ratio of the two bodies involved, we reply by deriving it from the application of classical particle mechanics to this system. I maintain that examination of any acceptable account of how the mass of a projectile might be determined would reveal

the same sort of dependence on an assumption that classical particle mechanics applied to the physical system used in making the mass determination.

According to Sneed, there are in CPM, as a matter of fact, exactly two CPM theoretical terms: mass (m) and force (f).[6] Be that as it may, in any sophisticated theory, certainly in developed economic theories, terms that are theoretical relative to that theory are expected to be found.

The existence of T-theoretical terms poses problems when someone tries to employ the set-theoretical predicate in order to produce empirical claims. For example, at first sight, an empirical assertion produced by means of the set-theoretical predicate that defined the models of CPM would consist of a sentence like the following:

(1) 'the motion of this brick along this inclined plane is a system of CPM'

or, in general, where letter σ denotes a concrete physical system,

(2) 'physical system σ is a system of CPM'.

Nevertheless, due to reasons already exposed in the previous section, a sentence of the form (2) can never be true because the predicate 'system of CPM' is true only of mathematical structures, and physical systems are *not* mathematical structures. It is clear that the subject of predication of empirical assertions has to be a being of the appropriate category.

An entity of the appropriate category that lends itself as a viable subject of predication is a possible model of the theory; i.e. a mathematical structure of the adequate type about which we ignore, in a first moment, whether it satisfies the laws of the theory. Recall that a possible model of CPM would be a structure $\mathfrak{A} = \langle P, T, s, m, f \rangle$ that satisfies the characterizations. The empirical assertion would consist precisely of the claim that $\mathfrak{A}$ satisfies, in addition, the laws of the theory; i.e. it would consist of the claim:

(3) '$\mathfrak{A}$ is a system of CPM'.

Suppose now that to each (putative) real-concrete mechanical system $\sigma \in \Sigma$ there corresponds a possible model $\mathfrak{A}_\sigma$ which can be considered as a candidate to represent concrete system σ. A mediated way of saying that CPM applies to σ would consist of affirming the sentence

(4) '$\mathfrak{A}_\sigma$ is a system of CPM'.

Now, in order to know the truth-value of sentence (4) we need to know the values of the functions in $\mathfrak{A}_\sigma$. The problem is that, since $\mathfrak{A}_\sigma$ contains CPM-theoretical functions, we cannot determine such functions unless we have good reasons to assume that a claim of the form '$\mathfrak{A}_{\sigma'}$ is a system of CPM' is true, where σ' can be the same concrete system σ or a different one. Therefore, we cannot have the required evidence to know whether $\mathfrak{A}_\sigma$ is system of CPM unless we have evidence to know whether $\mathfrak{A}_{\sigma'}$ is a system of CPM. Thus, we seem to be confronting a vicious circle or a *regressus ad infinitum*. This difficulty, which arises whenever we want to use a scientific theory in order to make an empirical claim, is what Sneed has called "the problem of theoretical terms" (which, again, has nothing to do with the logical-empiricist problem of the same name).

In order to solve this problem Sneed was led to the Ramsey sentence. As we have pointed out before, the non-T-theoretical part of a possible model is called a "partial potential model". Recall that in the case of CPM partial potential models are structures of the form $\langle P, T, s \rangle$.

If T is a scientific theory, let M be the class of its models, M_p the class of the potential models, and M_{pp} that of its partial potential models. Then we have the following relationships: $M \subset M_p$ and to each element of M_p there corresponds an element of M_{pp} which results from eliminating the theoretical components of the first. We can represent this correspondence by means of a "forgetful functor" or "cutting-off" function $\mathbf{r}: M_p \to M_{pp}$. If $\mathfrak{A} \in M_p$, $\mathbf{r}(\mathfrak{A}) \in M_{pp}$ shall be called the *reduct* of $\mathfrak{A}$. Suppose now, for the sake of the example, that to each real-concrete mechanical system $\sigma \in \Sigma$ there corresponds a collection of partial potential models $\{\mathfrak{A}_\sigma\}$ that can reasonably be considered as adequate representations of σ. If σ is, say, the sun-earth system, a typical element of $\{\mathfrak{A}_\sigma\}$ would be a structure that satisfies Kepler's laws. Hence, a *mediated* way of saying that (the regional theory of gravitation) of CPM applies to σ consists of asserting the Ramsey sentence

$$(5) \quad \exists \mathfrak{A} \, [\mathbf{r}(\mathfrak{A}) = \mathfrak{B}_\sigma \wedge \mathfrak{A} \in M],$$

where $\mathfrak{B}_\sigma \in \{\mathfrak{A}_\sigma\}$. The Ramsey sentence solves the problem of theoretical terms, since it only asserts that a structure made up of purely non-T-theoretical terms can be expanded to a structure that is a model of theory T.

Nevertheless, sentence (5) is at best incomplete. In the first place, it does not take into account the fact that diverse applications of the theory are interrelated by certain constraint, that is, certain conditions imposed upon the theoretical terms. An example of a constraint is the one that claims that the mass function of a body with constant mass must receive the same value in all the structures to whose universe it belongs, up to transformations of the system of units. In the second place, sentence (5) asserts a rather strong condition, since it implies that if $\mathfrak{B}_\sigma$ is an adequate representation of σ, produced independently of the theory T, then there is a model of T whose reduct coincides point by point with $\mathfrak{B}_\sigma$. This *may* turn out to be true but, usually, effectively produced models only match the observed data with a certain degree of approximation. We saw this in our example of the inclined plane, in which the model sets the motion of the brick in 2.198 seconds. Substituting this number for t in $(1/2)g(\sin\alpha - \mu\cos\alpha)t^2$ we get 49.99261248 cm, which represents a deviation of 7.875144×10^{-3} cm with respect to the value independently measured of the distance traversed by the brick. Hence, it is necessary to reformulate the Ramsey sentence.

Taking into account the former observations, we can express the proposition that theory T applies to real-concrete system σ by means of the sentence

(6) There is a model $\mathfrak{A}$ of T that satisfies the constraints, such that $\mathbf{r}(\mathfrak{A})$ approximates a non-T-theoretical description $\mathfrak{B}_\sigma \in M_{pp}$ of σ.

This shall be my first version of the empirical claims of a theory. These claims can be condensed in a single sentence which is usually called 'the empirical claim of the theory'. In order to be slightly more systematic, let me introduce some additional concepts.

3.5.1 Definition

A *theory core* is a list of classes M_p, M_{pp}, $\mathbf{r}$, M, C, such that, for fixed positive integers k, n, with $k < n$,

(1) M_p is the class of set-theoretical structures of a given similarity type;
(2) if structures in M_p are of the form

$$\mathfrak{A} = \langle D_1, \cdots, D_k, D_{k+1}, \cdots, D_n \rangle$$

M_{pp} is the set of all structures obtained from those in M_p by cutting off the last $n - k$ components of the elements of M_p;
(3) $\mathbf{r}: M_p \to M_{pp}$ is the cutting-off functor, such that

$$\mathbf{r}(\langle D_1, \cdots, D_k, D_{k+1}, \cdots, D_n \rangle) = \langle D_1, \cdots, D_k \rangle;$$

(4) $M \subset M_p$;
(5) C is the class of potential models that satisfy the constraints.

If T is a scientific theory, the structures in M_p are precisely those that satisfy the characterizations of the terms corresponding to $D_1, \ldots, D_k, D_{k+1}, \ldots, D_n$, and so M_p is a similarity type. M_{pp} turns out to be the class of all those structures that satisfy the characterizations that stipulate the meaning of the non-T-theoretical terms. M is the class of models of T; that is to say, of the structures in M_p that satisfy the nomological statements of T. C is the class of potential models that satisfy the constraints.

The notion of approximation is important in empirical science. Usually, when intra-theoretical approximation is discussed, the discussion is restricted merely to values of numerically-valued functions. It is said, for instance, that function f 'approximates' function g if the distance $|f(x) - g(x)|$ between the values of the functions is less than a specified positive real number ε. Each scientific theory T can be presumptively or effectively applied to a specified collection Σ of real-concrete systems, which can be described in a non-T-theoretical way. As a

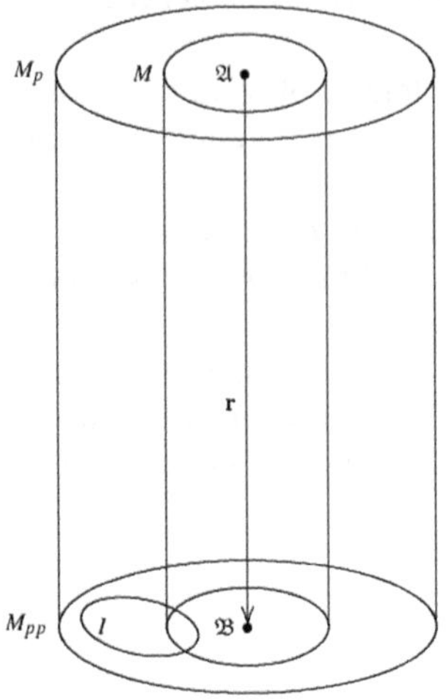

Figure 3.4 Structure of a theory-element

mater of fact, to each concrete system σ there may correspond several different representations (some better than others) in M_{pp}. Nevertheless, in order to simplify the exposition, I shall assume that to each $\sigma \in \Sigma$ there corresponds exactly one representation $\mathfrak{A}_\sigma \in M_{pp}$.

For each type of real-concrete systems $\boldsymbol{\sigma} = \{\sigma\}$, there exists an admissible approximation relation $\approx_{\boldsymbol{\sigma}}$. The admissible degree of approximation between an independent description $\mathfrak{B}_\sigma$ of σ and a partial potential model $\mathbf{r}(\mathfrak{A}) \in M_{pp}$, obtained out of a model $\mathfrak{A}$, depends upon several historical and pragmatic conditions, among which is found the degree of development of the theory, of the measurement instruments, or the type of application in question: It is obvious that the degree of approximation which is required when a small force in a spring is measured does not have to be the same as that demanded when planetary motion is being determined. Thus, for each type of independent description $\boldsymbol{\sigma}$ we define fuzzy set $A_{\boldsymbol{\sigma}}$ as the set of all partial potential models which are admissible approximations for structures describing phenomena of type $\boldsymbol{\sigma}$. If $\mathfrak{B} \in A_{\boldsymbol{\sigma}}$, we write $\mathfrak{B}_\sigma \approx_{\boldsymbol{\sigma}} \mathfrak{B}$. We are now in position to introduce one of the central notions of SVT.

3.5.2 Definition

A *theory-element* is a triple of classes K, $\mathcal{A}$, and I such that

(1) $K = \langle M_p, M_{pp}, r, M, C\rangle$ is a theory core;
(2) $\mathcal{A}$ is the class of all fuzzy sets;
(3) $I \subseteq M_{pp}$ is the class of all independently built structures representing real-concrete phenomena to which the theory presumptively applies.

Theory-elements constitute the metatheoretical representations of regional theories. Each regional theory is identified by means of a theory-element. From now on, without loss of generality, we shall assume that all models in M satisfy the constraints; i.e. $M \subset C$. Thus,

$$A(K) = \mathbf{r}(M)$$

is the class of all partial potential models obtained by 'derivation' from models of T. If $\sigma \in \boldsymbol{\sigma}$ is a real-concrete system, the claim that T applies to σ is a sentence expressing that to partial potential model $\mathfrak{B}_\sigma \in I$ there corresponds a partial potential model $\mathfrak{B} \in \mathbf{r}(M)$ such that $\mathfrak{B}_\sigma \approx_{\boldsymbol{\sigma}} \mathfrak{B}$. Hence, the aggregated empirical claim of theory T can be defined as follows.

3.5.3 *Definition*

For each type of real-concrete system $\boldsymbol{\sigma}$ to which the theory presumptively applies ($\mathfrak{B}_\sigma \in I$) there corresponds a partial potential model $\mathfrak{B} \in \mathbf{r}(M)$ such that $\mathfrak{B}_\sigma \approx_{\boldsymbol{\sigma}} \mathfrak{B}$

Within the framework of the $\mathcal{L}$-View, I characterized a scientific theory T as a sup-semilattice $\langle \mathcal{G}, \triangleright \rangle$, dominated by a supremum Γ_0 called basic theory-element of theory T. We can now redefine relation $\triangleright$ as a specialization relation among theory-elements.

3.5.4 *Definition*

If E and E' are theory-elements, then E' is a *specialization* of E ($E' \triangleleft E$) iff

(1) $M'_{pp} = M_{pp}$;
(2) $M'_p = M_p$;
(3) $\mathbf{r}' = \mathbf{r}$;
(4) $M' \subseteq M$;
(5) $I' \subseteq I$;
(7) $\mathcal{A}' = \{A_{\boldsymbol{\sigma}} \in \mathcal{A} | A_{\boldsymbol{\sigma}} \subset I')$;

The SVT notion corresponding to $\langle \mathcal{G}, \triangleright \rangle$ is that of a theory net, with which we close the present chapter.

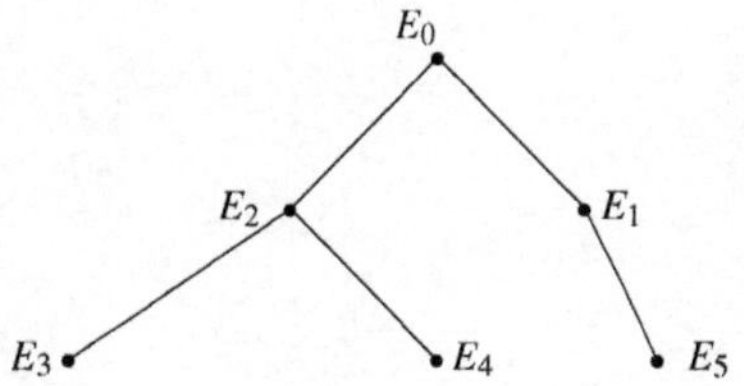

Figure 3.5 A theory net

3.5.5 Definition

A *theory net* T is a sup-semilattice $\langle \mathcal{E}, \lhd \rangle$, dominated by a supremum E_0 called *basic theory-element* of theory T.

Indeed, SVT intends to represent a scientific theory by means of a theory net. This notion is the basic Generality II we were looking for the theoretical practice consisting of the rational reconstruction of scientific theories. It is a good map of what a theory is, but it has to be refined further, since idealizations and ideal representations must be taken into account.

Notes

1 See this discussion in Suppes (2002), chapter 1, especially pp. 5–6.
2 For a review of the different kinds of axiomatizations than can be given, see Stegmüller (1976: 30–9).
3 For a criticism of the idea of the true and exact value of a magnitude, cf. Suppes (1984: 82ff).
4 Cf., for instance, Symon (1953), Spiegel (1967), or any advanced text of mechanics.
5 I am assuming that the length of the brick is 10 cm.
6 For an attempt to determine mass independently of CPM, see García de la Sienra (2015).

4 Idealization and concretization

4.1 Motivation

The aim of the present chapter is to deal, within a structuralist perspective, with the problem of the nature and types of idealization and concretization in (positive) economics. The most complete discussion of idealization from a structuralist perspective is due to De Donato (2011), but this work is concerned mainly with idealization in physics. Are the claims made about idealization in physics valid *mutatis mutandis* in economics? This is one of the leading questions of the chapter.

According to Balzer and Zoubek (1994: 57),

> The basic picture of concretization and idealization seems to be that there is 'the' real world which is described by human theories to more or less satisfactory degree. As the real world is very complex the theories describing it in the beginning provide very rough pictures, many real features are left out of account. Theories therefore are idealized. In the historical process more and more of the features originally ignored are incorporated into the theories which in this way become more accurate pictures of the world. This is the process of concretization.

Yet, even though Balzer and Zoubek recognize that "'the' real world seems to be necessary as a guide for concretization" for, without having it in view, "concretization has no 'direction' and becomes arbitrary, or so it seems", they nevertheless find problematic "the existence of a fully determined real world independent of human description" and so they conclude that "idealization and concretization should be regarded as ordinary intertheoretical relations between theories" (ibid.).

It is true that some philosophers have thought that some way of referring to concrete actual beings is necessary in order to develop a complete semantics of theories. A recent defense of this view was given by Muller (2011), who introduces the concept of concrete actual being in order to perform this task. Indeed, according to Marx's method of political economy, the subject (*das Subjekt*) of any science is real and concrete (*real und konkret*); it is an already given concrete organic whole (*ein gegebnes konkretes, lebendiges Ganzes*) that remains outside the head (*außerhalb des Kopfes*) independent of it (*in seiner Selbständigkeit bestehen*), and must always be kept in mind as a presupposition of the representation (*als Voraussetzung stets der Vorstellung vorschweben*), when the theoretical method (*theoretische Methode*) is employed.[1]

Even though Marx's *Subjekt* (in economics), as described according to his method, is far from being "a fully determined real world independent of human description", some extremely empiricist and instrumentalist philosophers would find it objectionable. Yet, some kind of conceptualization is necessary in order to fix the target system of any intended theorization, if only to know which empirical data or measurements might turn out to be relevant to its understanding, and indeed as a pre-condition to produce any idealized representation of it. Some philosophers have thought that nothing less than a full fledged metaphysical or ontological theory is required for this endeavor.[2] Marx's scientific practice seems to presuppose that only a certain minimal description of *das Subjekt*, the target system, is necessary in order to determine the real and concrete referent. This description is given by Marx, in the case of economics, in a language which contains general but not idealized terms. He says that, starting with a small number of determinant, abstract, general, and simple concepts (*einfachste Bestimmungen*) of aspects of the target system, a richer concept of the same is built by way of thought (*im Weg des Denkens*), as a concentration of many determinations (*Zussamenfassung vieler Bestimmungen*), as a unity of the diverse (*Einheit des Mannigfaltigen*). Clearly, this concept is not the real *Subjekt*, but only a 'spiritual' (*geistig*) reproduction of the same, just a concrete totality in thinking (*Gedankentotalität, als ein Gedankenkonkretum, in fact ein Produkt des Denkens*).

Marx claimed that in economics the real *Subjekt* always had to be seen as an *organisches Ganzes* and conceptualized, no matter which concrete real given economy was going to be studied, through four general categories: production, distribution, exchange, and consumption. These categories have to be further specified, seen in their mutual 'interaction', i.e. in their inner connections, and applied to given properties or relations of the economy under scrutiny. Clearly, the resulting *Gedankenkonkretum*, no matter to what extent the categories are specified, is still a general concept, but it is nevertheless far from being a theoretical model. Rather, it fixes a target system and opens the possibility of leading inquiries, probing into it, collecting empirical information (empirical data), making some measurements, and eventually the possibility of building idealized theoretical models of some of its aspects. The *Gedankenkonkretum* is the method by means of which the problems of the lost beings, unavailable stories, and lost content are tackled. In Chapter 6 I will present a map for the general representation of any economic system.

Hence, the construction of the *Gedankenkonkretum* by way of thought should not be confused with the process of concretization as understood by Leszek Nowak and some structuralists (as Balzer and Zoubek, quoted above, or De Donato 2011). Rather, idealization and concretization in this latter sense must be represented exclusively, in effect, as a relationship between theoretical models. But the reference to the *Gedankenkonkretum* is the required guide for concretization.

4.2 Empirical structures

By 'empirical structure' I mean a set-theoretic structure that records, in a systematic way, empirical observations about some aspect or aspects of a previously determined *Subjekt*. These can be data related to the aggregate production of a concrete economy during a certain period of time (e.g. the American economy from 1919 to 1929); tables reporting positions of "sparkling points" in the sky during a "long series of nights", or the data resulting from the comparison of several bodies, as to their weight, by means of an equal-arms balance. Other examples are given by tables recording the observation of business cycles or, more recently, by Patrick Suppes' record of electroencephalographic data collected in order to establish brain representations of words.[3]

It is not the case that the data collected by means of systematic observations are always recorded in order to test or apply a previously given theory; i.e. they are not necessarily embedded into a partial potential model of some theory *T*. For instance, in spite of their rich algebraic and computational tradition, the Babylonian astronomers did not produce anything that might be deemed as a 'theory' of planetary motion similar to that of Ptolemy. This situation is also typical in econometrics, where it is common the production of statistical correlations without the use of much theory. These correlations, normally obtained through the method of ordinary least squares, constitute an elementary form of idealization for which there is nothing resembling a concretization process. But this method is only one of the many methodologies used in order to interpret or organize quantitative observations: the wealth of data in the different sciences is so overwhelming, and the range of methodologies used in quantitative observations is so vast, "that in their full detail [they] are theoretically immeasurable" (cf. Suppes 2011: 119).

Essentially, empirical structures are sets of *n*-tuples $\langle x_1,\ldots, x_n\rangle$, whose coordinates are taken as belonging to certain empirical categories $X_1,\ldots, X_n$. For instance, X_1 may be required to be a set of consecutive years, X_2 the recorded annual GNP of a country during these years, and so on. These data are usually presented in tables and stored in databases.

Some empirical structures are built in order to serve the purposes of a given scientific theory. These purposes are varied: testing of a particular theoretical systematization, application, or computation of a particular magnitude. At a micrological level, sometimes a particular form of a magnitude is posited in order to explain some phenomenon, in which case empirical data are used to check the accuracy of that form. Sometimes, the point is not to check whether the theory is good, but just to apply it in order to obtain realizations useful for some particular purpose (for instance, information in order to put a satellite in a required orbit), or just to compute the value of some magnitude (like the mass of the sun).

A typical scientific endeavor is that of trying to imbed a data-structure into a partial potential model of a certain theory *T*. For the sake of the example, let us suppose that, out of the observation of the behavior of a consumer, we get a structure of data of the following form:

$$\mathfrak{D} = \langle X, F, \tilde{\eta} \rangle,$$

where X is a set of vectors representing the consumption vectors available to the agent, F is a finite subset of $P \times W$, P is the family of all possible price systems (vectors), W is the interval of all possible levels of wealth for the agent, and $\tilde{\eta}$ is a function defined over F recording the observed choice of the agent at each level of prices and wealth $(\mathbf{p}, w)$. Function $\tilde{\eta}$ is obviously finite and discrete, and can be presented as in Table 4.1.

If $\succsim$ is the preference relation of the agent (usually represented by some utility function $u\colon X \rightarrow \mathbb{R}$), the models of consumer choice theory T are of the form

$$\mathfrak{M} = \langle X, P, W, \eta, \succsim \rangle,$$

and are defined as those potential models that satisfy the law of utility maximization: $\eta(\mathbf{p}, w)$ is actually optimal within the set $\{\mathbf{x} \in X | \mathbf{px} \leq w\}$. Since $\succsim$ (and hence u) indeed smells like *T*-theoretical, the partial potential models of *T* have the following aspect:

$$\mathfrak{P} = \langle X, P, W, \eta \rangle = \mathbf{r}(\mathfrak{M}).$$

(Recall that **r** is the functor that eliminates the theoretical terms of the potential models of *T*.) Thus, the problem is to show that $\mathfrak{D}$ is 'approximately' imbedded in

$$\mathfrak{P} = \langle X, P, W, \eta \rangle;$$

that is to say, there exists a partial potential model

$$\hat{\mathfrak{P}} = \langle X, P, W, \hat{\eta} \rangle,$$

such that $\mathfrak{D}$ is imbedded in $\hat{\mathfrak{P}}$ and $\hat{\mathfrak{P}} \approx \mathfrak{P}$ (see Figure 4.1).

Table 4.1 Empirical structure D represented as a table

Argument	*Value of* $\tilde{\eta}$
$(\mathbf{p}^1, w^1)$	$\tilde{\mathbf{x}}^1 = \tilde{\eta}(\mathbf{p}^1, w^1)$
$(\mathbf{p}^2, w^1)$	$\tilde{\mathbf{x}}^2 = \tilde{\eta}(\mathbf{p}^2, w^2)$
$\vdots$	$\vdots$
$(\mathbf{p}^k, w^k)$	$\tilde{\mathbf{x}}^n = \tilde{\eta}(\mathbf{p}^k, w^k)$
$\vdots$	$\vdots$
$(\mathbf{p}^n, w^n)$	$\tilde{\mathbf{x}}^n = \tilde{\eta}(\mathbf{p}^n, w^n)$

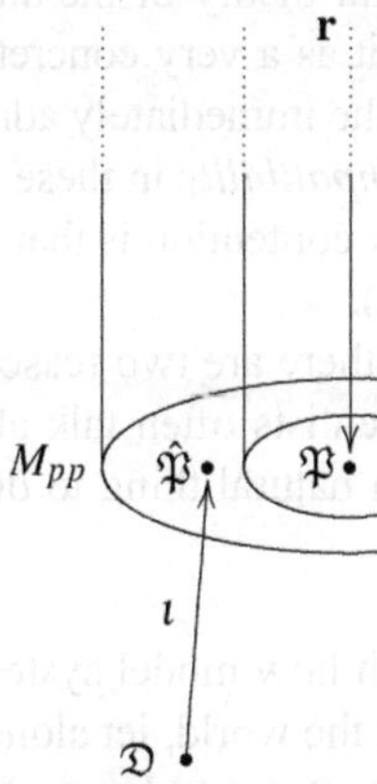

Figure 4.1 Approximated imbedding (ι) of empirical structure $\mathfrak{D}$ into $\mathfrak{P}$

4.3 Construction of idealized models

By 'model' economists usually understand a set of sentences describing a putative object, but I shall use the term here with a definite philosophical meaning. By 'model' I understand here, precisely, a set-theoretical structure seen as the realization of a set of sentences. In contradistinction to this notion, Frigg (2010) introduces the notion of 'model system' as a sort of idealized representation, *im Weg des Denkens*, of (an aspect of) some real concrete target system:

> Although [set-theoretic] structures do play an important role in scientific modeling, … model systems cannot be identified with structures. What is missing in the structuralist conception is an analysis of the physical character of model systems. The view of model systems that I advocate regards them as imagined physical systems, i.e. as hypothetical entities that, as a matter of fact, do not exist spatio-temporally but are nevertheless not purely mathematical or structural in that they would be physical things if they were real. If the Newtonian model system of sun and earth were real, it would consist of two spherical bodies with mass and other concrete properties such as hardness and colour, properties that structures do not have; likewise, the populations in the Lotka-Volterra model would consist of flesh-and-blood animals if they were real, and the agents in Edgeworth's economic model would be rational human beings.
>
> (Frigg 2010: 253)

Friggs attributes to Patrick Suppes the claim that model systems are to be identified with set-theoretical structures, but this attribution is unfair. Actually, Suppes acknowledges that many scientists think of their models as imagined concrete objects, different from set-theoretical structures. For instance, "many physicists want to think of a model of the orbital theory of the atom as being more than a set-theoretical entity. They envisage it as a very concrete physical thing built on the analogy of the solar system". But he immediately adds: "I think it is important to point out that *there is no real incompatibility* in these two viewpoints" (Suppes 1960: 290, emphasis added). His only contention is that "the set-theoretical usage is the more fundamental" (ibid.: 291).

Nevertheless, Frigg considers that there are two reasons to prefer 'his view' to the structuralist. "The first is that scientists often talk about model systems as if they were physical things, which is a natural thing to do if models are imagined physical entities" (Frigg 2010: 253).

> The second reason has to do with how model systems relate to the world. A structure is not about anything in the world, let alone about a particular target system. Those who take model systems to be structures suggest connecting structures to target systems by setting up a morphism between them (the most common morphism is isomorphism; other suggestions include partial isomorphism, homomorphism, and embedding). But a morphism holds between two structures and not between a structure and a part of the world per se. In order to make sense of the notion that there is a morphism between a model system and its target we have to assume that the target exemplifies a particular structure, and this cannot be had without bringing non-structural features into play.
>
> (Ibid.: 254)

Frigg observes that "in order for it to be true that a target system possesses a particular structure, a more concrete description must be true of the system as well", because "structural claims are abstract in the sense that they cannot be true unless some more concrete claims are true as well" and accepts that "this by itself would not have to worry the structuralist. The problem, and this is the second step, arises when we realise that the descriptions we choose to ground structural claims are almost never true descriptions of the target system" (ibid.). And he adds:

> Taken literally, descriptions that ground structural claims (almost always) fail to be descriptions of the intended target system. Instead, they describe a hypothetical system distinct from the target system. This has unfortunate consequences for the structuralist. If the descriptions employed to attribute a structure to a target system were just plain descriptions of that system, then the claim that model systems are just structures would appear at least prima facie plausible. But once we acknowledge that these descriptions describe hypothetical systems rather than real target systems, we also have to acknowledge that hypothetical systems are an important part of the theoretical apparatus we employ, and that they therefore have to be included in our analysis of how scientific modeling works.
>
> (Ibid.: 254–5)

In his interesting pretension theory Frigg distinguishes p-representations, which are representations of merely fictitious objects (like Don Quijote de la Mancha) from t-representations, which also intend to represent a certain target system:

> These two senses of 'representation' need to be clearly distinguished, and for this reason I call the former 'p-representation' ('p' for 'prop') and the latter 't-representation' ('t' for target). Using this idiom, the two acts mentioned in the introduction can be described as, first, introducing a p-representation specifying a hypothetical object and, second, claiming that this imagined object t-represents the relevant target system.
>
> (Ibid.: 264)

Frigg believes that "the apparent comparison with a nonexistent object eventually comes down to the unproblematic comparison of properties, and the statement making this comparison is true iff the statement comparing the properties with each other is true" (ibid.: 263–264). I would like to discuss, with a certain accuracy, by means of an example in economics, how this comparison is usually made, or should be made, and how both the target and the model system relate to set-theoretical structures used to make claims about both.

Accepting the distinction between model systems and set-theoretical structures, and acknowledging that model systems are an important part of the apparatus of empirical sciences, the first thing to be noticed is that model systems are idealizations par excellence. The following questions arise in a natural way: how are model systems used to make empirical claims about real target systems? What is the role in this task of the model systems and the empirical structures? How do model systems "t-represent" their respective target systems? Is there a place for p-representations in economic theory? What is the role of model systems in the process of idealization and concretization?

As I explained above, it is usual in economics to produce a *Gedankenkonkretum,* which is a non-idealized concept, stated in broad and general terms, of a class of target systems. A relatively simple and common example of such a concept is that of the consumer. Granted, Marx criticized the idea of the "individual and isolated" producer, a criticism that we may generalize to the notion of the individual and isolated economic agent. But, seen within the frame of a concrete capitalist economy (or of any other mode of production), it is possible to theorize over the specific determinations of the consumer. To attribute to the consumer a preference relation, or the capacity to make rational choices, does not mean that the consumer is a Robinson Crusoe, let alone a naturally independent, autonomous individual detached of all natural bonds (cf. Marx 1973: 83). For there is nothing in the theory of consumer choice that prevents accepting that the preference relation of the individual is the result of imbued traditions and tastes within a given community (like the family) that can be transformed by social forces (like advertisement). It is indeed a gross confusion to believe that Marx's view of the economic system as an organic whole conflicts with methodological individualism. Marx never denied that only individuals had the possibility of making choices. Rather, one of his complaints was that the conditions of the proletariat were such that the workers were forced to consume a restricted consumption basket, without many options. His claim that some social processes go on "behind the backs of the producers" (cf. Marx 1976: 135) is not meant to attribute agency to super-human entities, but rather to point out the fact that some social processes are unintended or unconscious consequences of current or previous individual decisions.

Hence, even though the typical human consumer lives within an organic social whole, it can be described as a normal human being, a psychophysical acting unit endowed with memory, able to store and process information, capable of performing arithmetic calculations, having preferences regarding the consumption of goods, able to make choices, and so on. Hence, the *Gedankenkonkretum* 'consumer' can be characterized by means of the conjunction of the following predicates:

(1′) x possesses information.
(2′) x has memory.
(3′) x is able to perform calculations.
(4′) x has preferences.
(5′) x is able to make choices.

The consumer – the story goes – has information about and remembers the available consumption menus within a determined set of commodity bundles X, there are several menus for him to choose from (X is nonempty and has more than one element), the amount of wealth w he has available to buy a menu is limited, this wealth can be applied to obtain any of the menus $\mathbf{x} \in X$ whose monetary value $\mathbf{px}$ (under a ruling system of prices $\mathbf{p}$) is not greater than w, and not all menus are equally indifferent to him. (This last condition is supposed to mean that the consumer has a non-trivial transitive preference relation $\succsim$ defined over X.) Among the menus within $B = \{\mathbf{x} \in X | \mathbf{px} \leq w\}$, the consumer always chooses one that is most preferred among those in B. This last condition can be expressed by means of the predicate

(6′) x is rational.

This concept of consumer can be applied to typical human persons under a situation in which they have to choose consumption baskets. It is not at all idealized. The concept seems roughly correct and applicable in general terms. Idealization starts when the economists demand more specification and the performance of measurements: it is then that the scientists become interested in constructing a quantitative theory to match the intuitive ideas of the original theory. But this requires mathematization: the introduction of more precise notions and the deformation of the original predicates attributed to the consumer, in order to match the demands of mathematical rigor. Mathematization is an engine driving idealization in the sense of model-system construction. Idealization is a way of creating a model system that is exactly described by the mathematical formalism required by the metrization of the original concepts. As Walras (1954: 71) put it:

> the mathematical method is not an *experimental* method; it is a *rational* method,....the pure science of economics should then abstract and define ideal-type concepts in terms of which it carries its reasoning. The return to reality should not take place until the science is completed and then only with a view to practical applications.

Let us call 'idealized concepts' (or, briefly, idealizations) the concepts obtained by deformation out of concepts which are truly predicable of real concrete beings if, in spite of this deformation, the same are meaningful – even if they are false – of these real objects, and keep an intension akin to those.

Idealizations obtained by deforming predicates (1′)–(6′) are the following

(1) x possesses perfect information.
(2) x has perfect recall.
(3) x has unlimited computational powers.
(4) x has regular preferences.
(5) x is able to make choices.
(6) x always chooses a menu that is optimal within

$$\{\mathbf{x} \in X | \mathbf{px} \leq w\} \text{ for any } (\mathbf{p}, w).$$

The conjunction of predicates (1)–(6) defines a type or ideal object – what we have called a model system – nonexistent in reality but required to channel mathematical reasoning. How is this model system related to set-theoretical structures?

First of all, perfect information and memory are required in order to postulate 'large' consumption sets, in fact as large as the nonnegative orthant of $\mathbb{R}^L$ (L a positive integer). Moreover, the consumer is supposed to produce or possess a quasiconcave, locally nonsatiated, continuously differentiable utility function representing his preference relation (this implies that the relation is connected and transitive). Given this function, the consumer is supposed to be able to maximize the utility function for any level $(\mathbf{p}, w)$ of prices and wealth. And he is indeed able, and sufficiently 'rational', to choose for consumption precisely the optimal menu.

Thus, on top of (1)–(6), the theory assumes the following axioms:

(7) x has as option set X the nonnegative orthant Ω of $\mathbb{R}^L$.
(8) x has kitschy tastes (since his preference relation is strictly convex, he strictly prefers combinations of variegated styles).

(9) x is nonsatiated; he always prefers to consume more to less.
(10) the rate of change of x's tastes, as he moves away from a consumption menu, is almost constant; i.e. the rate of change of his tastes is constant within an infinitesimal neighborhood of any of the consumption menus in the interior of Ω.

Axioms (1)–(10) delineate a very important idealization in economic theory, a model system depicting a very regular type of consumer. They also define a particular type of set-theoretical structure. By itself, they do not involve any empirical claim, but can be used to make empirical claims about real-concrete consumers (the theory requires that the utility functions be invariant with respect to monotonic increasing transformations; i.e. that they be ordinal).

Demetris Portides (2013) has pointed out that there are three kinds of idealization: isolation, stabilization, and decomposition. The first two kinds have been described by Uskali Mäki (1992, 1994), who distinguished among two types of idealizing assumptions: *nullifying idealizations and stabilizing idealizations.* Nullifying assumptions express that a certain factor, which is usually present affecting the powers of the isolated universal, is missing. If $p(x)$ is the degree in which factor p is present at x, a nullifying assumption can be expressed in the form $p(x) = 0$. A stabilizing assumption expresses that the rate of change of factor p at x is nullified, and is expressed as $\dot{p}(x)$. Additionally, decomposition, according to Portides, "is the conceptual act of setting apart factors, clusters of factors, processes, or mechanisms in our model descriptions; a rough way to put it, that decomposition is the conceptual act of abstracting from interconnection and interaction" (Portides 2013: 260). But we are in a position to see that these kinds of idealization are only particular cases of idealization. Another type of idealization, as important as the former, is deformation: the assumptions in this case do not mean that some factor is supposed nil or disconnected from others, but rather that the target system (or some of its parts) satisfies certain deformed predicates. Clearly, none of these kinds of idealization can be carried out if the target system – the *Subjekt* – has not been previously fixed by means of a *Gedankenkonkretum.*

A model system is an ideal system built by means of conjunctions of predicates expressing idealizations. The model system t-represents its respective target systems in the first place because the predicates defining the former are intelligible deformations of predicates which are literally true of the second. But this representation is conventional up to a point and it is deemed as such a representation just because it was built with the intention of representing that target system in the first place, the scientific community sees it that way, and that's the way it is presented in the textbooks of the discipline. If model system **S** is taken to represent target system σ, we write $\mathbf{S} \triangleq \sigma$, following a notation introduced by Bunge (1972). How well σ is represented with **S** is an empirical matter that has to be settled in terms of how well the set-theoretical structure $\mathfrak{A}$ associated to **S** matches the empirical data generated by σ.

4.4 Concretization

It is not unusual in the economic sciences to find that, far from being formulated in complete generality, scientific theories start with the concoction of a very special model system. This is the case, for instance, of the stylized capitalist economy Marx describes in *Capital*, where (among other things) labor is supposed to be homogeneous. It is also the history of game theory, where zero-sum, two-person games were the first to be formulated.

What this means, in structuralist terms, is that, historically, economic theories begin with some specialization and it is only later that their basic theory-element is determined (if at all). Whereas in physics certain magnitudes (like weights) are closely related to the senses and common practices, and in some cases simple operations can be performed to measure them, the opposite situation is true in economics. Economic value, in terms of public prices, can be observed without the development of much abstract theory. Nevertheless, the central magnitudes of important theories like the labor theory of value, game theory, or consumer choice are not that close to the experience of the common man. For instance, in order to prove the existence of labor-values, very stringent assumptions must be made on the structure of the productive system. Something analogous happens in game theory, where the calculation, or just the proof of the existence of expected utilities, can be very complex.

Concretization is in some 'virtual' sense the opposite of specialization. According to the structuralist view, specializations are seen as specializations of a previously given basic theory-element, defined by an explicit fundamental law. Specialization consists of the introduction of special laws or theoretical systematizations that describe with more detail putative specific applications of the theory. Historically, however, at least in economics, a very special theory-element appears first and then the problem is to find out that basic theory-element of which the special theory-element is a specialization. In other words, sometimes the special laws defining the typical theory-element – like Delphi's oracle – neither reveal nor conceal the general fundamental law, but give signs. Moulines is absolutely right when he says:

> From my own point of view, I consider approximation at least as fundamental for empirical science as idealization, and moreover I think that the two notions, though interrelated, have to be conceptually distinguished; they are in need of different explications – both from a logical and a methodological point of view. Very roughly speaking, idealization is rather connected with model construction, whereas approximation is a relationship between already constructed models.
>
> (Moulines 2007: 258–9)

As Walras has taught us, idealization has to do with the use of the mathematical method; it cares about nothing but the construction of model systems in which to carry out its reasoning. Once this problem has been solved, then it is possible to deal with the problem of better approximations, as part of the problem of the "return to reality".

But it is usual to apply even theory-elements that are very idealized. How good these theory-elements are is – as I said above – an empirical matter. Wade Hands pointed out that some intended applications of some economic theories are not 'concrete', in the sense in which "our solar system" is a concrete application of Newtonian mechanics or "the U.S. economy in 1960" is a concrete application of macroeconomic theory:

> While it may not be that general equilibrium theory is utterly devoid of such concrete intended applications, it is certainly safe to say "most" applications of the theory are not of this type. It seems that the sense in which general equilibrium is "empirical", that it has concrete applications, is much more complex than can be captured in the standard structuralist definition of the set of intended applications.
>
> (Hands 1985: 329)

Indeed, I have long stressed[4] that the cause of this problem is a confusion between the intended applications in the structuralist sense (which are set-theoretical structures) and the target systems the theory presumptively applies to. I have distinguished above between the *Gedankenkonkreten,* the intended applications (which are set-theoretical structures), the empirical structures (models of data; also set-theoretical structures), the model system precisely described by the theoretical systematizations of the theory-element (an idealized, imagined system), the target or real-concrete systems the model systems intend to represent, and how all these elements are combined to produce an empirical claim. I think this explains, in a detailed and thorough way, the complex sense in which economic theories (or any empirical theory, for that matter) has concrete applications. If there are theories which will never apply to any real-concrete system, not even in a remotely approximate way, then these theories are not empirical at all; they are not scientific theories. But the structuralist view is not to be blamed for their failure.

The structure of scientific theories, and the ways they relate to their putative real-concrete *Subjekte* is far from being simple. The typical narrative of normal scientific practice runs like this. Having in sight a real-concrete economic system or phenomenon σ described by means of a general concept **g** – a *Gedankenkonkretum* – the scientist wants to use theory T in order to explain certain empirical data related to σ recorded in an empirical structure $\mathfrak{D}$. Two ways are open here. The first one, let me call it 'parametrical', consists of trying to 'fit' (imbed) the data in $\mathfrak{D}$ into a partial potential model $\hat{\mathfrak{P}}$ of T in order to try to apply T (usually in an approximate way) to $\hat{\mathfrak{P}}$. The second consists of using the data in $\mathfrak{D}$ in order to directly determine the theoretical terms of *T*, by means of the laws or theoretical systematizations of *T*, build a model $\mathfrak{A}$ of *T*, and then to generate a reduct $\mathbf{r}(\mathfrak{A})$ into which the data are to be imbedded. The first way, the parametric one, was historically followed by Kepler, who intended to find curves (first circles and later ellipses) to fit the astronomical data left by Tycho Brahe. The second one has been proposed by Varian and other authors in order to determine the utility function of a consumer. The first method intends to obtain model $\mathfrak{A}$ by means of integration; the second method by means of a certain algorithm.[5]

Hands also believes that the structuralist view cannot account for the inverse process to 'virtual' specialization:

> Often theoretical progress occurs just in the reverse manner; the theory is made *not more specific, but more general.* Much of the history of general equilibrium theory can be characterized as a search for increasingly more general conditions which preserve the basic properties of the theory. This type of "generalizing" theoretical progress is outside the standard structuralist view of theoretical progress and thus represents one more way in which the fit seems less than perfect.
>
> (Hands 1985: 330)

Actually, the structuralist view is particularly suited to explain this process. It consists of postulating a theory-element T_0 of which the given, more idealized theory-element T_1 would be a specialization (in the usual structuralist sense). I claim, by the way, that *this is the most important sense of concretization.* Nowak's view can be seen as a case of concretization in which the special conditions defining T_1 are isolations. But sometimes concretization is not merely de-isolation: it must also figure out the form of the fundamental law defining the theory (and hence also T_0). All my effort in (García de la Sienra 1992) was devoted precisely to a task of this type,[6] namely to find a more general form of the law of value in order to generalize the (then) standard model systems of the labor theory of value, taking into account very general productive structures with heterogeneous labor.[7]

De Donato (2011: 83) proposes understanding idealization "basically as a relation between theory-elements just as any other intertheoretical relation". I think he is right, but his explication only accounts for the case in which idealized theory-elements are obtained by means of nullifying assumptions. Thus, it would seem that concretization consists simply of dropping the nullifying assumptions in order to obtain a more general theory-element. But, as I have been trying to stress, finding more general versions of the fundamental law implicitly involved in the definition of the idealized theory-element can be harder than what such a description suggests, as it may involve unsuspected conceptual transformations of the required notions.

Notes

1 Cf. "Die Methode der politischen Ökonomie" in Marx (1983); I follow closely the Penguin edition (Marx 1973).
2 I myself believed this when I wrote that a *philosophia de ente* was necessary to that end (cf. García de la Sienra 1990). Stigum (2003: 37ff) also seems to believe it when he introduces his "world of facts".
3 For a survey of this last project, cf. Crangle (2015).
4 For instance, García de la Sienra (1988: 77).
5 These methods will be discussed in Chapter 5 when I deal with the topic of measurement.
6 Cf. García de la Sienra (2007) for a survey of the approaches to the problem.
7 A similar case in biology has been reported by Lorenzano (2014).

5 Measurement

5.1 The nature of measurement

Some theoreticians define 'measurement' as the assignment of numbers to properties in such a way that the traits of the property are adequately represented by mathematical entities. This definition holds water if it is understood in a sufficiently wide sense, understanding by the assignment of numbers the assignment not only of isolated numbers, but also of arrangements of numbers (like vectors). This was actually the position held by Krantz, Luce, Suppes, and Tverski (KLST 1971: 1)[1] when they said that

> when measuring some attribute of a class of objects or events, we associate numbers (or other familiar mathematical entities, such as vectors) with the objects in such a way that the properties of the attribute are faithfully represented as numerical properties.

Another definition, that agrees with the former one, is due to Finkelstein:

> Measurement is the process of empirical, objective assignment of numbers to properties of objects or events of the real world in such a way as to describe them.
>
> (Finkelstein 1982: 6)

Nevertheless, in economics, it is sometimes necessary to measure properties of idealized objects, and so I would rather prefer to characterize measurement as the representation of an empirical or idealized property by means of a mathematical object belonging to some sort of mathematical system. Numbers, vectors, line segments, and so on can be and have been used for the purpose of measuring some object or magnitude. Actually, Eudoxo's theory of proportions represented irrational numbers by means of ratios of geometric segments. The methodology to inverse the procedure and represent ratios of segments by means of real numbers is intimated by Newton in his *Arithmetica universalis* (1761). But it is due to Hölder (1901) the rigorous axiomatization of the classical concept of magnitude in such a way that ratios of magnitudes (of which segments are an instance) could be expressed as positive real numbers.[2]

Historically, the first example of a numerical representation was analytic geometry, "which provides coordinate-vector representations for qualitative geometrical structures formulated in terms of such primitives as points, lines, comparative distances, and angles" (KLST 1989: 1). The discipline in charge of axiomatizing qualitative geometries is synthetic geometry, and the representation of qualitative geometries follows the same pattern of unidimensional measurement:

> a representation theorem shows how to embed a qualitative structure isomorphically into some family of numerical structures, and the corresponding uniqueness theorem describes the different ways that the embedding is possible.
>
> (Ibid.: 2)

Naturally, not any assignment of numbers to properties counts as measurement. The existence of a numerical representation requires that the properties satisfy certain conditions. The aim of the theory known as 'representational theory of measurement' (RTM) is to establish necessary and jointly sufficient conditions guaranteeing the *existence* and *uniqueness* (up to a certain class of transformations) of a numerical representation for a wide variety of possible measurement situations. These situations are represented by means of set-theoretical structures, and the conditions are formulated as axioms that these structures should satisfy in order to ensure the existence of the numerical representation. When the set-theoretical structures are entirely qualitative, in the sense that they do not contain results of any previous measurement (numbers), the resulting representation is called 'fundamental measurement'. Sometimes the representation is proven over structures that are defined in terms of numbers or other mathematical entities, as when the existence of utility functions is proven over sets of vectors intended to represent consumption menus. This one is a case of representational measurement which is not fundamental.

Some philosophers, like Brian Ellis (1966), believe that measurement is the assignment of numbers to quantities. He describes a quantity as a property with respect to which things can be compared in some way. And he clarifies:

> two things A and B are comparable in respect of a given quantity q if and only if one of the following relationships connects them:
>
> (i) A is greater in q than B (that is $A >_q B$);
> (ii) A is equal in q to B (that is $A =_q B$);
> (iii) A is less in q than B (that is $A <_q B$).
>
> Let us call such a set of relationships a set of quantitative relationships.
>
> (Ellis 1966: 25–6)

Ellis finds that the existence of a family of linear order relationships over a set of things A is at least necessary for the existence of a certain quantity. Thus, if the objects in A exhibit a certain quantity q, then there must be a relationship $\gtrsim$ over A such that $a \gtrsim b$ iff a is greater in q than b or a is equal in q to b for $a, b \in A$; in other words, if $\langle A, \gtrsim \rangle$ is a weak order. He even thinks that the existence of such ordering is also sufficient to grant the existence of a quantity in the objects so related (Ellis 1966: 32). This is not far-fetched, as we have seen that all at most countable weak orders are representable by a numerical function; but, at any rate, the community of scientists has to decide which properties of their objects are genuine quantities for the discipline in question.

Sydenham distinguishes a property from its "manifestations" and defines

$$Q = \{q_1, q_2, \cdots, q_i, \cdots\}$$

as the set of all its manifestations,

$$\Omega = \{w_1, w_2, \cdots, w_i, \cdots\}$$

as the class of all objects manifesting elements of Q, and

$$\mathcal{R} = \{R_1, R_2, \cdots, R_i, \cdots, R_N\}$$

as a set of empirical relations over Q. In order to provide a formal definition of measurement, Sydenham introduces class N of numbers, a set of relations

$$\mathcal{P} = \{P_1, P_2, \cdots, P_i, \cdots, P_N\},$$

and defines measurement as an "objective empirical operation" composed of two functions, $M{:}Q \to N$ and $F{:}\ \mathcal{R} \to \mathcal{P}$, such that $P_i = F(R_i)$ and

$$R_i(q_1, \cdots, q_n) \quad \text{iff} \quad P_i(M(q_1) \cdots M(q_n)).$$

In other words, $F(R_i)$ represents relation R_i and M maps homomorphically the instances of the property into the relations P_i. He then labels the structure

$$\mathfrak{S} = \langle Q, \mathcal{P}, N, \mathcal{R}, M, F \rangle$$

a *scale of measurement* and acknowledges that the representation is unique up to certain scale transformations. The image of q_i under M he calls the *measure of* q_i on scale $\mathfrak{S}$.

Given that Sydenham affirms that measurement is an objective empirical operation, one wonders why he introduces his concept of measurement as the assignment of numbers to *all* the manifestations of a property. How can anybody measure all the instances of a measurable property that are, were, and will ever be? Suppes and his collaborators were far more cautious when they introduced any given type of measuring structure: they supposed that any fundamental measuring situation would always be over a rather limited set of objects exhibiting the property, and not over all possible objects that will exhibit the property in the history of the universe. In other words, for Suppes and collaborators a fundamental measuring structure is a system consisting of a set A of objects exhibiting a given property and certain relations $R_1,\ldots R_n$ over A (operations can be seen as relations). The numerical representation is a homomorphism from A into some numerical set *cum* relations that preserves relations R_i. The proof of the representation is not considered complete until the kind of uniqueness of the representation is specified.

Once this proviso is made, it is fair to recognize that Sydenham's definition is more general than that of Ellis. For there are assignments of numbers to properties that are not quantities. For instance, KLST (1989: 84) introduce the betweenness relation $a|b|c$ among points of a line (it reads: b is between a and c) and prove that it can be represented by a real-valued function φ such that

$$a|b|c \quad \text{iff} \quad [\varphi(a) \leqslant \varphi(b) \leqslant \varphi(c) \quad \text{or} \quad \varphi(c) \leqslant \varphi(b) \leqslant \varphi(a)].$$

Clearly, the idea of betweenness does not convey any notion of greater or less and so it is not a quantitative relationship. Thus, we can define *metrization* as the demonstration of the existence of an assignment of numbers to objects that preserves specified relations over the objects and is unique up to a certain type of transformations.

I have introduced the term 'metrization' instead of 'measurement' in order to clear up certain confusions that recur in the literature on measurement. Indeed, one thing is to prove that a certain property is measurable (this is what I call 'metrization'), another one to actually specify a standard, a unit of measurement in order to measure the property, and a third one to actually measure a particular set of manifestations of the property.

5.2 Representational measurement

Regarding the aims of representational measurement theory (RTM), it is sufficiently obvious that nobody can find a nonexistent thing. No matter how hard he tried, Ponce de León was never able to find the Fountain of Eternal Youth. Analogously, the measuring of some magnitude may turn to be a sort of search for the Fountain of Eternal Youth if the existence of the appropriate representation is not warranted. RTM was developed since 1950 mainly in order to "modify in substantial ways the classical models of physical measurement to be better suited to psychological issues" (Luce and Suppes 2002: 1), for the extant ideas on measurement, imported from physics, were inappropriate for psychology. This had led a number of physicists and philosophers to conclude, by 1940, that the psychologists could not have an adequate basis for measurement.

> They concluded, correctly, that the classical measurement models were for the most part unsuited to psychological phenomena. But they also concluded, incorrectly, that no scientifically sound psychological measurement is possible at all.
>
> (Ibid.)

As Luce and Suppes (ibid.) show, the effort of RTM was mainly addressed to develop a deeper understanding of psychological measurement. Much of the the research done led to practical methods of measuring psychological properties in experimental subjects, but there is more to RTM than just devising measuring experiments.

The empirical claim of RTM, as I am prepared to construe it, is that any measurement whatsoever, in any discipline, can be represented as an imbedding of a relevant structure (representing some real or ideal object) into a numerical one. This not to say that any actual measuring procedure involves the construction of such an imbedding, that the imbedding has been explicitly formulated, but it is clear that any measurement presupposes some imbedding and, moreover, that the measurement is spurious if the property being measured does not satisfy the axioms required for the existence of the imbedding, as these axioms are *necessary* for its existence.

The empirical claim and aim of RTM has been misunderstood in opposite ways. In the first place, it has been confused with a set of methodologies devised to actually measure properties of concrete things. Suppes' beautiful example of measuring weights by means of a balance, as represented by a suitable set-theoretical structure, suggests that the representational theory of measurement involves a claim about measuring procedures (perhaps a form of instrumentalism), and that every measuring procedure consists of explicitly constructing some homomorphism. This can be misleading in two ways. It may suggest both that measurement structures are always empirical, in the sense that they are not describing idealized model systems, and also that RTM is a general theory of concrete empirical measuring procedures. The main criticisms against RTM begin by misconstruing it as a theory of measuring procedures, which it is not: it is a theory about the conditions that properties or relations of certain classes of systems must satisfy in order to be metrizable. It functions, thus, as a sort of ideal control for empirical measuring procedures (that sometimes is also suggestive of empirical measuring procedures). On the other hand, those unfamiliar with the motivation of the types of structures discussed by KLST may fall into the triple syndrome of the lost beings, unavailable stories and lost content, concluding (erroneously) that RTM is a sort of catalogue of mathematical theorems.

Actually, some have even come to say that the set-theoretical structures RTM makes use of, far from representing empirical instrumentalist measurement procedures, are not even about the 'natural world'. Michell (2007: 36), for one, writes that RTM

> is based upon an inconsistent triad: first, there is the idea that mathematical structures, including numerical ones, are about abstract entities and not about the natural world; second, there is the idea that representation requires at least a partial identity of structure between the system represented and the system representing it; and third, there is the idea that measurement is the numerical representation of natural systems. The second and third ideas imply that natural systems instantiate mathematical structures and when

the natural system involves an unbounded, continuous quantity, it provides an instance of the system of positive real numbers. Thus the second two refute the first idea, the principal *raison d'être* for the representational theory.

As I said above, by 'metrization of property *P*' I understand a demonstration, out of empirically meaningful conditions, of the fact that *P* is measurable. RTM accomplishes the metrization of *P* by building suitable set-theoretical structures and proving the existence of a certain homomorphism, which is a mathematical representation of *P*. By 'measuring procedure' I understand a procedure for actually finding the value of *P* for given objects, with respect to a unit of reference. It seems to me that RTM *does not* claim that every measuring procedure consists of explicitly constructing some homomorphism. What it *does* claim is that any (putative) magnitude *P* must satisfy certain conditions in order for it to be metrizable (Díez 2000: 20, n. 5). The task of the theory of fundamental metrization is to probe into the conditions that *P* must satisfy in order to guarantee the existence of such representation when the same does not presuppose any other previous metrizations. The fundamental measuring procedures determine specific empirical procedures for qualitative comparison of the specific property involved, and chooses a standard with which the assignment begins.

It is certain that RTM has never maintained the claim that "mathematical structures, including numerical ones, are about abstract entities and not about the natural world". Clearly, mathematical structures *are* abstract entities, insofar as they are set-theoretical structures. But I have explained in Chapter 4 how mathematical structures relate to real-concrete objects and empirical structures.

It is important at this point to stress that the RTM does *not* claim that every actual measurement procedure has to be performed by means of the proof of the existence of a homomorphism from a measurement structure into a numerical one. Patrick Suppes never pretended that every procedure of *effective determination* of a magnitude had to be achieved by means of the construction of a homomorphism. For instance, for the case of utility measurement, Suppes was very skeptical about the possibility of measuring utility of given agents by showing that their preference structures satisfy certain axioms. He relied instead on experimental methods that might, applying response theory, go beyond "the individual preference orderings to the environmental and constitutional conditions that produced them" (Suppes and Atkinson 1960: 233). RTM is relevant to establish the foundations of theories – especially psychological and economic theories – but not always provides methods to perform measurements of the properties it deals with. The role of the axioms defining the structures is to regulate the concepts, so to say, exhibiting the conditions that define them, but in order to determine an actual function it is often required to resort to other methods.

5.3 Measurement by means of theory

The main methodological tool of a scientific discipline is provided by its own theory. The view of theories as systems of set-theoretical structures naturally leads to a particular view of theory-application, measurement, and testing. Typically, to conceptualize a certain phenomenon means to 'apply' the conceptual apparatus of the theory, fleshing out the terms with a particular concrete meaning. For instance, in order to explain a target system σ, a real and concrete human consumer, demand theory (T) requieres that σ be represented by a certain model system $\boldsymbol{S}$, which is a consumer with unlimited memory that knows beforehand what would be his choice in confronting any budget set $\{\mathbf{x} \in X | \mathbf{px} \leq w\}$, where $\mathbf{p} \in P$ is a system of prices and $w \in W$ is his income. The information of this ideal consumer is represented in a set-theoretical structure by means of a demand function $\hat{\eta}: \mathcal{B} \to X$. If the Slutsky matrix corresponding to $\hat{\eta}$ is symmetric and negative semi-definite, $\boldsymbol{S}$ knows that $\hat{\eta}$ coincides with a Walrasian demand function η derived from a utility function that represents his preferences; moreover, since $\boldsymbol{S}$ has unlimited computational capabilities, he can determine instantaneously the preference relation from which $\hat{\eta}$ (which turns out to be equal to η) derives.

If the theory represents σ with $\boldsymbol{S}$, the scientist may try to apply T to σ. Whether T is applicable or not to σ is an entirely empirical matter. To say that it is applicable is a *claim* that has to be substantiated on the basis of empirical data. Varian (1983) has stressed that there are two approaches to this problem. One, the approach based upon calculus, originated in the works of Giovanni Battista Antonelli in 1886 (1971) and Slutsky (1915) derives necessary and sufficient conditions on the derivatives of the demand function $\hat{\eta}$. The second, originated in the work of Samuelson (1938, 1947, 1948) is called 'non-parametric' because it assumes no specific form whatsoever for $\hat{\eta}$.

> The distinction between the two approaches is very important in empirical work. The calculus approach assumes the entire demand function [our $\hat{\eta}$] is available for analysis, while the algebraic approach assumes only a finite number of observations on consumer behavior is available. Since all existing data on consumer behavior does consist of finite number of observations, the latter assumption is much more realistic.
>
> (Varian 1983: 99)

The parametric method proceeds in three stages. In the first one it builds an empirical structure out of observations of the behavior of the consumer. In the second stage it postulates a 'curve' that fits the data obtained in the first stage, an empirical demand function. In the third and last stage it 'integrates' the utility function out of the demand function making use of the fundamental law of the theory.

It is well known that any empirical demand function $\hat{\eta}$ that satisfies Samuelson's strong axiom of revealed preference (which is expressed in terms of conditions over the Slutsky matrix) can be rationalized by some utility function which is unique up to monotonically increasing transformations. Nevertheless, this condition is not constructive and does not give any clue as to how to obtain the utility function.

Thus, out of the observation of the behavior of the agent a structure of data

$$\mathfrak{D} = \langle X, F, \tilde{\eta} \rangle,$$

is obtained, where $\mathfrak{D}$ is as given in Chapter 3; i.e. $\tilde{\eta}$ is a record of observations over a finite set $F \subset P \times W$, precisely the set of pairs price-systems cum wealth under which the behavior of the consumer has been observed. The empirical demand function $\tilde{\eta}$ is obviously finite and discrete. The explanation proceeds then to build a partial potential model of consumer theory

$$\hat{\mathfrak{P}} = \langle X, F, \hat{\eta} \rangle,$$

for which there is an imbedding $\iota \colon \mathfrak{D} \to \hat{\mathfrak{P}}$. Finally, the theory is successfully applied to the consumer if there is a model $\mathfrak{M}$ of the theory such that $\mathbf{r}(\mathfrak{M}) \approx \hat{\mathfrak{P}}$. This means that $\mathfrak{M}$ is a structure

$$\mathfrak{M} = \langle X, P, W, \eta, \succsim \rangle,$$

where η is a Walrasian demand function.

The interesting point is that it is not possible to find the preference relation (or a utility function representing it) unless that function exists and we assume that the agent fulfills the fundamental law. RTM is in charge of providing us with the conditions under which that function exists, but not with the method to find it.

The parametric method, on the other hand, proceeds as follows. Let u be the function we are looking for, and let us suppose that the empirical data $\tilde{\eta}$ fit in the Cobb-Douglas function $\hat{\eta}(\mathbf{p}, w) = (\alpha p^{-1}w, (1-\alpha)q^{-1}w)$, where α is a number in (0, 1) (we consider the case in which $L = 2$ with $\mathbf{p} = (p, q)$ and $\mathbf{p}_0 = (p_0, q_0)$). Since the agent is assumed rational, the agent must maximize (the still unknown) utility function u for each pair $(\mathbf{p}, w)$, obtaining (among others) the indirect utility function $v(\mathbf{p}, w)$, which assigns to each such pair the level of utility obtained by the agent under such prices and level of wealth. Let μ be the compensation function which assigns to $(\mathbf{p}, \mathbf{p}_0, w)$ the minimum cost of reaching the (still unknown) utility level $v(\mathbf{p}_0, w)$ if the prevailing price system is $\mathbf{p}$.

Out of the integrability equations

$$\frac{\partial \mu(p, q; p_0, q_0, w)}{\partial p} = \hat{\eta}_1(p, q, \mu(p, q; p_0, q_0, w)) \tag{5.1}$$

$$\frac{\partial \mu(p, q; p_0, q_0, w)}{\partial q} = \hat{\eta}_2(p, q, \mu(p, q; p_0, q_0, w)) \tag{5.2}$$

$$\mu(p_0, q_0; p_0, q_0, w) = w \tag{5.3}$$

we can obtain a compensation function implicitly containing a compensation function and, out of it, it is possible to get the direct utility function solving the next problem:

$$\text{Minimize}_{(p,q)\geqq 0} \quad v(p,q,w)$$
subject to $px + qy = w$.

The unknown function to be determined is precisely μ. We can normalize prices in such a way that the price of good 2 is $q = 1$, being p the price of the first good, so that it is enough to solve equation 5.1 p. Substituting in 5.1 we get

$$\frac{d\mu}{dp} = \alpha p^{-1}\mu \tag{5.4}$$

or, equivalently,

$$\frac{d\mu}{dp} - \alpha p^{-1}\mu = 0. \tag{5.5}$$

The general solution of system 5.1–5.3 is

$$\mu = cp^{\alpha}q^{1-\alpha}. \tag{5.6}$$

Replacing in the initial condition we get $cp_0^{\alpha}q_0^{1-\alpha} = w$ or $c = p_0^{-\alpha}q_0^{\alpha-1}w$. Therefore,

$$\begin{aligned}\mu(p,q;p_0,q_0,w) &= p_0^{-\alpha}q_0^{\alpha-1}wp^{\alpha}q^{1-\alpha}\\ &= \left(\alpha^{\alpha}(1-\alpha)^{1-\alpha}p_0^{-\alpha}q_0^{\alpha-1}w\right)\left(\alpha^{-\alpha}(1-\alpha)^{\alpha-1}p^{\alpha}q^{1-\alpha}\right)\\ &= v(p_0,q_0,w)\cdot\left(\alpha^{-\alpha}(1-\alpha)^{\alpha-1}p^{\alpha}q^{1-\alpha}\right).\end{aligned}$$

Hence, for any system of prices (p_0, q_0), the indirect utility function is

$$\begin{aligned}v(p_0,q_0,w) &= \frac{\mu(p,q;p_0,q_0,w)}{\left(\alpha^{-\alpha}(1-\alpha)^{\alpha-1}p^{\alpha}q^{1-\alpha}\right)}\\ &= \alpha^{\alpha}(1-\alpha)^{1-\alpha}p_0^{-\alpha}q_0^{\alpha-1}w.\end{aligned}$$

Now we can then proceed to address the problem

$$\text{Minimize}_{(p,q)\geqq 0}\ \alpha^{\alpha}(1-\alpha)^{1-\alpha}p^{-\alpha}q^{\alpha-1}w$$
subject to $px + qy = w$,

whose solution is $(p', q') = (\alpha x^{-1}w, (1-\alpha)y^{-1}w)$. Substituting these values in the objective function we obtain, finally,

$$u(x,y) = v(p',q',w) = x^{\alpha}y^{1-\alpha}, \tag{5.7}$$

which is precisely the utility function we were looking for. Clearly, $\hat{\eta}$ turns out to be precisely the Walrasian demand function associated to u.

The non-parametric method, on the other hand, does not try to build directly the complete demand function $\hat{\eta}$, but rather uses an algorithm to build directly a utility function that 'rationalizes' the data, provided that structure $\mathfrak{D}$ satisfies any of the conditions of the following theorem.

5.3.1 Theorem

(AFRIAT) *The following conditions are equivalent:*

(1) There exists a nonsatiated utility function that rationalizes the data.
(2) The data satisfy the general [strong] axiom of revealed preference.
(3) There are numbers U^i, $\lambda^i > 0$ $(i = 1,\ldots, N)$ that satisfy Afriat's inequalities:

$$U^i \leq U^j + \lambda^j \mathbf{p}^j(\mathbf{x}^i - \mathbf{x}^j)$$

for $i, j = 1,\ldots, N$.
(4) There is a concave, monotonic, continuous, and nonsatiated utility function that rationalizes the data.[3]

(The proof is omitted.)

Afriat (1967) and Varian (1982) provided algorithms by means of which it is possible to build a utility function u that rationalizes the data of structure $\mathfrak{D}$. This is "jumping", so to say, from a model of data to the theoretic function u. Then it is possible to imbed $\mathfrak{D}$ into the partial structure consisting of the Walrasian demand function η induced by u. That is to say, η restricted to F coincides with $\tilde{\eta}$. The parametric method, on the other hand, tries first to determine the non-theoretic demand function $\hat{\eta}$ without involving u and afterward tries to recover u out of $\hat{\eta}$.

The upshot of this example is that there are some applications of economic theories that require methods other than those of RTM in order to flesh out the terms of the theory, to actually measure the magnitudes referred to by the terms of the theory. Suppes himself used methods more similar to this (fleshing out the magnitudes out of models of data) in his classical experiments on learning theory.[4]

Hence, more than a method to flesh out the terms of a theory in empirical application or testing, in economics RTM seems to be rather a methodology to establish the existence of metrizations, sometimes for idealized magnitudes.

5.4 Measurement without theory

Measurement without theory is possible, provided that the property to be measured is actually measurable (there are properties, like beauty for instance, that are hardly measurable), that the person in charge of the measurement has a fair representation of the real-concrete thing and the property that is being measured, and that the measuring does not require sophisticated theory or instruments. Measurement does not always necessarily require a full-fledged theory, but just a

Gedankenkontrum, some concept of the target system to be measured, or sheer common sense.

Men have performed measurements at least since they started allocating goods and labor, trading, building, and delimiting parcels of land. According to Struik (1954: 1), "our first conceptions of number and form date back to times as far removed as the Old Stone Age, the Paleolithicum". Nevertheless, "numerical terms – expressing some of 'the most abstract ideas which the human mind is capable of forming,' as Adam Smith has said – came only slowly into use" (ibid.: 3) since the fifth millenium BC. Trade, in particular, required, on top of mere counting, to compare weights, lengths and volumes. The use of the balance in order to measure weights is very ancient, as Jammer (1964: 16–17) points out; it is mentioned in the Book of the Dead and in the biblical narrative of Genesis 23:16. As a matter of fact in Moses' law (Leviticus 19:35–6) there is a demand to be fair in the measurement of weights, lengths, and volumes:

> 'You shall do no injustice in judgment, in measurement of length, weight, or volume. 'You shall have just balances, just weights, a just ephah, and a just hin.

Nevertheless, the first theory of equal-arms balance measurement appeared much later; it is due to Archimedes, specifically in Book I of *On the Equilibrium of Planes*.[5] The point is that the practice of measurement, at least in some cases, did not have to wait for abstract theories in order to be carried on.

Econometrists are very prone to measure things without much appeal to theory. Famous vocal defenders of the practice of measurement without theory were Burns and Mitchell (1946). Koopmans (1947) described the approach of these authors as empirical, in the following sense:

> The various choices as to what to "look for", what economic phenomena to observe, and what measures to define and compute, are made with a minimum of assistance from theoretical conceptions or hypotheses regarding the nature of the economic processes by which the variables studied are generated.
>
> (Koopmans 1947: 161)

This agrees well with Suppes description of econometric work, where 'models' are "usually of a relatively simple character without substantial theoretical deductions from the model itself" (Suppes 1976: 440).

Actually, an econometric 'model' is sometimes no more than a set of linear equations. Some econometrists distinguish an econometric model from an economic one in that the latter consists of mathematical equations describing diverse relationships used to test economic theories. Thus, the difference would be that the latter is obtained out of a theory as a sort of specification of its axioms, whereas the former is "not derived from any more fundamental assumptions, nor is it the consequence of elementary qualitative assumptions or of some deeper running formulation of economic theory" (Suppes 1976: 441); that is to say, it is postulated without necessarily appealing to any economic theory. At any rate, if the econometric 'model' is not built as an application or testing of an economic theory, it is a model of probability theory, as we shall see in Chapter 12.

Koopmans criticized the pretension of performing econometric measurements "without theory", on the ground that it is impossible to choose the relevant aspects of a phenomenon without some theoretical preconceptions:

> even for the purpose of systematic and large scale observation of such a many-sided phenomenon [as business cycles], theoretical preconceptions about its nature cannot be dispensed with.
>
> (Koopmans 1947: 163)

What I have claimed is that such preconceptions need not belong to a systematic abstract theory, but may proceed from a general concept of the phenomenon under interest. In Chapter 6 I will develop a map, a schema devised to generate *Gedankenkonkreten*, descriptions of what the econometricians call 'data generation processes' (DGP), which are previous to the development of idealized models of the same.

Aris Spanos (1986: 11) has pointed out that the most important issue in econometric modelling is "the connection between estimated equations using observed data and the theoretical relationships postulated by economic theory". Spanos himself has an interesting doctrine about such relationships that I will formalize with some detail below, in Chapter 12, from the point of view of SVT.

Summing up, measurement sometimes can or must be performed by means of a theory, making essential use of the theoretical systematizations, in particular nomological sentences, in order to find the value of a particular function. This is especially the case when the function is *T*-theoretical. Sometimes measurement is grounded in ancient traditions and common sense, and performed all of the time as a practical matter. Sometimes measurement is carried on by means of the application of the apparatus of probability theory and statistics, without much recourse to economic theory, and just based upon some understanding of the target system by means of a general concept of the same. And in all cases it can be proven that behind any measurement there must needs be a homomorphism of some kind of structure. What seems far-fetched is the idea of a theory of measurement that takes into account all the messy details involved in every possible measuring situation, since there is no science of the particular, as the Philosopher pointed out.[6]

Notes

1 I will refer to this group of authors as KLST from now on.
2 I shall make use of Hölder's methodology in Chapter 7, in order to prove the existence of differentiable utility functions.

3 For a proof see Varian (1983).
4 For a description of these see García de la Sienra (2011).
5 The text is published in English in Heath (2010). The first edition of this work saw the light in 1897. Suppes (1971, 1980) reconstructs this theory by means of his concept of a conjoint structure in order to illustrate the use of fundamental measurement concepts in the history of science.
6 Aristotle, *Prior Analytics*, bk. II, chap. 21; also *Posterior Analytics*, bk. I, chapter 1. Cf. Barnes (1984, vol. 1: 39–166).

6 A general concept of an economy

6.1 Fixing the reference of economic theories

Theorization in economics is about real-concrete systems, processes, or phenomena, which must be identified before any idealized model of the same is built. Econometricians call these real concrete entities 'data generation processes' (DGP), and use this term in order

> to designate the phenomenon of interest which a theory purports to explain. The concept is used in order to emphasize the intended scope of the theory as well as the source of the observable data. Defined this way, the concept of the actual DGP might be a real observable phenomenon or an experimental-like situation depending on the intended scope of the theory.
>
> (Spanos 1986: 661)

I have designated the DGPs by means of the Greek letter σ. The intended scope of the theory is historically fixed by the community of scientists as a certain time-dependent set $\{\sigma\}$, which is classified into types $\boldsymbol{\sigma}_1, \ldots, \boldsymbol{\sigma}_n$ of real-concrete phenomena. Each of these types, in turn, is represented by partial potential models collected in the set $I = \{\mathfrak{B}_{\sigma_1}, \ldots, \mathfrak{B}_{\sigma_n}\}$ of intended applications of the theory.

The reference to the DGPs is basically fixed by a general term expressing a certain *Gedankenkonkretum*, not by the theoretical models. This means that *we do have*, indeed, a theory-independent way of referring to the phenomena the theory intends to deal with.

6.2 A general concept of an economic system

Even in primitive and undifferentiated societies human life manifests in activities – actions – of different kinds: familiar, ecclesiastical, agricultural, educational, artisanal, political, artistic, and so on. The realization of these activities requires inputs – goods and labor services – whose production requires skills and specialized capabilities. Human activities are carried out in economics units, which can be production units or households, being the case that there may be overlapping among these. An economic unit is *self-sufficient* if it produces all the inputs and services required to exist and reproduce itself. But even from remote times economic units are not self-sufficient, since they require inputs from other units in order to perform their activities. This leads to a social division of labor and the interconnection of economic units, which in this form integrate systems. An *economic system* is a family of interrelated economic units providing goods to the others and receiving inputs from them.

A cycle of an economic system involves choices in the bosom of each economic unit. What to consume? How much? What to produce and in what amounts? The functioning of an economic system requires coordination, because the set of actions available to a given unit depends upon the actions carried out by the others. That is to say, if there are κ units in the system, and the actions of units other than unit $\boldsymbol{\kappa}$ are $a_1, \ldots, a_{k-1}, a_{k+1} \ldots, a_\kappa$, we can represent these actions by means of a vector $\boldsymbol{a} = (a_1, \ldots, a_{k-1}, z_k, a_{k+1} \ldots, a_\kappa)$, where z_k is a generic action available to k, and we can denote by means of $\boldsymbol{\varphi}_k(\boldsymbol{a})$ the set of options that the actions of the other units make available to unit k.

In order to describe the choices of the agents in the different environments (profiles), we introduce a choice function for each agent. Given the profile $\boldsymbol{a} = (a_1, \ldots, a_\kappa) \in A$, the effectively feasible actions for agent k are in the set $\boldsymbol{\varphi}_k(\boldsymbol{a})$. Therefore, his choice $\eta_k(\boldsymbol{a})$ must be restricted to $\boldsymbol{\varphi}_k(\boldsymbol{a})$; that is to say, it must be that $\eta_k(\boldsymbol{a}) \in \boldsymbol{\varphi}_k(\boldsymbol{a})$. If k is a consumer, $\eta_k(\boldsymbol{a})$ is a consumption menu feasible for k; if k is a producer, $\eta_k(\boldsymbol{a})$ is a production process feasible for k.

A profile of choices $\boldsymbol{a} = (a_1, \ldots, a_\kappa)$ is *feasible* iff $\boldsymbol{a}_k \in \boldsymbol{\varphi}_k(\boldsymbol{a})$; that is to say, if $\boldsymbol{a}$ is fixed point of the product correspondence

$$\boldsymbol{\varphi}(\boldsymbol{a}) = \bigtimes_{k=1}^{\kappa} \boldsymbol{\varphi}_k(\boldsymbol{a})$$

(cf. Nash 1950). Notice that this is not an *equilibrium* condition, but rather one of *feasibility*.

Every economy must be seen as an *organisches Ganzes*, an organic whole, in which four facets are articulated, even though economic theory eventually abstracts from them in order to consider only one aspect (as it is done, for example, by consumer theory):

(1) Production: the production of goods by means of goods and labor power, with nature as a resource.
(2) Distribution: the allocation of products as a prerequisite for production, as production means (according to the division of labor) or as goods for final consumption.
(3) Exchange: the exchange of goods or labor among the individuals after allocation has taken place, for instance by means of barter or money.
(4) Final consumption: the use of natural goods and products of human labor in order to sustain the different types of labor capabilities.

Production in a determinate society in a given moment consists of the implementation of certain production processes at a certain level of operation. A production process can be represented as a combination

$$\tilde{\mathbf{y}} = [\mathbf{y}, \underline{\mathbf{y}}, \bar{\mathbf{y}}]$$

of labor inputs (represented here by means of vector $\mathbf{y}$), production means, tools and raw or prime materials ($\underline{\mathbf{y}}$), and products ($\bar{\mathbf{y}}$) A production process represented in this way is said to be in stock version. It is sometimes convenient to represent production processes in flow version, namely as

$$\check{\mathbf{y}} = [-\mathbf{y}, \hat{\mathbf{y}}],$$

where $\hat{\mathbf{y}} = \bar{\mathbf{y}} - \underline{\mathbf{y}}$ is the vector of net outputs. If we assume that there is a number λ of types of goods, and a number v of trades, vector $\mathbf{y}$ has dimension v and vectors $\underline{\mathbf{y}}$ and $\bar{\mathbf{y}}$ will have dimension λ. The household consumption menus, which I shall denote below by means of letters $\mathbf{x}$ with or without subindexes, shall also be of dimension λ, even though some goods are useful only in production.

A production technology set is a collection Y of production processes. Some agents have at their disposal technologies that can operate. Let $\boldsymbol{\chi} = \{1, \ldots, \chi\}$ be the set of such agents. The set of production possibilities for agent $j \in \boldsymbol{\chi}$ is denoted by Y_j. Hence, the available technologies for society in a given moment are represented by means of a list $Y_1, \ldots, Y_\chi$. The production processes that are going to be operated must be chosen by someone, which involves allocating labor power, as well as production means, to different production processes. In an extreme case, there is a central planner in the other, all agents are independent producers.

The form of distribution is determined by the production mode; it is a set of actually operating rules that determines who receives what out of production; that is to say, who is or are the immediate owners of the outputs of production. In private ownership economies, for instance, the owner of the production means is also the owner (by default) of the products emanating from the production processes that he operates. But there can be and there have been economies with different allocation rules. The map we are aiming at must make room for all the different modes of production, with their respective distribution systems.

Marx distinguishes the allocation that results from exchange from distribution properly speaking. Exchange takes place, for instance, when the owner of the product of a production process sells it in the market, or when the worker who gets paid in kind trades part of his payment for other goods. It is logically possible the existence of societies in which there is no exchange, if all agents are content with what distribution assigns to them (perhaps this took place in some primitive societies). These societies would lack a market properly speaking.

Final consumption is distinguished from productive consumption even though, actually, it is part of it, because it is necessary in order to reproduce the labor power. Marx believed that the proleratiat was doomed to the consumption of a subsistence basket rigidly determined, but this restriction is not necessary. In modern capitalist societies nothing prevents the attribution to each consumer of a preference relation and the possibility of choosing different menus within his budget restrictions. I shall represent the family of consumption menus available to consumer i by means of symbol X_i, where i is an element of set $\iota = \{1, \ldots, \imath\}$.

The hierarchy of ends and needs of agent i induces a preference ordering over X_i, merely a binary relation over X_i, that does not have to be connected or transitive. There is a minimum consumption required to guarantee the subsistence of consumer i, represented by a vector $\mathbf{s}_i$ distinct of $\mathbf{0}$; that is to say, a feasibility condition of the system is that i can choose a menu $\mathbf{x}_i$ such that $\mathbf{s} \leqq \mathbf{x}_i$ for every $i \in \iota$. Arrow and Debreu (1954) chose to omit any menu not satisfying this condition but I don't find convenient to do that here. Nevertheless, I will introduce in Chapter 10 an analogous notion, the worker's subsistence basket.

The total resources of the economy at the beginning of the productive cycle can be represented by means of a λ-dimensional vector $\boldsymbol{\omega}$, where λ is the number of types of goods produced in the economy. Debreu (1959: 74–5) characterizes $\boldsymbol{\omega}$ in the following manner:

> The *total resources* of an economy are the *a priori given* quantities of commodities that are made available to (or by) its agents. Quantities made available to (resp. by) the agents of the economy are represented by positive (resp. negative) numbers. ... They include the capital of the economy at the present instant, i.e., all the land, buildings, mineral deposits, equipment, inventories of goods,... now existing and available to the agents of the economy. All these are a legacy of the past; they are *a priori* given.

The use of words like 'commodities' or 'capital' in this quote is due to the fact that Debreu was thinking mainly on capitalist economies. In some economies it would not be correct to call 'capital' the means of production or 'commodities' the goods, but it is easy to introduce the pertinent corrections to the definition. Besides, it is importante to take into account also the available labor-power. In order to start the productive cycle it is required to allocate not only material inputs, machinery or tools, but also labor-power to the production processes that are going to be operated. That is why it is also required another vector of *total labor resources*, let us call it $\boldsymbol{l}$, that represents the amounts of labor hours (of all kinds) available in the economy. I shall suppose that there are v kinds of labor, so that labor is heterogeneous.[1]

Debreu (1959) characterizes an economy as a structure

$$\mathfrak{A} = \langle (X_1, \succsim_1), \cdots, (X_\imath, \succsim_\imath), Y_1, \cdots, Y_\chi, \boldsymbol{\omega} \rangle.$$

But a more complete characterization of an economy requires also the specification of $\boldsymbol{l}$, the distribution rules, and the choices of the agents. Debreu (1959: 78–9) specifies the distribution rules by means of concept of share and price of the 'good' labor (salary). But that presupposes the existence of money and prices in the economy, and there might be economies where no such institutions exist.

A distribution rule is a stipulation (it does not have to be formal or belong to an explicit juridical system) that establishes who are the immediate owners of the goods integrating the total social resources (and, in a slave-based economy also part of the labor power). As the goods can be pooled, the rule stipulates what part of the total resources do correspond to each pool. A *pool* is an element of the power set of $\boldsymbol{\imath}$ having more than one element. If $\mathcal{M}$ is the family of all nonempty subsets of $\boldsymbol{\imath}$, a *distribution rule* is a function $\boldsymbol{\omega}: \mathcal{M} \to \mathbb{R}^{\lambda}$ that assigns to each individual (singleton) and to each pool $M \in \mathcal{M}$ a share of the total resources. The rule must satisfy the following conditions:

$$\omega(M) \geqq \mathbf{0}; \quad \sum_{M \in \mathcal{M}} \omega(M) = \boldsymbol{\omega}.$$

The producers are individuals (singletons of $\mathcal{M}$) or organized groups (pools) for the production of some family of goods. In order to unify the notation, from now on the producers will be $\imath + 1, \ldots, \imath + \chi$ and a generic agent (consumer or producer) will be denoted by k. Thus, $\boldsymbol{\kappa} = \{1, \ldots, \imath, \imath + 1, \ldots, \imath + \chi\}$ and κ will be equal to $\imath + \chi$. A_k shall denote the set of possible actions for agent $k \in \boldsymbol{\kappa}$, whether he is a consumer or a producer. The set $A_1 \times \cdots \times A_\kappa$ of all profiles of actions of the agents will be denoted by A. It will be convenient to think of the agents $\imath + 1, \ldots, \imath + \chi$ as individuals or pools and redefine $\boldsymbol{\omega}$ as a function dividing the total resources among the elements of $\boldsymbol{\kappa}$. In other words, we shall convene that $\imath + 1, \ldots, \imath + \chi$ is a numeration of the individuals and the pools and suppose that $\boldsymbol{\omega}$ has as domain the set $\boldsymbol{\kappa}$. The conditions that $\boldsymbol{\omega}$ must satisfy are reformulated as follows:

$$\text{for every } k \in \boldsymbol{\kappa}, \quad \omega(k) \geqq \mathbf{0}; \quad \sum_{k \in \boldsymbol{\kappa}} \omega(k) = \boldsymbol{\omega}.$$

From now on we shall write $\boldsymbol{\omega}(k)$ as usual, as $\boldsymbol{\omega}_k$.

Given the initial social endowments of material resources and labor-power, $\boldsymbol{\omega}$ and $\boldsymbol{l}$, the initial distribution $\boldsymbol{\omega}$ determines the consumptions available to the consumers and the process that the producers can operate.

6.2.1 Definition

A *feasible social choice* is a list $\boldsymbol{a}$ of actions of the agents such that

(0) $\boldsymbol{a} = (\mathbf{x}_1, \ldots, \mathbf{x}_\imath, \tilde{\mathbf{y}}_{\imath+1}, \ldots, \tilde{\mathbf{y}}_\kappa)$;
(1) $\forall i \in \boldsymbol{\imath}$, $\mathbf{x}_i \in X_i$ and $\mathbf{x}_i \leqq \boldsymbol{\omega}_i$;
(2) $\forall j \in \{\imath + 1, \ldots, \kappa\}$, $\tilde{\mathbf{y}} \in Y_j$ with $\underline{\mathbf{y}}_j \leqq \boldsymbol{\omega}_j$;
(3) $\sum_j \mathbf{y}_j \leqq \boldsymbol{l}$.

Axiom (1) stipulates that the initial endowment of agent *i* is enough to feed his family. Axiom (2) expresses that the initial endowment of producer *j* is enough to operate a production process within his technological possibilities. Axiom (3) expresses that the production processes chosen do not require more labor-power than that socially available.

The problem is that the said processes can be insufficient in order to reproduce the system, or even to guarantee the subsistence of the whole labor-power. It can also happen that there is a disequilibrium in the economy, so that too much of a good is produced and too little of another which is essential. This opens the problem of economic coordination. There have been several forms of coordination, beside the market, and it is important to stress here that no one is feasible that does not allow the reproduction of the system. That requires the transmission of information and may require some form of exchange of the goods, or reallocation of the labor power.

An economy is reproducible if production can reconstitute, at least, the wealth available at the beginning of the cycle, in the sense clarified by the following definition.

6.2.2 *Definition*

A *reproducible social choice* is a feasible social choice

$$(\mathbf{x}_1, \cdots, \mathbf{x}_\iota, \tilde{\mathbf{y}}_{\iota+1}, \cdots, \tilde{\mathbf{y}}_\kappa)$$

such that

$$\sum_{j=\iota+1}^{\kappa} \bar{\mathbf{y}}_j \geqq \boldsymbol{\omega}.$$

There may be reproducible social choices but it can happen that the choice realized by the agents within the restrictions imposed by the prevalent allocation of resources is not reproducible. In such a case exchange – the market – becomes a drastic economic need.

There are empirically countless forms in which exchange can be carried on but, as the Philosopher said, there is no science of the particular. Exchange can be realized by means of barter, familiar agreements, the use of a general equivalent (as the cocoa seed in Prehispanic Mexico), etc. At the present level of generality, the only thing that matters is to highlight that exchange has the effect of a reallocation of the initial endowments represented by $\boldsymbol{\omega}$. If we designate by means of letter Ω the set of all possible allocations; that is to say

$$\Omega = \left\{ (\boldsymbol{\omega}_1 \cdots, \boldsymbol{\omega}_\kappa) \in \mathbb{R}^{\lambda\kappa} : \sum_{k \in \kappa} \boldsymbol{\omega}_k = \boldsymbol{\omega} \right\},$$

then we can represent the *result* of the social exchange process by means of a transformation $\tau\colon \Omega \to \Omega$.

Exchange can be seen as a reallocation of originally distributed goods. This reallocation is realized by means of barter, or the money form if it exists, and generates a market. Hence, in societies where the only way of allocating is distribution there is no market.

We can formulate in a compact way the general concept of an economy in the following terms:

6.2.3 *Definition*

An *economy* is a structure

$$\mathfrak{A} = \langle \{(X_i, \succsim_i)\}_{i\in\iota}, \{Y_j\}_{j\in\chi}, \boldsymbol{t}, \boldsymbol{l}, \Omega, \hat{\boldsymbol{\omega}}, \tau, \{\eta_k\}\rangle.$$

such that

(1) For each $i \in \boldsymbol{\iota}$, X_i is a set of nonnegative λ-dimensional vectors representing possible consumption menus for consumer i during the period in which the economic process is going to be studied. Any of these menus guarantees the subsistence of the consumer (and his family). $\succsim_i$ is the consumer's preference relation. It is usually assumed to be connected and transitive, but these conditions may fail to hold.

(2) For each $j \in \chi$, Y_j is the production technology set for agent j. This agent may be an individual consumer or a conglomerate or pool of consumers. The elements of Y_j are vectors of the form $[\mathbf{y}, \underline{\mathbf{y}}, \bar{\mathbf{y}}]$ that represent production processes, where $\mathbf{y}$ is a vector of dimension ν that represents the labor power employed in the process, $\underline{\mathbf{y}}$ is vector of dimension λ representing the means and objects of labor of the process, and $\bar{\mathbf{y}}$ is a vector, also of dimension λ, representing the product that emanates from the process.

(3) $\boldsymbol{t}$ is a vector of dimension λ that represents the total material resources of the economy at the beginning of the cycle under study.

(4) $\boldsymbol{l}$ is ν-dimensional vector representing the total labor-power available at the beginning of the cycle under study.

(5) Ω is the set of all possible allocations of the material resources to all the agents in the economy at the beginning of the cycle.

(6) $\hat{\boldsymbol{\omega}}$ represents the initial endowment, which results from the allocation that turns out according to the reigning production mode. Clearly, $\hat{\boldsymbol{\omega}} \in \Omega$.

(7) $\tau\colon \Omega \to \Omega$ is a function representing the possible results of the exchange process. If there is no trade, $\hat{\boldsymbol{\omega}}$ is a fixed point of τ: $\tau(\hat{\boldsymbol{\omega}}) = \hat{\boldsymbol{\omega}}$.

(8) For each $k \in \boldsymbol{\kappa}$, η_k is the choice function of agent k, which describes the choice actually made by agent k, if the final allocation resulting from trade is $(\boldsymbol{\omega}_k) = \tau(\hat{\boldsymbol{\omega}})$. That is to say, $\eta_k(\boldsymbol{\omega}_k) \in B(\boldsymbol{\omega}_k) = \{\mathbf{x} \in X_k | \mathbf{x} \leqq \boldsymbol{\omega}_k\}$ with $\eta_k(\boldsymbol{\omega}_k) \succsim_i \mathbf{x}$ for every $\mathbf{x} \in B(\boldsymbol{\omega}_k)$.

The clauses of this definition of an economy are not restrictive and have full generality. The definition is applicable to any economy: it is not restricted to modern or capitalist economies. It provides a map, an outline that allows the fixation of the *Subjekt*, topic, target system or DGP of any economic theoretization, through the fleshing out of the terms. This is, roughly, what Marx called "raising from the abstract to the concrete" (*vom Abstrakten zum Konkreten aufzusteigen*).

Note

1 Debreu (1959) introduces the labor resources as 'services' in the vector of total resources, as he introduces labor services within the consumption vectors.

7 Preference and utility

A **ratio** is a sort of relation in respect of size between two magnitudes of the same kind.

Euclid, Elements Book V, Definition 3

7.1 Introduction

This chapter deals with the foundations of individual rational choice, specifically with the foundations of consumer theory. Neoclassical consumer theory requires that the behavior of the consumer be explained by means of a preference relation, and that all the required properties of the corresponding utility representation be derived from the properties of this relation. Yet, it is not clear what is the meaning of the property of the preference relation required in order to show that it is representable by means of a continuously differentiable (C^1) utility function. The aim of the present chapter is to propose an explanation of such property and to prove the existence of a C^1 representation.

Just as classical dynamics purports to explain the motion of bodies by means of the concept of force, rational choice theory proposes to explain the behavior of the agents by means of the concept of preference. This is done by taking, as a starting point, a regular preference structure defined by axioms that actually attribute empirically meaningful (even though idealized) properties to the preference relation. Among these properties, strict convexity, non-satiation, or continuity can be mentioned. Restrictions on preference relations translate into restrictions on the form of the utility functions. For instance, if the preference relation is strictly convex, the corresponding utility representation is strictly quasi-concave; if the relation is nonsatiated, the corresponding utility representation is monotonically increasing; if the relation is continuous, the corresponding utility representation is also continuous. Certain specializations of the theory require, additionally, that the utility function representing the preference relation be differentiable, in order to apply methods of nonlinear programming to the derivation of the demand functions.

Even though some of the aforementioned properties are deemed as "non-substantial" and "technical" by economists of a positivist and instrumentalist philosophical persuasion, nonetheless the tendency has been to formulate them by means of natural and intuitive conditions that depict an idealized consumer described by set-theoretical structures into which the empirical data can be imbedded.[1] For the actual meaning of the axioms defining the structures is important: the more idealized they are, the less precise are the empirical consequences of the same, and it is impossible to check intuitively their degree of idealization if their economic meaning is unknown. I think that the reason why it is said (for instance by Barten and Böhm 1981: 385–6) that even though "Axioms 1–3 [reflexivity, transitivity and completeness] describe order properties of a preference relation that have intuitive meaning in the context of the theory of choice…[this] is much less so with the topological conditions which are usually assumed as well" is that the language of topology obscures such intuitive meaning altogether because it is not suitable to express the economic meaning of such properties.

It is not really difficult to formulate conditions like continuity or convexity in intuitive terms, but the differentiability condition has turned out to be more resilient to such treatment. Certainly, Gerard Debreu (1983a, 1983b) and Andreu Mas-Colell (1985) have provided conditions over a preference relation that imply the existence of continuously differentiable utility functions. The problem is that – in contradistinction to the properties I referred to previously – these conditions are admittedly not intuitive. The first aim of the present chapter is to propose a language in which all the usual properties attributed to the preference relation, including differentiability, can be formulated in a natural, intuitive way. Even if differentiability is deemed as a mere technical computational convenience, without any actual empirical meaning, the condition presented here is mathematically simpler (once the language has been assimilated) than the ones presented by Debreu and Mas-Colell (which rely upon the heavy machinery of differential topology), and is formulated within the framework of a unified language and conceptual apparatus that clarifies its relationship with the concept of preference strength.

After discussing, in the second section, the conditions proposed by Gerard Debreu (1983a, 1983b) and Andreu Mas-Colell (1985), in the third I will motivate and state, in intuitive numerical terms, the required differentiability condition. The fourth section will be devoted to introduce the algebraic theory of difference as a preparation to present, in the fifth section, the conceptual and linguistic apparatus required to provide a geometric theory of preference strength within which differentiability (actually all the usual) conditions can be formulated in an intuitive way. The sixth section contains a development of preference theory within the proposed conceptual apparatus, up to the proof of the existence of a C^1 utility function for the preference relation. The seventh section introduces the differentiability condition and the eight and final one discusses the relevance and importance of having a continuously differentiable utility function. The chapter ends with a reflection on the convenience of formulating a non-standard version of Hölder's theory in order to formulate the differentiability condition in an even more intuitive way.

7.2 The conditions of Debreu and Mas-Colell

According to Mas-Colell, Whinston, and Green (1995: 49) "it is possible to give a condition purely in terms of preferences", implying the existence of a utility representation of the same:

> Intuitively, what is required is that indifference sets be smooth surfaces that fit together nicely so that the rates at which commodities substitute for each other depend differentially of the consumption levels.
>
> (Ibid.)

The problem is that it is not at all clear which empirically meaningful (even if idealized) property must the preference relation of a consumer have so that its indifference sets "fit together nicely". What is worse, C^2 differentiability is restrictive because some demand functions that are derivable do not come from a C^2 utility function, as the same authors have noticed (Mas-Colell, Whinston, and Green 1995: 95, n. 33). Furthermore, as Debreu (1983a: 201) has pointed out, it is enough for the utility function to be C^1 in order to guarantee that the corresponding Walrasian demand function be also C^1. Is it possible to find a condition that can be considered sufficiently natural and general for that purpose? My claim is that it is possible, and I intend to substantiate this claim by means of the intuitive discussion motivating Definition 7.7.1.

The differentiability condition has been interpreted by Mas-Colell in terms of the concept of a differentiable manifold, giving rise to the following important result.

[Mas-Colell 1985]. *Let X be an open set of $\mathbb{R}^L$ and R a locally nonsatiated preference relation over X, with connected indifference sets. Then, for $k \geq 1$, R is representable by a C^k utility function with no critical point iff the frontier of R is a C^k manifold.* (Cf. Mas-Colell 1985: 64)

In terms of the Gaussian curvature of the indifference curve in each point, Debreu obtained the following result.

[Debreu 1972]. *Let X be an open set of $\mathbb{R}^L$ and R a regular preference relation over X which is monotonic, continuous, and such that its frontier is a C^2 manifold. If the indifference sets of R do not intersect the frontier of X, then there exists a demand function φ of class C^1 iff the Gaussian curvature is different from zero in each point of the indifference surfaces.* (Cf. Debreu 1983a: 194–199)

I would like to conclude the present section with a reflection on the meaning of these conditions. In the first place, the definition of Gaussian curvature proposed by Debreu (taken from Hicks 1965, sec. 2.2) presupposes *de facto* that the indifference surfaces are already differentiable manifolds (actually, Debreu assumes that they are of class C^2), and so the condition only translates the problem to a deeper level. For the question is, precisely, What is the property that must be attributed to the consumer in order to guarantee that the indifference surfaces are differentiable manifolds? In Debreu's definition, the question whether the Gaussian curvature of the manifold is different from zero or not arises once the first problem has been solved. It seems clear that Mas-Colell's condition is just a modified generalization of Debreu's and so analogous considerations apply to it.

7.3 Motivation

The problem we are concerned with can be formulated thus: is it possible to find an (idealized) empirically meaningful property over a (cardinal) preference relation that enables a continuously differentiable utility representation of the same?

In order to discuss this question let us recall that, according to consumer theory, the satisfaction of a given agent at a certain consumption menu (i.e. when the menu constitutes his current consumption) reaches a certain level. This level normally changes as he moves from that menu to another one (i.e. when he changes his consumption from the previous menu to a new one). If his preferences are continuous, to small changes in his consumption menu there correspond small changes in his satisfaction level. Hence, it makes sense to ask: How fast is his satisfaction changing as he moves from one consumption menu to another nearby? Let $\mathbf{x}$ be an interior point of Ω, the nonnegative orthant of vector space $\mathbb{R}^L$, and notice that, since $\mathbf{x}$ is an interior point of Ω, it is possible to move away from $\mathbf{x}$ a little in any direction without abandoning Ω.[2] As he moves from $\mathbf{x}$ to $\mathbf{x} + \varepsilon\mathbf{u}$ (say), where ε is a small number and $\mathbf{u}$ is a unit vector in a fixed direction, his satisfaction may change at different speeds. If ε is infinitesimal and his preferences are continuous, the change $\Delta\varphi$ in his satisfaction level is indeed infinitesimal, but the order of this infinitesimal can be different from that of ε. Moreover, even if $\Delta\varphi$ is of the same order as ε, it might be of a different order for a different choice of ε. Sheer differentiability requires not only that $\Delta\varphi$ be of the same order for any choice of ε, but that the quotients $\Delta\varphi/\varepsilon$ be all infinitely close to one and the same real number. This real number measures the speed at which the satisfaction level changes at $\mathbf{x}$ as the agent changes his consumption slightly in the direction of $\mathbf{u}$. The given condition does not guarantee, however, the continuity of the directional derivative $[\partial\phi/\partial\mathbf{u}](\mathbf{x})$.

Continuous differentiability at a vector $\mathbf{x} \in \Omega$ in the direction of $\mathbf{u}$ means that the rate of satisfaction change along $\mathbf{u}$ is continuous. What this means is that the rates $[\partial\phi/\partial\mathbf{u}](\mathbf{x}_1)$ and $[\partial\phi/\partial\mathbf{u}](\mathbf{x}_2)$ approximate each other as menus $\mathbf{x}_1$ and $\mathbf{x}_2$ get closer.

It is indeed impossible to formulate this condition within the conceptual apparatus of ordinal preference theory, or even within the usual apparatus of cardinal preference theory. This is due to the fact that the notion of differentiability requires the comparison of intervals of the same kind but different interpretation. It requires the comparison of lengths of satisfaction intervals with lengths of geometric intervals; i.e. the comparison of the distance in satisfaction between menus $\mathbf{x}_1$, $\mathbf{x}_2$ with the geometric distance $\| \mathbf{x}_1 - \mathbf{x}_2 \|$ among them. The problem is that the difference relation R falls short of providing the linguistic and conceptual resources to make this comparison.

But there is an indirect way of making claims about R, of attributing (idealized) empirically meaningful properties to R, using the geometric analogy involved in the notion of a satisfaction 'interval'. Actually, the very notion of difference comparison is built upon this analogy: When the agent compares the difference in satisfaction (for him) between the pair of menus $\mathbf{x}_1$, $\mathbf{x}_2$ and the pair $\mathbf{x}_3$, $\mathbf{x}_4$, he is somehow comparing 'distances' between them. That the agent actually thinks or feels that the distance between $\mathbf{x}_1$, $\mathbf{x}_2$ is at least as long as that between $\mathbf{x}_3$, $\mathbf{x}_4$ is expressed by the theoretician in economics by means of the formula '$\mathbf{x}_1\mathbf{x}_2R\mathbf{x}_3\mathbf{x}_4$'. Hence, it is not far-fetched, but rather natural, for the theoretician to represent this distance by means of a geometric entity of the obvious sort: An interval within a straight line. It seems to me that a fully general theory of cardinal preference must be grounded upon such a representation. I will try to show below how such a theory would be like, but it will be convenient to start considering the axioms required for the usual numerical representation of relation R. I will use in the presentation the first letters of the alphabet, a, b, c, d, in order to make it more readable.

7.4 The algebraic theory of difference

There is no doubt that every consumer has an idea of the satisfaction differences between the consumption menus among which he has to make a choice. Hence, the comparison of these differences is only natural. As we already indicated, it is usual to express this comparison by means of a difference relation R among pairs of consumption menus (represented by points in the nonnegative orthant Ω of $\mathbb{R}^L$). The simplest such relation is defined as follows.

7.4.1 Definition

A *difference relation* R over $\Omega \times \Omega$ is a connected and transitive binary relation over $\Omega \times \Omega$; i.e. a weak ordering. If R is a difference relation over $\Omega \times \Omega$, we say that $\langle \Omega \times \Omega, R \rangle$ is a *difference structure.*

Write $abEcd$ if $abRcd$ and $cdRab$; $abPcd$ if $abRcd$ but not $cdRab$.

In the interpretation we are interested in here, formula '$abRcd$' means that the change from menu a to menu b is preferred by the agent to the motion from c to d. The change from one to the other can be an improvement or a worsening for the agent. To fix ideas, if we think of the menus as amounts of money, and the agent prefers to have more money to less, a motion from (say) nine thousand (a) to twelve thousand (b) dollars is better than one from ten thousand (c) to eleven thousand (*d*). But, if the agent is to lose money, it is preferable for him to fall from eleven (*d*) to ten (*c*) than from twelve (*b*) to nine (*a*) thousand dollars. Thus, we shall assume (below) that

$abRcd$ iff $dcRba$.

It will be necessary to introduce, also, the operation of composition of motions. For instance, we can compose the motion from nine thousand (*a*) to twelve thousand (*b*) with the motion from twelve thousand (*b*) to eight thousand (*c*). The result will be a motion from nine thousand (*a*) to eight thousand (*c*), a net loss of one thousand dollars. I will define below, in general terms, the required composition operation among intervals.

In order to formulate axiomatic conditions over *R*, say that interval $ab \in \Omega^2$ is positive ($ab \in A^+$) iff $abPcc$ for any *c*, which means that moving from *a* to *b* is an improvement for the agent. Interval *ab* is *negative* ($ab \in A^-$) iff *ba* is positive. *ab* is *null* ($ab \in A^0$) iff *ab* is neither positive nor negative. It is easy to show, out of the axioms that will be introduced below, that all null intervals are equivalent among themselves; i.e. $abEcd$ for any null intervals *ab*, *cd*; it can be seen also that, if *ab* is null, then *ba* is also null.

We shall denote with symbol ⊞ the operation of composition of motions. Its meaning depends upon several conditions that we can put together in six cases. In the first case, both *ab* and *bc* are positive, so that *ab* represents an improvement and *bc* another one. In this case, $ab \boxplus bc$ is *ac*, which is also positive. In the second case, we have that *ab* is positive and *bc* negative, but the distance between *a* and *b* is larger than that between *b* and *c*; thus, the net advance $ab \boxplus bc$ is positive and equal to *ac*. In the third case, *ab* is positive and *bc* again negative, but this time the loss represented by *bc* is greater than the win represented by *ab*; hence, $ab \boxplus bc = ac$ is negative. In the fourth case, *ab* is negative and *bc* positive, but distance *ab* is greater than distance *bc*, and so $ab \boxplus bc = ac$ is negative. In the fifth case, *ab* is negative and *bc* positive, but the distance between *a* and *b* is lesser than that between *c* and *b*, and so $ab \boxplus bc = ac$ is positive. Finally, in the last case, both *ab* and *bc* are negative, and so $ab \boxplus bc = ac$ is negative. Summing up, $ab \boxplus bc$ is always congruent with *ac* but this interval may be of any direction. Definition 7.4.2 provides a formal definition of operation ⊞.

7.4.2 *Definition*

Let *R* be a difference relation over Ω^2. For any options $a, b, c \in \Omega$, operation ⊞ over pairs of the form *ab*, *bc* is defined as follows:

(1) If $ab \in A^+$ ($ab \in A^-$), $bc \in A^-$ ($bc \in A^+$), and $abEbc$, then $ab \boxplus bc$ is the null interval.
(2) If $ab, bc \in A^+$ then $ab \boxplus bc = ac \in A^+$.
(3) If $ab \in A^+$, $bc \in A^-$, and $abPcb$, then $ab \boxplus bc = ac \in A^+$.

(4) If $ab \in A^+$, $bc \in A^-$, and $cbPab$, then $ab \boxplus bc = ac \in A^-$.
(5) If $ab \in A^-$, $bc \in A^+$, and $baPbc$, then $ab \boxplus bc = ac \in A^-$.
(6) If $ab \in A^-$, $bc \in A^+$, and $bcPba$, then $ab \boxplus bc = ac \in A^+$.
(7) If ab, $bc \in A^-$ then $ab \boxplus bc = ac \in A^-$.

Notice that operation ⊞ is not defined for all pairs of intervals, but only for those that have one option in common and have the indicated form.

A *standard sequence* of elements of Ω is a set $\{a_k\}_{k \in K}$, where K is an initial segment of the set $\mathbb{Z}^+$ of positive integers (or the whole set), such that $a_{k+1}a_kEba$ for all a_k, a_{k+1} in the sequence, and it is not the case that $baEaa$. The sequence is *strictly bounded* if there exist a', $a'' \in \Omega$ such that $a'a''Pa_kaPa''a'$ for all $k \in K$.

I will assume that relation R satisfies the conditions specified in the following definition.

7.4.3 Definition

Difference structure $\langle \Omega^2, R \rangle$ is an *algebraic-difference structure*[3] iff, in addition to being a weak order, it satisfies the following axioms for every a_1, a_2, a_3, a_4, a_5, a_6, a', b', $c' \in \Omega$:

(1) If the motion from a to b is at least as good (bad) as the motion from c to d, then the motion from d to c is at least as bad (good) as the motion from b to a. In symbols, if $abRcd$ then $dcRba$.
(2) If the motion from a to b is as good (bad) as the motion from a' to b', and the motion from b to c is as good (bad) as the motion from b' to c', then the motion from a to c is as good (bad) as that from a' to c'; i.e. if $abRa'b'$ and $bcRb'c'$, then $acRa'c'$.
(3) If ab and cd are segments such that the motion from a to b is at least as good (bad) as the motion from c to d, it is possible to find a menu $b' \in \Omega$, slightly less satisfactory than b, or just as satisfactory, such that the motion from a to b' matches the motion from c to d. In the same token, it is possible to find a menu $a' \in \Omega$ slightly more satisfactory than a, or just as satisfactory, such that the difference between a' and b matches the difference between c and d. In symbols, if $abRcdRaa$, then there exist a', $b' \in \Omega$ such that $ab'Ecd$ and $cdEa'b$.
(4) Every strictly bounded sequence is finite; i.e. for each strictly bounded standard sequence $\{a_k\}_{k \in K}$ of elements of Ω, there exists a number $N \in \mathbb{Z}^+$ such that $k < N$ for each $k \in K$.

It can be proven[4] that, for any algebraic-difference structure $\langle \Omega^2, R \rangle$, there exists a real-valued function ϕ on Ω such that, for all a, b, c, $d \in \Omega$,

$$abRcd \quad \text{iff} \quad \phi(b) - \phi(a) \geq \phi(d) - \phi(c).$$

ϕ, which is a utility function, is unique up to a positive linear transformation; i.e. if ϕ' is another such utility function, then there are real constants α, β, $\alpha > 0$, such that $\phi' = \alpha u + \beta$. This means that ϕ is, indeed, a cardinal utility function.

7.5 The geometric theory of difference

It is nearly impossible to formulate differentiability conditions over R within the language and conceptual apparatus of the algebraic theory of difference. What is required is a certain 'intermediate' language. In order to introduce this language, let us suppose that a good straight Euclidean line is given in its purity. Following Hölder (1996, 1997), I shall assume that intervals within this straight line are of two kinds, such that any interval is of one and only one kind.

> Intervals of the same kind are called "of the same direction,"[5] and intervals of different kinds are called "of opposite direction." The intervals AB and BA are always of opposite direction. Let the intervals of one kind be called "intervals of the first direction" and the fact that AB is an interval of the first direction be expressed as $A \prec B$ or $B \succ A$.
>
> (Hölder 1997: 346)

Equality (congruence) of intervals AB and $A'B'$ will be expressed as $AB \doteq A'B'$. Clearly, $\doteq$ is an equivalence relation over the set Λ of all intervals within the straight line. Intervals of the first direction with endpoints A, B, $A \prec B$, will be denoted as $\overrightarrow{AB}$. Intervals of the second direction with endpoints A, B, $A \prec B$ will be denoted as $\overleftarrow{AB}$. Notice that $\overrightarrow{AB} \doteq \overleftarrow{AB}$, but the intervals are not equal, as they are of opposite directions. In Hölder's notation, the interval congruent to $\overrightarrow{AB}$ (AB) but of opposite direction is denoted as BA. Since notation AB does not indicate in itself what is the direction of interval AB, I decided to introduce notations $\overrightarrow{AB}$ and $\overleftarrow{AB}$ in order to let the reader know at a glance the direction of the intervals.

I assume that points and intervals satisfy Hölder's axioms up to the definition of interval numbers (see 1997: 351; §23, equations 53 and 54). Hence, we take for granted that there are arbitrarily designated points N and E, with $N \prec E$ such that interval $\overrightarrow{NE}$ is taken as unit. We will denote interval NE eventually as $\vec{1}$.

On top of $\doteq$, I will use symbols $\leqslant$, $<$, or their counterparts $\geqslant$ and $>$, to express the congruence comparisons among intervals. The sum of intervals of the first direction (for its definition, see Hölder 1997: 347) is denoted by Hölder with symbol $+$. Notice that what Hölder (1996) calls 'magnitudes' are congruence classes of line intervals ('distances') of the first direction in the interpretation intended here. This same interpretation is developed by Hölder (1997: 346–7, §19). I will introduce symbol $\oplus$ as a 'sum' operation defined over (equivalence classes of) intervals of *both* directions.

It is possible, and it will turn out to be convenient, to express the properties that are attributed to R in terms of relations among geometric intervals within the given Euclidean straight line. What this means is that *we, as theoreticians*, can represent the comparison of the differences felt by the consumer, expressed by symbol 'R', by means of comparisons among intervals in Λ. My proposal is to build the theory of relation R by means of these comparisons, trying to express intuitive, empirical (idealized) properties of R in terms of such comparisons.

To that end, let me introduce the function $\sigma\colon \boldsymbol{\Omega}^2 \to \boldsymbol{\Lambda}$, as an application that assigns to each satisfaction interval ab the equivalence class of all the line intervals whose length is intended to represent the distance that the agent associates to ab (how 'far' is a from b in terms of satisfaction), and whose direction is intended to represent whether the motion from a to b would be an improvement, a worsening, or indifferent for the agent. In particular, σ will assign to any interval aa in the diagonal the (equivalence class of the) null line interval, which of course does not exist but we can create by a convenient *fiat*.

If $\mathfrak{l}$ represents (on the straight line) the motion from option a to b, and $\mathfrak{m}$ represents that from b to a, the addition of $\mathfrak{l}$ and $\mathfrak{m}$ must be the null interval. The sum of any equivalence class $\mathfrak{l}$ with the null segment must leave $\mathfrak{l}$ invariant. There are three cases of addition of non-congruent intervals. In the first case, both intervals are of the first direction, in the second they are of opposite directions, in the third both are of the second direction. The second case has two subcases: the interval of the second direction is greater in length that that of the first, or the other way round; thus, we have to consider four cases overall.

7.5.1 Definition

Let $\boldsymbol{\Lambda}$ be the family of equivalence classes of elements of Λ modulo $\doteq$, including the class of the null vector AA, which we shall denote as $\mathfrak{e}$. We define the binary operation $\oplus$, closed over $\boldsymbol{\Lambda}$, by means of the following conditions:

(1) $\mathfrak{l} \oplus \mathfrak{e} = \mathfrak{e} \oplus \mathfrak{l} = \mathfrak{l}$.

(2) If $\mathfrak{l} = \llbracket \overrightarrow{AB} \rrbracket$ and $\mathfrak{m} = \llbracket \overleftarrow{AB} \rrbracket$, then $\mathfrak{l} \oplus \mathfrak{m} = \mathfrak{e}$.

(3) If $\mathfrak{l} = \llbracket \overrightarrow{AB} \rrbracket$ and $\mathfrak{m} = \llbracket \overrightarrow{DE} \rrbracket$ are not null, let C be the point such that $\overrightarrow{DE} = \overrightarrow{BC}$. We then have $A \prec B \prec C$ and we define $\mathfrak{l} \oplus \mathfrak{m}$ as the set $\llbracket \overrightarrow{AC} \rrbracket$.

(4) If $\mathfrak{l} = \llbracket \overrightarrow{AB} \rrbracket$ and $\mathfrak{m} = \llbracket \overleftarrow{ED} \rrbracket$ are not null, with $\overleftarrow{ED} \lessdot \overrightarrow{AB}$, let C be the point such that $\overleftarrow{ED} = \overleftarrow{CB}$. We then have $A \prec C \prec B$ and we define $\mathfrak{l} \oplus \mathfrak{m}$ as the set $\llbracket \overrightarrow{AC} \rrbracket$.

(5) If $\mathfrak{l} = \llbracket \overrightarrow{AB} \rrbracket$ and $\mathfrak{m} = \llbracket \overleftarrow{ED} \rrbracket$ are not null, with $\overleftarrow{ED} \gtrdot \overrightarrow{AB}$, let C be the point such that $\overleftarrow{ED} = \overleftarrow{CB}$. We then have $C \prec A \prec B$ and we define $\mathfrak{l} \oplus \mathfrak{m}$ as the set $\llbracket \overleftarrow{CA} \rrbracket$.

(6) If $\mathfrak{l} = \llbracket \overleftarrow{AB} \rrbracket$ and $\mathfrak{m} = \llbracket \overleftarrow{DE} \rrbracket$ are not null, let C be the point such that $\overleftarrow{DE} = \overleftarrow{BC}$. We then have $A \prec B \prec C$ and we define $\mathfrak{l} \oplus \mathfrak{m}$ as the set $\llbracket \overleftarrow{CA} \rrbracket$.

Relation $\preccurlyeq$ among intervals induces in a natural way an order relation among their equivalence classes. If $\mathfrak{l}, \mathfrak{m} \in \mathbf{\Lambda}$, we write $\mathfrak{l} \preccurlyeq \mathfrak{m}$ if there exist segments $AB \in \mathfrak{l}$ and $CD \in \mathfrak{m}$ such that $AB \preccurlyeq CD$.

7.5.2 *Theorem*

Structure $\langle \mathbf{\Lambda}, \oplus, \mathfrak{e} \rangle$ *is an Abelian group totally ordered by* $\preccurlyeq$, *with* $\mathfrak{e}$ *as identity element.*

PROOF: A rigorous proof can be given using Definition 7.5.1 and the conceptual apparatus and axioms of Hölder's theory (Hölder 1996, 1997), a task that is involved, as it requires lengthy arguments and the consideration of several cases. For example, the proof that $\oplus$ is associative is tedious, as eight cases need to be considered. The first case is when $\mathfrak{l}, \mathfrak{m}, \mathfrak{n} \in A^{+}$. Without loss of generality we may let $\mathfrak{l} = \overrightarrow{AB}$, $\mathfrak{m} = \overrightarrow{BC}$ and $\mathfrak{n} = \overrightarrow{CD}$. By 7.5.1 (3), $\mathfrak{l} \oplus \mathfrak{m}$ is the set $[\![\overrightarrow{AC}]\!]$, and so, by the same tenet, $(\mathfrak{l} \oplus \mathfrak{m}) \oplus \mathfrak{n}$ is $[\![\overrightarrow{AD}]\!]$. On the other hand, $\mathfrak{m} \oplus \mathfrak{n}$ is the set $[\![\overrightarrow{BD}]\!]$, and therefore $\mathfrak{l} \oplus (\mathfrak{m} \oplus \mathfrak{n})$ is $[\![\overrightarrow{AD}]\!]$. Hence, $(\mathfrak{l} \oplus \mathfrak{m}) \oplus \mathfrak{n} = \mathfrak{l} \oplus (\mathfrak{m} \oplus \mathfrak{n})$. The remaining cases are proven in an analogous way and are left to the enthusiastic reader.

The proof of the two following conditions is also tedious:

if $\mathfrak{l} \preccurlyeq \mathfrak{m}$ then $\mathfrak{l} \oplus \mathfrak{n} \preccurlyeq \mathfrak{m} \oplus \mathfrak{n}$;
if $\mathfrak{l} \preccurlyeq \mathfrak{m}$ then $\mathfrak{n} \oplus \mathfrak{l} \preccurlyeq \mathfrak{n} \oplus \mathfrak{m}$.

For the case in which the elements of $\mathfrak{l}$, $\mathfrak{m}$ and $\mathfrak{n}$ are are of the first direction, assume that $\mathfrak{l} \preccurlyeq \mathfrak{m}$. If $\mathfrak{l} = [\![\overrightarrow{AB}]\!]$, $\mathfrak{m} = [\![\overrightarrow{CD}]\!]$, and $\mathfrak{n} = [\![\overrightarrow{EF}]\!]$, we have $\overrightarrow{AB} \preccurlyeq \overrightarrow{CD}$ and there exist points G and H on the line such that $\overrightarrow{BG} \doteq \overrightarrow{DH} \doteq \overrightarrow{EF}$. Since $\overrightarrow{AB}$, $\overrightarrow{CD}$, $\overrightarrow{BG}$ and $\overrightarrow{DH}$ are magnitudes, the sums $\overrightarrow{AG} = \overrightarrow{AB} \oplus \overrightarrow{BG}$ and $\overrightarrow{CH} = \overrightarrow{CD} \oplus \overrightarrow{DH}$ are also magnitudes. It follows that $\overrightarrow{AG} \preccurlyeq \overrightarrow{CH}$ (cf. Hölder 1996: 238; §2, sec. 2), and so $\mathfrak{l} \oplus \mathfrak{n} \preccurlyeq \mathfrak{m} \oplus \mathfrak{n}$. The remaining cases are proven in an analogous way. □

In order to represent distances among options, I have introduced function $\sigma\colon \mathbf{\Omega}^2 \rightarrow \mathbf{\Lambda}$, which maps each satisfaction interval ab into an equivalence class of intervals (modulo $\doteq$) of the same direction – an element of $\mathbf{\Lambda}$ – but occassionally we shall use expression $\sigma(ab)$ in order to designate one of them in particular, which will be identified with its extreme points. Thus, $\sigma(ab)$ will be an interval of the line whose length represents the distance that the agent associates to ab (i.e. how 'far' is a from b in terms of satisfaction, with respect to a fixed distance taken as unit), whose direction represents the value of the motion from a to b for the agent; that is to say, if it is an improvement, a worsening, or none of these. In particular σ will map any interval of the form aa into the null interval. The following definition introduces correspondence σ in a formal way (see Table 7.1).

Table 7.1 Representation of motions by means of σ

CORRESPONDENCE σ				
Case	$\sigma(ab)$	$\sigma(bc)$	*Order*	$\sigma(ab) \oplus \sigma(bc)$
$ab,\ cd \in A^+$	$\overrightarrow{AB}$	$\overrightarrow{BC}$	$A \prec B \prec C$	$\overrightarrow{AC}$
$ab \in A^+,\ cd \in A^-$	$\overrightarrow{AB}$	$\overleftarrow{CB}$	$A \prec C \prec B$	$\overrightarrow{AC}$
$ab \in A^+,\ cd \in A^-$	$\overrightarrow{AB}$	$\overleftarrow{CB}$	$C \prec A \prec B$	$\overleftarrow{CA}$
$ab,\ cd \in A^-$	$\overleftarrow{BA}$	$\overleftarrow{CB}$	$C \prec B \prec A$	$\overleftarrow{CA}$

7.5.3 Definition

Let $\langle \Omega^2, R \rangle$ be a difference structure. A function $\sigma\colon \Omega^2 \to \boldsymbol{\Lambda}$ is a *geometric representation of* R iff it satisfies the following conditions for every a, b, c and d in Ω:

(1) (Any element of) $\sigma(ab)$ is an interval of the first direction iff ab is positive.
(2) (Any element of) $\sigma(ab)$ is an interval of the second direction iff ab is negative.
(3) (The unique element of) $\sigma(ab)$ is the null interval iff ab is null.
(4) $abPcd$ iff either both ab and cd are positive or null and $\sigma(ab) > \sigma(cd)$; or both ab and cd are negative and $\sigma(ab) < \sigma(cd)$; or $\sigma(ab)$ is of the first direction, or null, and $\sigma(cd)$ is negative.
(5) $abEcd$ iff both $\sigma(ab)$ and $\sigma(cd)$ are of the same direction and $\sigma(ab) \doteq \sigma(cd)$.
(6) $\sigma(ac) \doteq \sigma(ab) \oplus \sigma(bc)$.
(7) If $\overrightarrow{AB} \doteq \sigma(ab)$ for some ab, then, for any interval $\overrightarrow{CD} \leqslant \overrightarrow{AB}$ (or $\overleftarrow{CD} \geqslant \overleftarrow{AB}$), there exist a', $b' \in \Omega$ such that $\sigma(ab') \doteq \overrightarrow{CD} \doteq \sigma(a'b)$.

The following result is immediate, as it is based upon the existence of the already mentioned numerical representation.

7.5.4 Theorem

If $\langle \Omega^2, R \rangle$ *is an algebraic difference structure then there exists a geometric representation* $\sigma\colon \Omega^2 \to \boldsymbol{\Lambda}$ of R.

PROOF: Consider any numerical representation ϕ of R. If ab is positive, $\psi(ab) = \phi(b) - \phi(a)$ is a positive real number and so there are points A, B on the line such that $A \prec B$ and $\psi(ab)$ is equal to the interval number (cut) $[\overrightarrow{AB} : \vec{1}]$. Let ρ be the

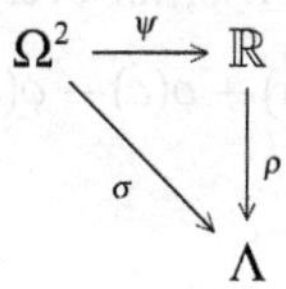

Figure 7.1 σ is the composition $\rho \oplus \psi$: $\Omega^2 \to \Lambda$

application mapping $[\mathfrak{l} : \vec{1}]$ into $\mathfrak{l}$, and define σ as follows (cf. Hölder 1997: 351–2):

$$\sigma(ab) = \begin{cases} \overrightarrow{AB} & \text{if} \quad [\overrightarrow{AB} : \vec{1}] = \psi(ab) > 0 \\ AA & \text{if} \quad \psi(ab) = 0 \\ \overrightarrow{BA} & \text{if} \quad [\overrightarrow{AB} : \vec{1}] = \psi(ba) > 0 \end{cases}$$

Clearly, by construction, $\sigma(ab)$ is of the first direction iff *ab* is positive; of the second iff it is negative; and null iff it is neither. Since $\overrightarrow{AB} \doteq \overrightarrow{BA}$, notice that $\sigma(ab) \doteq \sigma(ba)$.

Suppose that *ab* and *cd* are nonnegative and let *A*, *B*, *C*, *D* be points such that $\psi(ab) = [\overrightarrow{AB} : \vec{1}]$ and $\psi(cd) = [\overrightarrow{CD} : \vec{1}]$. Then we have

$$\begin{aligned} abPcd &\Leftrightarrow \psi(ab) > \psi(cd) \\ &\Leftrightarrow [AB : \vec{1}] > [CD : \vec{1}] \\ &\Leftrightarrow \overrightarrow{AB} > \overrightarrow{CD} \\ &\Leftrightarrow \sigma(ab) > \sigma(cd) \end{aligned}$$

If both *ab* and *cd* are negative, *ba* and *dc* are positive and we have

$$\begin{aligned} abPcd &\Leftrightarrow dcPba \\ &\Leftrightarrow \sigma(dc) \geqslant \sigma(ba) \\ &\Leftrightarrow \sigma(ab) \leqslant \sigma(cd) \end{aligned}$$

Given *abPcd* when the intervals are of opposite signs, the case when *ab* is negative and *cd* is nonnegative is excluded because in such a case we would have

$$cdRaa \wedge aaPab,$$

and so *cdPab*. Hence, the only case remaining is when *ab* is nonnegative and *cd* is negative.

It has to be shown that $\sigma(ac) \doteq \sigma(ab) \oplus \sigma(bc)$. I refer the reader to Table 7.1, as I shall consider case by case. Keep in mind that it is always true that

$$[a : \vec{1}] + [a' : \vec{1}] = [a \oplus a' : \vec{1}]$$

(cf. Hölder 1996: 243; eqn. 19). Also, for every a, b, $c \in \Omega$,

$$\begin{aligned}\psi(ab) + \psi(bc) &= \phi(b) - \phi(a) + \phi(c) - \phi(b) \\ &\phi(c) - \phi(a) \\ &\psi(ac)\end{aligned}$$

In all cases, let $\psi(ab) = [\overrightarrow{AB} : \vec{1}]$ and $\psi(bc) = [\overrightarrow{BC} : \vec{1}]$. It will suffice to show that $[\overrightarrow{AC} : \vec{1}] = \psi(ac)$.

Case 1: $A \prec B \prec C$. We have

$$[AC : \vec{1}] = [\overrightarrow{AB} : \vec{1}] + [\overrightarrow{BC} : \vec{1}]$$

and so

$$\begin{aligned}[AC : \vec{1}] &= [\overrightarrow{AB} : \vec{1}] + [\overrightarrow{BC} : \vec{1}] \\ &= \psi(ab) + \psi(bc) \\ &= \psi(ac).\end{aligned}$$

Case 2: $C \prec A \prec B$. We have

$$[\overrightarrow{AC} : \vec{1}] + [\overrightarrow{CB} : \vec{1}] = [\overrightarrow{AB} : \vec{1}]$$

and so

$$\begin{aligned}[\overrightarrow{AC} : \vec{1}] &= [\overrightarrow{AB} : \vec{1}] - [\overrightarrow{CB} : \vec{1}] \\ &= [\overrightarrow{AB} : \vec{1}] + [\overrightarrow{BC} : \vec{1}] \\ &= \psi(ab) + \psi(bc) \\ &= \psi(ac).\end{aligned}$$

Case 3: $C \prec A \prec B$. We have

$$[\overrightarrow{CA} : \vec{1}] + [\overrightarrow{AB} : \vec{1}] = [\overrightarrow{CB} : \vec{1}]$$

or

$$[\overrightarrow{CA} : \vec{1}] = [\overrightarrow{CB} : \vec{1}] - [\overrightarrow{AB} : \vec{1}]$$

and so

$$\begin{aligned}[\overrightarrow{AC} : \vec{1}] &= [\overrightarrow{AB} : \vec{1}] - [\overrightarrow{CB} : \vec{1}] \\ &= [\overrightarrow{AB} : \vec{1}] + [\overrightarrow{BC} : \vec{1}] \\ &= \psi(ab) + \psi(bc) \\ &= \psi(ac).\end{aligned}$$

Case 4: $C \prec B \prec A$. We have

$$[\overrightarrow{CB}:\vec{1}]+[\overrightarrow{BA}:\vec{1}]=[\overrightarrow{CA}:\vec{1}]$$

and so

$$\begin{aligned}[\overrightarrow{AC}:\vec{1}] &= [\overrightarrow{AB}:\vec{1}]+[\overrightarrow{BC}:\vec{1}]\\ &= \psi(ab)+\psi(bc)\\ &= \psi(ac).\end{aligned}$$

Hence, at any rate, $\sigma(ac)=\overrightarrow{AC}$ and so axiom (6) of Definition 7.5.3 is shown to be satisfied.

Finally, assume that *abRcd* and let $[\overrightarrow{CD}:\vec{1}]=\psi(cd)$, so that $\sigma(cd)=\overrightarrow{CD}$. By axiom 3 of Definition 7.4.3, there exist a' and b' such that $ab'Ecd$ and $cdEa'b$. Setting $\overrightarrow{CD}\doteq\sigma(ab')\doteq\sigma(a'b)$, condition 7 of Definition 7.5.3 is satisfied. □

We have shown the existence of a geometric representation of an algebraic difference structure. The point of having this representation is that it provides a conceptual and linguistic apparatus adequate to express the differentiability condition we are looking for. Moreover, it can be shown that the existence of a geometric representation for a difference structure $\mathfrak{D}=\langle\Omega^2,R\rangle$ guarantees that $\mathfrak{D}$ is an algebraic difference structure. For we can express the properties defining the concept of an algebraic difference structure purely in terms of the geometric representation, and show that the structure has these properties out of the axioms regulating σ. The wages of doing this is that we can also express in terms of the geometric representation all the properties of an algebraic difference structure, plus the required differentiability condition, and establish in this way the existence of a C^1 numerical representation of *R*.

I will prove in what follows that the existence of a geometric representation of difference structure $\mathfrak{D}$ implies that $\mathfrak{D}$ is an algebraic difference structure. The following four lemmas, all of which share the assumption that such representation exists, are devoted to this end. I will introduce later the differentiability condition. For the sake of brevity, from now on, that an interval is of the first direction will be expressed by saying that "it is I"; and that "it is II" if it is of the second direction. The null interval will be denoted as $\vec{0}$.

7.5.5 Lemma

If abRcd then dcRba.

PROOF: Suppose that both *ab* and *cd* are in $A^+\cup A^0$. This means that both $\sigma(ab)$ and $\sigma(cd)$ are I or null, with $\sigma(ab)\geqslant\sigma(cd)$. Hence, $\sigma(ba)$ and $\sigma(dc)$ are II or null, with $\sigma(ba)\geqslant\sigma(dc)$. It follows that *dcRba*.

If both are II, *abRcd* implies that $ab\leqslant cd$ and that *ba* and *dc* are I. Hence, again, *dcRba*.

Notice that $abRcd$ implies that cd cannot be I or null if ab is II. Hence, the only remaining case is when ab is I or null, and cd is II. In this case, ba is II or null and dc is I. It follows that $dcPba$ and so, finally, $dcRba$. □

7.5.6 *Lemma*

If $abRa'b'$ and $bcRb'c'$ *then* $acRa'c'$.

PROOF: The proof of this lemma is easy but laborious, since there are several cases to be considered. Excluding the cases precluded by the hypothesis of the proposition, there are still nine cases to consider. They are given in Table 7.2. The proof is interesting because it yields more insight into the meaning of the geometric representation.

Case 1 is straightforward because all intervals are I or null and so $abRa'b'$, and $bcRb'c'$ is tantamount to $\sigma(ab) \geqslant \sigma(a'b')$ and $\sigma(bc) \geqslant \sigma(b'c')$. We have

$$\sigma(ac) \doteq \sigma(ab) \oplus \sigma(bc) \quad \text{and} \quad \sigma(a'c') \doteq \sigma(a'b') \oplus \sigma(b'c').$$

Hence, by Hölder's (1996: 238) conclusion 2,

$$\sigma(ac) > \sigma(a'c')$$

or, equivalently,

$$acRa'c'.$$

In case 4 there is nothing to prove because $\sigma(ac)$ is I or null and $\sigma(a'c')$ is II.

In cases 2 and 3, $\sigma(a'c')$ can be I or null, or II. When it is II, we are done, because $\sigma(ac)$ is I or null. When $\sigma(a'c')$ is I or null, we have

$$\sigma(a'c') \doteq \sigma(a'b') \oplus \sigma(b'c') \leqslant \sigma(a'b') \leqslant \sigma(ab) \leqslant \sigma(ac)$$

Table 7.2 Feasible cases in Lemma 7.5.6

FEASIBLE CASES IN LEMMA 7.5.6						
Case	$\sigma(ab)$	$\sigma(bc)$	$\sigma(a'b')$	$\sigma(b'c')$	$\sigma(ac)$	$\sigma(a'c')$
1	I or null	I or null	I or null	I or null	I or null	I or null
2	I or null	I or null	I or null	II	I or null	any
3	I or null	I or null	II	I or null	I or null	any
4	I or null	I or null	II	II	I or null	II
5	I or null	II	I or null	II	any	any
6	I or null	II	II	II	any	II
7	II	I or null	II	I or null	any	any
8	II	I or null	II	II	any	II
9	II	II	II	II	II	II

Figure 7.2 $A \prec A' \langle B = B'$

if $\sigma(b'c') \lessdot \vec{0}$, or

$$\sigma(a'c') \doteq \sigma(a'b') \oplus \sigma(b'c') \leqslant \sigma(a'b') \leqslant \sigma(bc) \leqslant \sigma(ac)$$

if $\sigma(a'b') \lessdot \vec{0}$.

In case 5 we have $\sigma(ab) \geqslant \sigma(a'b')$ and $\sigma(bc) \leqslant \sigma(b'c')$. We have five subcases, setting $B = B'$ (see Figure 7.2).

Subcase (5.1). $A \prec A' \prec C'C \prec B = B'$. In this case we have that both $\sigma(ac)$ and $\sigma(a'c')$ are I or null with

$$\sigma(ac) \doteq \overrightarrow{AC} \geqslant \overrightarrow{A'C'} \doteq \sigma(a'c').$$

It follows that $acRa'c'$.

Subcase (5.2). $A \prec C' \prec A' \prec C \prec B = B'$.

Subcase (5.3). $A \prec C' \prec A' \prec A' \prec B = B'$.

Subcase (5.4). $C' \prec A \prec C \prec A' \prec B = B'$.

In cases (5.2)–(5.4), $AC \doteq \sigma(ac)$ is I or null, whereas $A'C' \doteq \sigma(a'c')$ is II. It is immediate that $acRa'c'$ in these cases.

Subcase (5.5). $C' \prec C \prec A \prec A' \prec B = B'$. In this final case, both $AC \doteq \sigma(ac)$ and $A'C' \doteq \sigma(a'c')$ are II but $\sigma(ac) \leqslant \sigma(a'c')$, and so $acRa'c'$.

Case 7 is entirely analogous to case 5.

In cases, 6 and 8 $\sigma(ac)$ can be I, null, or II. If it is I or null, we are done. If $\sigma(ac)$ is II, in case 6 we have $C \prec A \prec B$ and $C' \prec B' \prec A'$ with

$$\begin{aligned}
\sigma(a'c') &\doteq \sigma(c'a') \\
&\doteq C'A' \\
&\doteq \sigma(c'a') \\
&\doteq \sigma(c'b') \oplus \sigma(b'a') \\
&\geqslant \sigma(c'b') \\
&\geqslant \sigma(cb) \\
&\doteq CB \\
&\doteq CA \oplus AB \\
&\geqslant CA \\
&\doteq \sigma(ca) \\
&\doteq \sigma(ac)
\end{aligned}$$

Thus, $acRa'c'$. An analogous argument leads to the same conclusion in case 8.

Finally, in case 9, all segments are II and we have both $\sigma(ab) \leqslant \sigma(a'b')$ and $\sigma(bc) \leqslant \sigma(b'c')$. Hence, $\sigma(a'c') \geqslant \sigma(ac)$ and so $acRa'c'$. □

7.5.7 **Lemma**

If abRcd, then there exist $a', b' \in \Omega$ *such that* $ab'Ecd$ *and* $cdEa'b$.

PROOF: Assume that $abRcd$. If $abEcd$, there is nothing to prove, and so we may suppose that $abPcd$.

Let $CD \doteq \sigma(cd)$. By axiom 7 of Definition 7.5.3, there exist menus a', b' such that $\sigma(a'b) \doteq CD \doteq \sigma(ab')$. It follows that $a'bEcd$ and $cdEab'$. □

7.5.8 **Lemma**

Every strictly bounded sequence is finite.

PROOF: Let (a_k) be a bounded standard sequence and $a, a' \in \Omega$ be such that $aa'Paa_k$ for all a_k in the sequence. Let $AB = \sigma(a_k a_{k+1})$ and $CD = \sigma(aa')$. Then $\overrightarrow{CD} > k\overrightarrow{AB}$ for every k such that a_k is in the sequence. But, if (a_k) were not finite, there would be one such positive integer k with $k\overrightarrow{AB} > \overrightarrow{CD}$ (cf. Hölder 1996: 239). □

Using the previous lemmas and Theorem 7.5.4, we can establish the following proposition.

7.5.9 **Theorem**

There exists a geometric representation of a difference structure $\mathfrak{D}$ *iff* $\mathfrak{D}$ *is an algebraic-difference structure.*

Hence, the existence of a geometric representation of $\mathfrak{D}$ is necessary and sufficient for $\mathfrak{D}$ to be an algebraic-difference structure, and indeed implies the existence of a numerical representation of $\mathfrak{D}$. Yet, as the reader shall presently see, the geometric language has more expressive power than the algebraic one.

7.6 The theory of preference

A preference relation among consumption menus in Ω can be defined out of the difference relation. As we said, if $\mathbf{x}_1\mathbf{x}_2$ is I or null, $\mathbf{x}_2$ is weakly preferred by the agent to $\mathbf{x}_1$. We may express this preference relation by means of symbol $\succsim$.

7.6.1 **Definition**

For consumption menus $\mathbf{x}_1$, $\mathbf{x}_2$ in Ω, say that $\mathbf{x}_1$ is *weakly preferred* to $\mathbf{x}_2$, and write $\mathbf{x}_1 \succsim \mathbf{x}_2$, iff $\mathbf{x}_2\mathbf{x}_1$ is I or null.

The kin notions of strict preference and indifference, denoted by symbols $\succ$ and $\sim$, are defined as usual. Clearly, ϕ as characterized by the numerical representation of the difference relation is a utility function representing $\succsim$, for we have

$$
\begin{aligned}
\mathbf{x}_1 \succsim \mathbf{x}_2 &\Leftrightarrow \mathbf{x}_2\mathbf{x}_1 P\mathbf{x}\mathbf{x} \quad \text{or} \quad \mathbf{x}_2\mathbf{x}_1 E\mathbf{x}\mathbf{x} \\
&\Leftrightarrow \mathbf{x}_2\mathbf{x}_1 R\mathbf{x}\mathbf{x} \\
&\Leftrightarrow \phi(\mathbf{x}_1) - \phi(\mathbf{x}_2) \geq \phi(\mathbf{x}) - \phi(\mathbf{x}) \\
&\Leftrightarrow \phi(\mathbf{x}_1) - \phi(\mathbf{x}_2) \geq 0 \\
&\Leftrightarrow \phi(\mathbf{x}_1) \geq \phi(\mathbf{x}_2)
\end{aligned}
$$

Actually, all the properties that have been attributed to the preference relation in microeconomic textbooks can be defined in terms of relations among geometric intervals within the given Euclidean straight line, just as we did with the properties of the difference relation. This shows that the language of intervals, being more powerful than the usual language used in economic theory, is a suitable way of expressing the theories of difference and preference. I hope the reader will find natural this way of expressing the properties of R (some usual ones are given below), particularly the one implying differentiability. We keep assuming that $\langle \Omega^2, R\rangle$ is an algebraic-difference structure.

7.6.2 Definition

$\succsim$ is *monotonic* iff, for all $\mathbf{x}_1, \mathbf{x}_2 \in \Omega$, $\mathbf{x}_1 \geq \mathbf{x}_2$ implies that $\sigma(\mathbf{x}_2,\mathbf{x}_1)$is an interval of the first direction.

7.6.3 Definition

$\succsim$ is *continuous* at $\mathbf{x}_0 \in \Omega$ iff, for every interval $\mathfrak{l} \in \Lambda$, as small as you wish, there is a $\delta > 0$ such that $\mathbf{x}_0 + \mathbf{h} \in \Omega$ and $\sigma(\mathbf{x}_0(\mathbf{x}_0 + \mathbf{h})) \lessdot \mathfrak{l}$ whenever $\|\mathbf{h}\| < \delta$.

7.6.4 Definition

$\succsim$ is *strictly convex* iff, for every $\alpha \in [0.1]$ and menus $\mathbf{x}_1, \mathbf{x}_2 \in \Omega$, $\mathbf{x}_1 \neq \mathbf{x}_2$, $\alpha\mathbf{x}_1 + (1-\alpha)\mathbf{x}_2 \in \Omega$ and $\sigma(\alpha\mathbf{x}_1 + (1-\alpha)\mathbf{x}_2)$ is of the first direction whenever $\sigma(\mathbf{x}_1\mathbf{x}_2)$ is of the first direction.

The great advantage of the language of intervals over the languages typically used to formulate preference theories is that it provides resources by means of which we can also express natural, intuitive differentiability conditions for the preference relation. We turn now to these.

7.7 The empirical meaning of differentiability

Derivates are, and cannot be, but ratios between homogeneous magnitudes. That is why it is necessary to represent satisfaction differences by means of intervals within the same geometric space in which distances among consumption vectors are represented. Notice that there is a natural mapping τ from the segments within Ω into Λ, namely $\tau(\mathbf{x}_1\mathbf{x}_2)$ is (the equivalence class of) that interval in Λ whose Euclidean norm is $\| \mathbf{x}_1 - \mathbf{x}_2 \|$. Notice that the cut $[\tau(\mathbf{x}_1\mathbf{x}_2) : \vec{1}]$ is precisely $\| \mathbf{x}_1 - \mathbf{x}_2 \|$. Using Hölder's interval numbers (cuts) or measure-numbers (Hölder 1996: 242), as we did in the proof of Theorem 7.5.4, it is possible to map the Ω-segments into Λ. In particular all segments of length 1 are mapped by τ into segment $\vec{1} \doteq NE$ in Λ.

Recall that a real-valued function defined on an open subset D of $\mathbb{R}^L$ is continuously differentiable at $\mathbf{x} \in D$ iff all its partial derivatives exist throughout a neighborhood of $\mathbf{x}$ and are continuous at $\mathbf{x}$. Hence, our aim is to find conditions over the satisfaction differences (or their proxies in Λ) implying the existence of a function ϕ fulfilling these requirements.

The empirical meaning of the differentiability condition is that the agent's tastes have a certain sort of stability. That is to say, the rate of change of the agent's satisfaction is almost constant within a small vicinity of any consumption menu $\mathbf{x}$ and, at any rate, it varies continuously in any given direction. This means that, within the infinitesimal neighborhood of $\mathbf{x}$ (within the 'halo' or 'monad' of $\mathbf{x}$) the rate of change of satisfaction of the agent is 'almost' constant. This implies, in particular, that in an arbitrarily given direction, determined by the unit vector $\mathbf{u}$, the ratio of the satisfaction difference between any two menus to their physical difference is 'almost' constant. How can this condition be expressed in a formal way?

Let $\mathbf{x}$ be an arbitrary point in the interior of Ω and $\mathbf{u}$ a unit vector in a given fixed direction. Following Newton's conception of the theory of proportions, the ratio of one magnitude to another of the same kind is to be expressed as a real positive number,[6] and so the required condition is that, for any infinitesimal number ε, the ratio of the satisfaction segment $\sigma(\mathbf{x}(\mathbf{x} + \boldsymbol{\varepsilon}\mathbf{u}))$ to the quantity segment $\tau(\mathbf{x}(\mathbf{x} + \boldsymbol{\varepsilon}\mathbf{u}))$ be infinitely close to a certain positive real number which we can conveniently identify with the cut $[\Delta(\mathbf{x}) : \vec{1}]$. Naturally, we want to identify the cut $[\Delta(\mathbf{x}) : \vec{1}]$ with a certain directional derivative. Hence, the condition we are looking for can be formulated, in the language of intervals, in the following way.

If $\mathbf{x}_1$, $\mathbf{x}_2$ are menus in Ω, let us denote with $\lceil \mathbf{x}_1, \mathbf{x}_2 \rceil$ the set

$$\{\mathbf{x} \in \Omega | \mathbf{x} = \alpha\mathbf{x}_1 + (1 - \alpha)\mathbf{x}_2 \text{ for some } \alpha \in (0, 1)\}.$$

Notice that the points in $\lceil \mathbf{x}_1, \mathbf{x}_2 \rceil$ are interior points of Ω whenever at least one of the two points $\mathbf{x}_1$, $\mathbf{x}_2$ is an interior point (see Figure 7.3).

7.7.1 Definition

$\succsim$ is *uniformly differentiable* or *smooth* on $\lceil \mathbf{x}_1, \mathbf{x}_1 \rceil$ if there is a function

$$\Delta : \lceil \mathbf{x}_1, \mathbf{x}_2 \rceil \to \Lambda$$

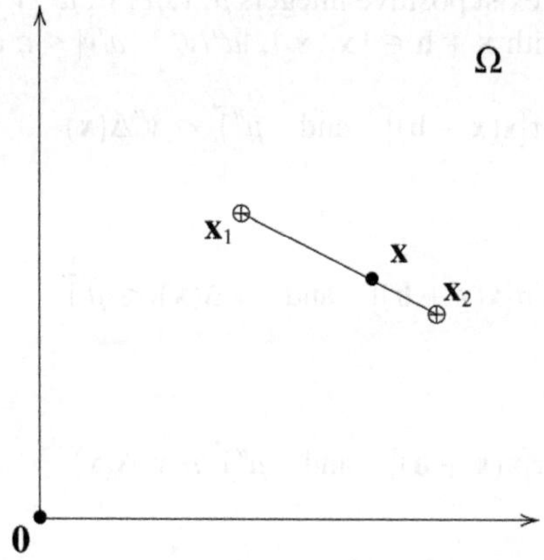

Figure 7.3 The segment ($\mathbf{x}_1$, $\mathbf{x}_2$) and a point $\mathbf{x}$ within it. Notice that the extremes, $\mathbf{x}_1$, $\mathbf{x}_2$, do not belong to the segment

such that, for any menus $\mathbf{x}_3, \mathbf{x}_4 \in \lceil \mathbf{x}_1, \mathbf{x}_2 \rceil$, any $\mathbf{x} \in \lceil \mathbf{x}_3, \mathbf{x}_4 \rceil$ and $\varepsilon > 0$, there exist positive integers μ, ν, μ', ν', μ'', ν'' and $\delta > 0$ such that, whenever $\| \mathbf{h} \| < \delta$ with $\mathbf{x} + \mathbf{h} \in \lceil \mathbf{x}_1, \mathbf{x}_2 \rceil$, $|\mu''/\nu'' - \mu/\nu| < \varepsilon$ and

$$\nu\sigma[\mathbf{x}(\mathbf{x}+\mathbf{h})] \lessdot \mu\tau[\mathbf{x}(\mathbf{x}+\mathbf{h})] \quad \text{and} \quad \mu''\vec{1} \lessdot \nu''\Delta(\mathbf{x})$$

if

$$\mu'\tau[\mathbf{x}(\mathbf{x}+\mathbf{h})] \lessdot \nu'\sigma[\mathbf{x}(\mathbf{x}+\mathbf{h})] \quad \text{and} \quad \nu'\Delta(\mathbf{x}) \lessdot \mu'\vec{1};$$

or

$$\nu\sigma[\mathbf{x}(\mathbf{x}+\mathbf{h})] \gtrdot \mu\tau[\mathbf{x}(\mathbf{x}+\mathbf{h})] \quad \text{and} \quad \mu''\vec{1} \gtrdot \nu''\Delta(\mathbf{x})$$

if

$$\mu'\tau[\mathbf{x}(\mathbf{x}+\mathbf{h})] \gtrdot \nu'\sigma[\mathbf{x}(\mathbf{x}+\mathbf{h})] \quad \text{and} \quad \nu'\Delta(\mathbf{x}) \gtrdot \mu'\vec{1}.$$

We say that $\succsim$ is *uniformly differentiable* iff it is uniformly differentiable on every set $\lceil \mathbf{x}_1, \mathbf{x}_2 \rceil$ with at least one of $\mathbf{x}_1$, $\mathbf{x}_2$ being an interior point of Ω.

7.7.2 ***Theorem***

If $\succsim$ is uniformly differentiable, then there exists a utility function representing $\succsim$ which is continuously differentiable in the interior of Ω.

PROOF: We will show, first, that there is a uniformly differentiable function $\hat{\phi}$ on any open interval. Let $\lceil \mathbf{x}_1, \mathbf{x}_2 \rceil$ be any such interval, $\mathbf{x}_3$, $\mathbf{x}_4$ any menus in $\lceil \mathbf{x}_1, \mathbf{x}_2 \rceil$ with $\mathbf{x}_3 \neq \mathbf{x}_4$, $\mathbf{x}$ any menu in $\lceil \mathbf{x}_3, \mathbf{x}_4 \rceil$, and ε any positive number, as small as you wish.

It follows that there exist positive integers μ, ν, μ', ν', μ'', ν'' and $\delta > 0$ such that, whenever $\| \mathbf{h} \| < \delta$ with $\mathbf{x} + \mathbf{h} \in \ulcorner \mathbf{x}_1, \mathbf{x}_2 \urcorner$, $|\mu''/\nu'' - \mu/\nu| < \varepsilon$ and

$$\nu\sigma[\mathbf{x}(\mathbf{x}+\mathbf{h})] \lessdot \mu\tau[\mathbf{x}(\mathbf{x}+\mathbf{h})] \quad \text{and} \quad \mu''\vec{1} \lessdot \nu''\Delta(\mathbf{x})$$

if

$$\mu'\tau[\mathbf{x}(\mathbf{x}+\mathbf{h})] \lessdot \nu'\sigma[\mathbf{x}(\mathbf{x}+\mathbf{h})] \quad \text{and} \quad \nu'\Delta(\mathbf{x}) \lessdot \mu'\vec{1};$$

or

$$\nu\sigma[\mathbf{x}(\mathbf{x}+\mathbf{h})] \gtrdot \mu\tau[\mathbf{x}(\mathbf{x}+\mathbf{h})] \quad \text{and} \quad \mu''\vec{1} \gtrdot \nu''\Delta(\mathbf{x})$$

if

$$\mu'\tau[\mathbf{x}(\mathbf{x}+\mathbf{h})] \gtrdot \nu'\sigma[\mathbf{x}(\mathbf{x}+\mathbf{h})] \quad \text{and} \quad \nu'\Delta(\mathbf{x}) \gtrdot \mu'\vec{1};$$

Assume that

$$\mu'\tau[\mathbf{x}(\mathbf{x}+\mathbf{h})] \lessdot \nu'\sigma[\mathbf{x}(\mathbf{x}+\mathbf{h})] \quad \text{and} \quad \nu'\Delta(\mathbf{x}) \lessdot \mu'\vec{1},$$

let $\psi(\mathbf{x}_1\mathbf{x}_2) = [\sigma(\mathbf{x}_1\mathbf{x}_2) : \vec{1}]$, and choose ϕ with $\phi(\mathbf{x}_2) - \phi(\mathbf{x}_1) = \psi(\mathbf{x}_1\mathbf{x}_2)$. Since

$$[\vec{1} : \mathfrak{l}] = 1/[\mathfrak{l} : \vec{1}]$$

for any segment $\mathfrak{l} \in \Lambda$ (cf. Hölder 1996: 244),

$$\begin{aligned}
&[[\sigma[\mathbf{x}(\mathbf{x}+\mathbf{h})] : \tau[\mathbf{x}(\mathbf{x}+\mathbf{h})]] \\
&\quad = \left[[\sigma[\mathbf{x}(\mathbf{x}+\mathbf{h})] : \vec{1}\right] \cdot \left[\vec{1} : \tau[\mathbf{x}(\mathbf{x}+\mathbf{h})]\right] \\
&\quad\quad = \psi(\mathbf{x}(\mathbf{x}+\mathbf{h})) \cdot 1/[\tau[\mathbf{x}(\mathbf{x}+\mathbf{h})] : \vec{1}] \\
&\quad\quad\quad = \psi(\mathbf{x}(\mathbf{x}+\mathbf{h})) \cdot (1/ \| \mathbf{x}+\mathbf{h}-\mathbf{x} \|) \\
&\quad\quad\quad\quad = \psi(\mathbf{x}(\mathbf{x}+\mathbf{h})) \cdot (1/ \| \mathbf{h} \|) \\
&\quad\quad\quad\quad\quad = \frac{\phi(\mathbf{x}+\mathbf{h}) - \phi(\mathbf{x})}{\| \mathbf{h} \|}.
\end{aligned}$$

If we let $\hat{\phi}$ be the function defined by condition

$$\hat{\phi}(\mathbf{x}) = [\Delta(\mathbf{x}) : \vec{1}],$$

it follows that

$$\mu''/\nu'' < \hat{\phi}(\mathbf{x}) < \mu'/\nu' < \frac{\phi(\mathbf{x}+\mathbf{h}) - \phi(\mathbf{x})}{\| \mathbf{h} \|} < \mu/\nu.$$

with

$$\frac{\mu v'' - \mu'' v}{v v''} < \varepsilon.$$

Hence,

$$0 \leq \frac{\phi(\mathbf{x}+\mathbf{h}) - \phi(\mathbf{x})}{\| \mathbf{h} \|} - \hat{\phi}(\mathbf{x}) < \varepsilon.$$

The assumption that

$$\mu'\tau[\mathbf{x}(\mathbf{x}+\mathbf{h})] \gg v'\sigma[\mathbf{x}(\mathbf{x}+\mathbf{h})] \quad \text{and} \quad v'\Delta(\mathbf{x}) \gg \mu'\vec{1}$$

leads, by an analogous argument, to

$$0 \leq \hat{\phi}(\mathbf{x}) - \frac{\phi(\mathbf{x}+\mathbf{h}) - \phi(\mathbf{x})}{\| \mathbf{h} \|} < \varepsilon.$$

Thus, at any rate,

$$\left| \frac{\phi(\mathbf{x}+\mathbf{h}) - \phi(\mathbf{x})}{\| \mathbf{h} \|} - \hat{\phi}(\mathbf{x}) \right| < \varepsilon.$$

This establishes that ϕ is uniformly differentiable on the interval $\ulcorner \mathbf{x}_1, \mathbf{x}_2 \urcorner$ (with derivative $\hat{\phi}(\mathbf{x})$ at point $\mathbf{x}$) and, therefore, the derivative of any point within the interval is continuous.

Consider now, for any interior point $\mathbf{x}_0$ of Ω, in particular, intervals of the form $\ulcorner \mathbf{x}_0 - \alpha \mathbf{e}_l, \mathbf{x}_0 + \alpha \mathbf{e}_l \urcorner \subset \Omega$, where $\mathbf{e}_l$ is the canonical vector in direction l. The derivative of ϕ at $\mathbf{x}_0$ is then nothing but the partial derivative of ϕ with respect to x_l evaluated at $\mathbf{x}_0$:

$$\frac{\partial \phi}{\partial x_l}(\mathbf{x}_0).$$

Since this derivative is continuous for every l ($l = 1, \ldots, L$), we may conclude that ϕ is continuously differentiable at $\mathbf{x}_0$. As $\mathbf{x}_0$ was arbitrarily chosen, we may conclude that ϕ is continuously differentiable in the interior of Ω. □

7.8 New foundations of preference theory

The previous argument shows that we can provide a new conceptual apparatus for preference theory by means of which all the usual properties of the preference relation, as well as the differentiability condition, can be expressed. Is it possible to find another conceptual apparatus that allows the expression of some differentiability condition? That is unlikely because differentiability requires the comparison of satisfaction distances with quantity distances within the same space. At any rate, it is incumbent upon those who believe that it is feasible to do so to produce such an apparatus.

By Theorem 7.5.9, a difference structure $\mathfrak{D}$ is an algebraic-difference structure iff $\mathfrak{D}$ admits a geometric representation. Hence, the new conceptual apparatus for preference theory can be briefly summarized as follows. I use the term 'geometric-difference' to avoid confusion.

7.8.1 Definition

$\mathfrak{D}$ is a *geometric-difference structure* iff there exist Ω, R and σ such that

(1) $\mathfrak{D} = \langle \Omega^2, R \rangle$;
(2) $\langle \Omega^2, R, \rangle$ is a weak order;
(3) $\sigma : \Omega^2 \to \Lambda$ is a geometric representation of R.

As pointed out in section 6 above, the preference relation $\succsim$ can be defined in terms of σ and all the properties usually attributed to it can be expressed using the language of geometric intervals (see the examples there). The novelty – as I have just shown – is that the smoothness condition can also be so expressed. Thus, using the notion introduced in Definition 7.7.1 we can define the concept of a smooth preference structure.

7.8.2 Definition

$\mathfrak{A}$ is a *smooth preference structure* iff there exist Ω and $\succsim$ such that

(1) $\mathfrak{A} = \langle \Omega^2, \succsim \rangle$;
(2) $\succsim$ is a preference relation induced by a geometric-difference structure;
(3) $\succsim$ is smooth.

By virtue of Theorem 7.7.2, there is a continuously differentiable utility function $\phi : \Omega \to \mathbb{R}$ representing $\succsim$. The relevance and usefulness of having such a function lies in that it allows the application of non-linear programming techniques in order to find the optimal points.

It would be desirable, because the empirical condition would be even more intuitive, to formulate entirely the smoothness condition in non-standard language, by means of the notion of an infinitesimal segment, as intimated in the informal discussion preceding the formal introduction of the condition. That is entirely feasible because Euclid's Archimedian axiom is logically independent of the rest,[7] but that would require a complete reformulation of Hölder's theory, as well as of the theory of algebraic-difference measurement.

Notes

1 See, for instance, Katzner (1970), Barten and Böhm (1981), and Mas-Colell, Whinston, and Green (1995).

2 Because the dimension of Ω is L, which is the same as that of $\mathbb{R}^L$. This implies that the relative interior of Ω with respect to the linear space $\mathbb{R}^L$ is nonempty and so, for

sufficiently small $\varepsilon > 0$, the open ball $B_\varepsilon(\mathbf{x})$ centered at $\mathbf{x}$ is contained in Ω. For a discussion of the notion of relative interior that relates it to economic theory, see Koopmans (1951), especially p. 45.

3 Precisely in the sense of Definition 3 in KLST (1971: 151).

4 See Theorem 2 in KLST (1971: 151); see p. 158 for a proof.

5 *Von gleicher Richtung* in the original.

6 Cf. Hölder 1996: 241, §8.

7 Cf. Hilbert (1950: 21–2); Fleuriot (2001, ch. 4).

8 The logical structure of game theory

8.1 Introduction

The literature on game theory (GT) is usually concerned with providing formulations of the same that are enough to consider specific applications (almost always in economics or political science), or to prove the existence of equilibria. In contradistinction, this chapter is devoted to provide a systematic logical reconstruction of GT whose aim is to determine its basic theory-element through the formulation of its fundamental law. After defining the concepts of strategy, it proceeds to show how any behavioral strategy determines a probability space over the histories of the game, as a prolegomenon to the definition of the concept of game and the treatment of the problem of its empirical applicability.

The basic theory-element of "neoclassical economics" is obtained, as a specialization, out of some axiomatic formulation of the concept of a dynamic game. My main aim in this chapter is to offer a rather general, rigorous and abstract formulation of this concept. This is tantamount to an extrinsic characterization of the models of game theory. The second is to discuss the meaning of the fundamental law of game theory, seen as a positive discipline. The third is to discuss its empirical applicability and to show that the conditions usually known as "axioms of revealed preference" (Samuelson 1938, 1947) are nothing but special cases of a certain constraint (in the sense of SVT).

The class of dynamic games is sufficiently general for almost all economic applications. Their temporal horizon can be finite or infinite, their temporal sequence discrete or continuous, but I will consider here only the structure of games with finite horizon and discrete time for two reasons. The first is that a first approach to the logical structure of the concept of a dynamic game does not need to get involved with the details of continuous time or infinite horizon; the second is that the generalization is straightforward through the theorem of Kolmogorov-Bochner (cf. Rao 1981: 9, and chapter III).

After introducing the conceptual apparatus required to define such games, I will discuss the concepts of strategy. Behavioral strategies determine probability measures over events that have as members, as elementary events, feasible histories of the game. I shall explain in detail how those measures are defined over the sets of such events.

Another central concept of the theory is that of equilibrium. The usual literature of game theory proceeds to find sufficient conditions for the existence of equilibria, but a general formulation of the logical foundations of a theory should not try to provide some set of such conditions, but rather to formulate the fundamental law that all games should satisfy. I will formulate this law before discussing the constraints of the theory and the general form of its empirical claim.

8.2 Finding the (lost) beings, stories and narratives

In order to grasp the sense of the mathematical concepts, the reader may imagine that game theory deals with ideal agents endowed with unlimited computational powers, as well as with abiding utility functions. These agents, moreover, have perfect knowledge of the strategies available to the other players, as well as of the probability spaces induced by them, even though not necessarily perfect memory; that is to say, in a given stage of the game, information about the precise moves that the other players have actually made. The theory pretends that the social equilibria found in reality are determined by some strategic equilibrium, which consists of a system (profile) of choices of strategies of the agents such that any of them is a best response to the others. In other words, the agents behave as they do because they have chosen respective behavioral strategies that jointly form an equilibrium.

I will prove in a detailed and rigorous way that behavioral strategies determine a probability measure μ over the space of all possible histories of the game, making some histories more probable than others. On the other hand, the empirical observation of the actual behavior of the agents is to be represented by an histogram or Pearson curve v, over the same space of possible histories, that exhibits some of them as being more probable than others. It is important to stress that μ is obtained out of the assumption of a system (profile) of strategies of the agents, whereas v is empirically obtained and is logically independent of μ. The fundamental law of the theory expresses precisely that both are related in a certain way, to wit, that v must be equal or approximately equal to μ. That is to say, the observed behavior can be rationalized as strategic behavior in equilibrium. That is why it might be said that μ is subjectively determined, while v is obtained out of empirical data. The law of the theory might be interpreted as expressing that any observed histogram is the result of strategic rational behavior (that possibly takes into account probable states of nature).

It might be thought that the constraint (which is a generalization of Samuelson-Houthakker's strong axiom of revealed preference) is too rigid in insisting that the utility function of any of the agents must be assumed identical throughout every application of the theory to the same agents. Nevertheless, this condition is a condition of possibility of comparative statics, for it is required in order to obtain the function of Walrasian demand. It must be considered as an implicit definition of 'same agent'.

8.3 Conceptual prolegomena

Let us consider $\imath$ or $\imath + 1$ players in a set $\boldsymbol{\imath} = \{1, \ldots, \imath\}$ or $\boldsymbol{\imath} = \{0, 1, \ldots, \imath\}$, among which 1,..., $\imath$ are personal and 0 is fate (or nature, which appears as a factor only in some games). To say that $\boldsymbol{\imath}$ excludes 0 means that in some applications 'nature' is not taken into account. Index i will run exclusively upon this set.

Let us consider also the temporal horizon $\boldsymbol{\tau}$, which is a set of stages $\{1,..., \tau\}$. Index t will run exclusively upon set $\boldsymbol{\tau}$, even though letter k will also be used to refer to elements of this set.

Each player i has a space X_{it} of possible actions in stage t. X_{it} must be seen as a sample space with events in set $\mathcal{F}_{it}$, which is a σ-algebra over X_{it}. If player i has no move at stage t, we shall set $X_{it} = \mathbf{n}$, where $\mathbf{n}$ is the instruction "do nothing".

Just about to begin stage 1, starting the game, each player is prompted to choose one of the actions in his corresponding space of possible actions X_{i1}, or else to choose a probability distribution over such space. At this stage, all possible actions are feasible, and so the set of all feasible results at stage $t = 1$ is $X_1 = \times_{i=0}^{\imath} X_{i1}$. A typical element of X_1 is a $(\imath + 1)$-tuple of the form $\mathbf{x}_1 = (x_{01}, x_{11}, \ldots, x_{\imath 1})$, where $x_{i1} \in X_{i1}$ $(i = 0, 1,..., \imath)$. Any of these tuples is a possible initial history of the game (of length 1).

In contradistinction to stage $t = 1$, where all the possible actions are feasible, in stages other than this some possible results may turn out to be not feasible, depending upon the history of the game up to the previous stage. The set of all possible actions at stage t is $X_t = \times_{i=0}^{\imath} X_{it}$. The set of all feasible actions for agent i at t is denoted by $A_{it}[\mathbf{h}_{t-1}]$, where $\mathbf{h}_{t-1} = (\mathbf{x}_1, \ldots, \mathbf{x}_{t-1})$.

$H = \times_{t=1}^{\tau} X_t$ shall denote the set of all possible histories. A *complete history* is an element of H. An *initial history up to stage t* − 1 is a sequence of choices $(\mathbf{x}_1, \mathbf{x}_2, \ldots, \mathbf{x}_{t-1})$. Given history $\mathbf{h} \in H$, the results up to stage $t - 1$ within that history are denoted by

$$\mathbf{h}_{t-1} = \mathfrak{a}_{t-1}(\mathbf{h}) = (\mathbf{x}_1, \mathbf{x}_2, \cdots, \mathbf{x}_{t-1}).$$

We agree that $\mathfrak{a}_0(\mathbf{h})$ is the singleton of null history $\mathbf{o}$. The sequence of results from stage t on is denoted by

$$\mathfrak{b}_t(\mathbf{h}) = (\mathbf{x}_t, \mathbf{x}_{t+1}, \cdots \mathbf{x}_\tau).$$

As I said above, what actions are feasible for a player at stage t depends upon the initial history of the game up to that stage, and so it depends upon $\mathfrak{a}_{t-1}(\mathbf{h})$. This requires that a correspondence

$$A_{it} \circ \mathfrak{a}_{t-1} \colon H \to X_{it}$$

be defined for each player i and each stage t, that assigns to each initial history $\mathfrak{a}_{t-1}(\mathbf{h})$ up to stage $t - 1$ the set of all feasible actions $A_{it}[\mathfrak{a}_{t-1}(\mathbf{h})]$ for i in t. I shall assume that $A_{it}[\mathfrak{a}_{t-1}(\mathbf{h})] \in \mathcal{F}_{it}$ – that the set of all feasible actions at t for agent i is $\mathcal{F}_{it}$-measurable.

The initial history $\mathfrak{a}_{t-1}(\mathbf{h})$ is *feasible* iff, for every k $(1 \leq k \leq t-1)$ and $i \in \iota$

$$x_{i(k+1)} \in A_{i(k+1)}[\mathfrak{a}_k(\mathbf{h})].$$

If the initial history $\mathfrak{a}_{t-1}(\mathbf{h})$ up to stage $t-1$ is not feasible, then $A_{it}[\mathfrak{a}_{t-1}(\mathbf{h})] = \varnothing$ for every $i \in \iota$, and so correspondence A_{it} is not empty only over the set of initial histories that are feasible until stage $t-1$.

Let $F \subseteq H$ be the set of all histories that are feasible in the game. Then any $\mathbf{h} \in F$ satisfies the consistency requirement: for every i,

$$x_{i(k+1)} \in A_{i(k+1)}[\mathfrak{a}_k(\mathbf{h})] \quad \text{for all} \quad k \geq 1.$$

The set of feasible histories given initial history $\mathfrak{a}_{t-1}(\mathbf{h})$ is

$$F_{+}[\mathfrak{a}_{t-1}(\mathbf{h})] = \{\mathbf{h}' \in X | \mathbf{h}' \in F \text{ and } \mathfrak{a}_{t-1}(\mathbf{h}') = \mathfrak{a}_{t-1}(\mathbf{h})\}.$$

The set of histories feasible up to stage $t-1$ is

$$\mathfrak{a}_{t-1}(F) = \left\{\mathfrak{a}_{t-1}(\mathbf{h}) | x_{i(k+1)} \in A_{i(k+1)}[\mathfrak{a}_k(\mathbf{h})] \text{ for all } k \leq t-1 \text{ and } i \in \iota\right\}.$$

Remember that, in particular, $\mathfrak{a}_0(F)$ is defined and is equal to $\{\mathbf{o}\}$. Its definition is required in order to define the types of strategies. I shall assume that

$$\bigcup_{\mathbf{h} \in F} A_{it}[\mathfrak{a}_{t-1}(\mathbf{h})] = X_{it}$$

for every i y t.

8.4 Concepts of strategy

A *pure strategy for player i* at stage t is a function s_{it}: $\mathfrak{a}_{t-1}(F) \rightarrow X_{it}$ that assigns to each feasible initial history $\mathfrak{a}_{t-1}(\mathbf{h})$ of length $t-1$ a point of $A_{it}[\mathfrak{a}_{t-1}(\mathbf{h})] \subseteq X_{it}$. In particular, for $t = 1$, s_{i1} is a function from $\mathfrak{a}_0(F) = \{\mathbf{o}\}$ into X_{i1}. A *pure strategy* of player i is a function s_i: $\bigcup_{t=1}^{\tau} \mathfrak{a}_{t-1}(F) \rightarrow X_{i1} \cup \ldots \cup X_{i\tau}$ such that $s_i(\mathfrak{a}_{t-1}(\mathbf{h})) \in A_{it}[\mathfrak{a}_{t-1}(\mathbf{h})]$. Clearly, the restriction of s_i to $\mathfrak{a}_{t-1}(F)$ is a pure strategy of player i at stage t. Hence, a pure strategy can be seen as a set of instructions indicating which option to choose before any initial feasible history that shows up. The set of all pure strategies of i is denoted by S_i. A *profile of pure strategies* of the players is a list $(s_0, \ldots, s_\iota) \in S_0 \times \cdots \times S_\iota$.

The definition of mixed and behavioral strategies requires the introduction of standard probability spaces. A subset of an m-dimensional space is called *standard* if it is either finite or denumerable with the discrete structure (i.e. all subsets are measurable), or if it is isomorphic with $\mathfrak{I} = [0, 1]$. According to Aumann (1964: 633–4), the intuitive justification for taking all sample spaces appearing in game theory as standard is that

> every "real-life" random device is either "discrete," "continuous," or a combination of the two; that is, the sample space involved must either be finite or denumerable, or it must be a copy of $\mathfrak{I}$ (with a measure that is not necessarily Lebesgue measure). All such random devices can be represented by random variables whose sample space is actually [a standard space].

From now on, $\langle \Omega_{it}, \mathfrak{b}_{it}, \lambda_{it} \rangle$ shall designate the probability space representing the sample space for agent i at stage t.

A *mixed strategy of player i at stage t* is a couple of functions (ρ_{it}, σ_{it}) such that $\rho_{it}{:}\Omega_{it} \to S_{it}$ associates to each elementary event of Ω_{it} an instruction $\rho_{it}(\omega) \in S_{it}$, and $\sigma_{it}\colon \Omega_{it} \times \mathfrak{a}_{t-1}(F) \to X_{it}$ associates to the event $\omega \in \Omega_{it}$ and initial history $\mathfrak{a}_{t-1}(\mathbf{h})$ the point $\sigma_{it}(\omega, \mathfrak{a}_{t-1}(\mathbf{h})) = s_{it}[\mathfrak{a}_{t-1}(\mathbf{h})])$, where $s_{it} = \rho_{it}(\omega)$. ρ_{it} represents a random mechanism (as a roulette or a pair of dice) that associates to each elementary event of this mechanism a pure strategy. Function $\sigma_{it}(\cdot, \mathfrak{a}_{t-1}(\mathbf{h}))$ is required to be $\mathcal{F}_{it}$-measurable. A sequence of pairs of functions $\{(\rho_{it}, \sigma_{it})\}_{t=1}^{\tau}$ is a *system of mixed strategies* of player i. A *profile of mixed strategies* is a list $(\{(\rho_{1t}, \sigma_{1t}\}_{t=1}^{\tau}), \ldots, \{(\rho_{it}, \sigma_{it})\}_{t=1}^{\tau})$.

A *behavioral strategy of player i at stage t* associates to each feasible initial segment $\mathfrak{a}_{t-1}(\mathbf{h})$ a probability measure $\mu_{it}[\mathfrak{a}_{t-1}(\mathbf{h})]$ over the algebra of events $\mathcal{F}_{it}$ that assigns mass 1 to the feasible actions in $\mathfrak{a}_{t-1}(\mathbf{h})$; i.e.

$$\mu_{it}[\mathfrak{a}_{t-1}(\mathbf{h})](A_{it}[\mathfrak{a}_{t-1}(\mathbf{h})]) = 1$$

and $\mu_{it}[\mathfrak{a}_{t-1}(\mathbf{h})](B_{it}) = 0$ if $B_{it} \cap A_{it}[\mathfrak{a}_{t-1}(\mathbf{h})] = \varnothing$ (i.e. $A_{it}[\mathfrak{a}_{t-1}(\mathbf{h})]$ is a set of full measure in $\mathcal{F}_{it}$).

This assignment takes place in the following way. A behavioral strategy for i in t is a measurable function $b_{it}\colon \Omega_{it} \times \mathfrak{a}_{t-1}(F) \to X_{it}$, such that $b_{it}(\omega, \mathfrak{a}_{t-1}(\mathbf{h})) \in A_{it}[\mathfrak{a}_{t-1}(\mathbf{h})]$ for each $\omega \in \Omega_{it}$. If $B_{it} \in \mathcal{F}_{it}$,

$$\mu_{it}[\mathfrak{a}_{t-1}(\mathbf{h})](B_{it}) = \lambda_{it}\{\omega \in \Omega_{it} | b_{it}(\omega, \mathfrak{a}_{t-1}(\mathbf{h})) \in B_{it}\}$$

is the probability of event B_{it}. A sequence $\{b_{it}\}_{t=1}^{\tau}$ is a *system of behavioral strategies* for player i. A *profile of behavioral strategies* is a list $(\{b_{0t}\}_{t=1}^{\tau}, \ldots, \{b_{it}\}_{t=1}^{\tau})$.

A pure strategy s_{it} is a particular case of a behavioral strategy b_{it} if, for each $\mathfrak{a}_{t-1}(\mathbf{h}) \in \mathfrak{a}_{t-1}(F)$, $b_{it}(\omega, \mathfrak{a}_{t-1}(\mathbf{h})) = s_{it}(\mathfrak{a}_{t-1}(\mathbf{h}))$ for every $\omega \in \Omega_{it}$. Nevertheless, it is not true in general that mixed strategies are particular cases of the behavioral ones, even though in games of perfect recall to each mixed strategy there corresponds a behavioral one which is equivalent to the first in some sense (this is Kuhn's famous theorem; cf. Kuhn 1953 and Aumann 1964).

8.5 Probability spaces induced by behavioral strategies

A behavioral strategy b_{it} determines a probability measure over $\mathcal{F}_{it}$ for each feasible initial history $\mathfrak{a}_{t-1}(\mathbf{h})$ in $\mathfrak{a}_{t-1}(F)$. Suppose that the agents (nature included) have 'chosen' a profile of behavioral strategies $(\{b_{it}\})$. At stage $t = 1$ strategy b_{i1} (for any i) determines a probability measure μ_{i1} over $\mathcal{F}_{i1}$, and this is the only measure derived from b_{i1} at this stage.

$\imath + 1$ probability spaces

$$\langle X_{01}, \mathcal{F}_{01}, \mu_{01}\rangle, \langle X_{11}, \mathcal{F}_{11}, \mu_{11}\rangle, \ldots, \langle X_{\imath 1}, \mathcal{F}_{\imath 1}, \mu_{\imath 1}\rangle$$

are so obtained. Due to the manner in which strategies are built, any event in $\mathcal{F}_{i1}$ is stochastically independent of any event in $\mathcal{F}_{i'1}(i \neq i')$, and therefore it is legitimate to build the product space $\langle \times_{i=0}^{\imath} X_{i1}, \mathcal{F}_1, \mu_1\rangle$ in the usual way. But notice that $X_1 = \times_{i=0}^{\imath} X_{i1}$ is nothing but the set of feasible histories in $t = 1$; i.e. $\times_{i=0}^{\imath} X_{i1} = \mathfrak{a}_1(F)$. I have just shown that the system of behavioral strategies determines a probability space over $\mathfrak{a}_1(F)$. The reader may convince himself that μ_1 is a σ-aditive measure.

At $t > 1$ the analysis is more complicated, since the behavioral strategies of agent i determine a probability space for each feasible initial history $\mathfrak{a}_{t-1}(\mathbf{h}) \in \mathfrak{a}_{t-1}(F)$, namely the space

$$\langle X_{it}, \mathcal{F}_{it}, \mu_{it}[\mathfrak{a}_{t-1}(\mathbf{h})]\rangle.$$

All these spaces combine in order to give rise to a new space, whose elementary events are all combinations in $X_t = \times_{i=0}^{\imath} X_{it}$, but the feasible events are found in subset $A_t[\mathfrak{a}_{t-1}(\mathbf{h})] = \times_{i=0}^{\imath} A_{it}[\mathfrak{a}_{t-1}(\mathbf{h})] \subseteq X_t$. The corresponding space of events is the product algebra $\mathcal{F}_t = \otimes_{i=0}^{\imath} \mathcal{F}_{it}$, and the resulting probability measure is the product measure $\mu_t[\mathfrak{a}_{t-1}(\mathbf{h})]$ of the $\mu_{it}[\mathfrak{a}_{t-1}(\mathbf{h})]$. In this manner is obtained, in each stage t and for each $\mathbf{h}_{t-1} \in \mathfrak{a}_{t-1}(F)$ the space $\langle X_t, \mathcal{F}_t, \mu_t[\mathbf{h}_{t-1}]\rangle$.

In order to define the probability measure that any behavioral strategy determines over the space of feasible histories of the game, it is convenient to define the sequence of measurable spaces $\{\mathfrak{H}_t\}_{t=1}^{\tau}$, where $\mathfrak{H}_t = \langle H_t, \mathcal{H}_t\rangle$ and the sets H_t and $\mathcal{H}_t$ are recursively defined as follows: $H_1 = X_1$, $H_t = H_{t-1} \times X_t$, and $\mathcal{H}_t$ is the σ-algebra generated by rectangles of the form $B_{t-1} \times B_t$, with $B_{t-1} \in \mathcal{H}_{t-1}$ and $B_t \in \mathcal{F}_t$. Clearly, $F \subseteq H = H_\tau$ and we can establish the following propositions.

8.5.1 Lemma

Let $B_{t-1} \times B_t$ be a rectangle, with $B_{t-1} \in \mathcal{H}_{t-1}$ and $B_t \in \mathcal{F}_t$, and assume that μ_{t-1} is a σ-additive probability measure over $\mathfrak{H}_{t-1}$. Then the integral

$$\int_{B_{t-1}} f[B_t](\mathbf{h}_{t-1})\, \mathrm{d}\mu_{t-1},$$

such that $f[B_t](\mathbf{h}_{t-1}) = \mu_t[\mathbf{h}_{t-1}](B_t)$, *is well defined, is not negative, and assigns* 1 *to* $H_{t-1} \times X_t$.

PROOF: For any $\mathbf{h}_{t-1} \in H_{t-1}$, $f[B_t](\mathbf{h}_{t-1}) = \mu_t[\mathbf{h}_{t-1}](B_t) \in [0,1]$. Hence, $f[B_t]$ $(B_{t-1}) \subseteq [0, 1]$ and $f[B_t]$ is bounded, and so integrable, in B_{t-1}. Besides, as $f[B_t](\mathbf{h}_{t-1}) \geq 0$, the integral is not negative. Finally, for every $\mathbf{h}_{t-1} \in H_{t-1}, f[X_t] \times$ $(\mathbf{h}_{t-1}) = 1$ and we have

$$\int_{H_{t-1}} f[X_t](\mathbf{h}_{t-1})\, \mathrm{d}\mu_{t-1} = \int_{H_{t-1}} \mathrm{d}\mu_{t-1} = \mu_{t-1}(H_{t-1}) = 1. \square$$

Let $\hat{\mathcal{H}}_t \subseteq \mathcal{H}_t$ be the set of rectangles $B_{t-1} \times B_t$, with $B_{t-1} \in \mathcal{H}_{t-1}$ and $B_t \in \mathcal{F}_t$. We define the set function $\hat{\mu}$: $\hat{\mathcal{H}}_t \to \mathbb{R}$ as the function assigning to each rectangle $B_{t-1} \times B_t$ the number $\int_{B_{t-1}} f[B_t](\mathbf{h}_{t-1})\, \mathrm{d}\mu_{t-1}$.

It is easy to see that the set $\hat{\mathcal{H}}_t \subseteq \mathcal{H}_t$ of rectangles $B_{t-1} \times B_t$, with $B_{t-1} \in \mathcal{H}_{t-1}$ and $B_t \in \mathcal{F}_t$, is a semiring with unit $H_t = H_{t-1} \times \times_t$. A less obvious result is the following.

8.5.2 Lemma

$\hat{\mu}_t$ *is additive.*

PROOF: Let $B_{t-1} \times B_t$ be any element of $\hat{\mathcal{H}}_t$ and let $(B^1_{t-1} \times B^1_t) \cup \ldots \cup (B^n_{t-1} \times B^n_t)$ any decomposition of $B_{t-1} \times B_t$ in pairwise disjoint rectangles. It is required to show that

$$\hat{\mu}(B_{t-1} \times B_t) = \sum_{k=1}^{n} \hat{\mu}(B^k_{t-1} \times B^k_t).$$

Since $B^1_{t-1}, \ldots, B^n_{t-1} \in \mathcal{H}_{t-1}, B^1_t, \ldots, B^n_t \in \mathcal{F}_t$, and both $\mathcal{H}_{t-1}$ and $\mathcal{F}_t$ are semirings (for any σ-algebra is so), there exist pairwise disjoint sets $C^1_{t-1}, \ldots, C^p_{t-1} \in \mathcal{H}_{t-1}$ such that each B^k_{t-1} can be represented as the union of some C_{t-1}; and there exist also pairwise disjoint sets $C^1_t, \ldots, C^q_t \in \mathcal{F}_t$ such that each B^k_t can be represented as the union of some C^k_t. If L_k is the set of all indexes l such that $B^k_{t-1} = \bigcup_{l \in L_k} C^l_{t-1}$, and M_k the set of the m with $B^k_t = \cup_{m \in M_k} C^m_t (L_k \subseteq \{1, \ldots, p\} = L, M_k \subseteq \{1, \ldots, q\} = M)$, it is true that two sets L_k and $L_{k'}$ – or M_k and $M_{k'}$ – need not be disjoint, but the the products $M_k \times L_k$ are so because, if $M_k \times L_k$ y $M_{k'} \times L_{k'}$ had a point in common, $B^k_t \times B^k_t$ y $B^{k'}_t \times B^{k'}_t$ would not be disjoint, which contradicts the hypothesis. In other words, $M_1 \times L_1, \ldots, M_n \times L_n$ is a partition of $M \times L$.

Since

$$B_{t-1} \times B_t = \left(\bigcup_{l \in L} C_{t-1}^l \right) \times \left(\bigcup_{m \in M} C_t^m \right),$$

$$\begin{aligned}
\hat{\mu}_t(B_{t-1} \times B_t) &= \int_{\bigcup_{l \in L} C_{t-1}^l} f\left[\bigcup_{m \in M} C_t^m\right](\mathbf{h}_{t-1})\, \mathrm{d}\mu_{t-1} \\
&= \int_{\bigcup_{l \in L} C_{t-1}^l} \left[\mu_t[\mathbf{h}_{t-1}]\left(\bigcup_{m \in M} C_t^m\right)\right] \mathrm{d}\mu_{t-1} \\
&= \int_{\bigcup_{l \in L} C_{t-1}^l} \left[\sum_{m \in M} \mu_t[\mathbf{h}_{t-1}](C_t^m)\right] \mathrm{d}\mu_{t-1} \\
&= \int_{\bigcup_{l \in L} C_{t-1}^l} \sum_{m \in M} f\left[C_t^m\right](\mathbf{h}_{t-1})\, \mathrm{d}\mu_{t-1} \\
&= \sum_{m \in M} \int_{\bigcup_{l \in L} C_{t-1}^l} f\left[C_t^m\right](\mathbf{h}_{t-1})\, \mathrm{d}\mu_{t-1} \\
&= \sum_{m \in M} \sum_{l \in L} \int_{C_{t-1}^l} f\left[C_t^m\right](\mathbf{h}_{t-1})\, \mathrm{d}\mu_{t-1} \\
&= \sum_{(m,l) \in M \times L} \hat{\mu}_t(C_{t-1}^l \times C_t^m) \\
&= \sum_{k=1}^{n} \sum_{(m,l) \in M_k \times L_k} \hat{\mu}_t(C_{t-1}^l \times C_t^m) \\
&= \sum_{k=1}^{n} \sum_{m \in M_k} \sum_{l \in L_k} \int_{C_{t-1}^l} f[C_t^m](\mathbf{h}_{t-1})\, \mathrm{d}\mu_{t-1} \\
&= \sum_{k=1}^{n} \sum_{m \in M_k} \int_{\bigcup_{l \in L_k} C_{t-1}^l} f[C_t^m](\mathbf{h}_{t-1})\, \mathrm{d}\mu_{t-1} \\
&= \sum_{k=1}^{n} \int_{B_{t-1}^k} \sum_{m \in M_k} \mu_{t-1}[\mathbf{h}_{t-1}](C_t^m)\, \mathrm{d}\mu_{t-1} \\
&= \sum_{k=1}^{n} \int_{B_{t-1}^k} \mu_{t-1}[\mathbf{h}_{t-1}](B_t^k)\, \mathrm{d}\mu_{t-1} \\
&= \sum_{k=1}^{n} \hat{\mu}_t(B_{t-1}^k \times B_t^k). \; \square
\end{aligned}$$

8.5.3 *Lemma*

The set function $\hat{\mu}_t\colon \hat{\mathcal{H}}_t \to \mathbb{R}$ is a σ-additive measure.

PROOF: Let $B_{t-1} \times B_t$ be any rectangle in $\hat{\mathcal{H}}_t$ and $\{B^k_{t-1} \times B^k_t\}_{k=1}^{\infty}$ any partition of the same. In order to derive that $\hat{\mu}_t(B_{t-1} \times B_t) = \sum_{k=1}^{\infty} \hat{\mu}_t(B^k_{t-1} \times B^k_t)$ we observe, in the first place, that

$$\sum_{k=1}^{\infty} \hat{\mu}_t(B^k_{t-1} \times B^k_t) \leq \hat{\mu}_t(B_{t-1} \times B_t), \qquad (*)$$

because $\hat{\mu}_t$ is additive.

For each positive integer k, let $C^k_t = B^k_t / \bigcup_{l=1}^{k-1} B^l_t$. Then the C^k_t are pairwise disjoint, $C^k_t \subseteq B^k_t$ for each k, and $\bigcup_{k=1}^{\infty} C^k_t = B_t$.

For $\mathbf{h}_{t-1}$ arbitrary but fixed, we define for each k a function ϕ_k over the set B_{t-1} as follows:

$$\phi_k(\mathbf{z}) = \begin{cases} \mu_t[\mathbf{h}_{t-1}](C^k_t) & \text{if } \mathbf{z} \in B^k_{t-1}; \\ 0 & \text{if } \mathbf{z} \notin B^k_{t-1}. \end{cases}$$

We then have that $\phi_k(\mathbf{z}) \geq 0$ and that, for any n, since

$$\bigcup_{k=1}^{n} (B_{t-1} \times C^k_t) = B_{t-1} \times \left(\bigcup_{k=1}^{n} C^k_t \right),$$

$\bigcup_{k=1}^{n} (B_{t-1} \times C^k_t)$ is in fact a rectangle in $\hat{\mathcal{H}}_t$. Since $\hat{\mu}_t$ is additive over $\hat{\mathcal{H}}_t$, it holds for every n that

$$\begin{aligned} \sum_{k=1}^{n} \int_{B_{t-1}} \phi_k(\mathbf{z})\, \mathrm{d}\mu_{t-1} &= \sum_{k=1}^{n} \hat{\mu}_t(B_{t-1} \times C^k_t) \\ &= \hat{\mu}_t\left(\bigcup_{k=1}^{n} (B_{t-1} \times C^k_t) \right) \\ &\leq 1, \end{aligned}$$

and so $\sum_{k=1}^{\infty} \int_{B_{t-1}} \phi_k(\mathbf{z})\, \mathrm{d}\mu_{t-1} < \infty$. Therefore, the series $\sum_{k=1}^{\infty} \phi_k(\mathbf{z})$ converges almost everywhere in B_{t-1}, from where it follows:

$$\begin{aligned} \sum_{k=1}^{\infty} \int_{B_{t-1}} \phi_k(\mathbf{z})\, \mathrm{d}\mu_{t-1} &= \int_{B_{t-1}} \sum_{k=1}^{\infty} \phi_k(\mathbf{z})\, \mathrm{d}\mu_{t-1} \\ &= \int_{B_{t-1}} \sum_{k=1}^{\infty} \mu_t[\mathbf{h}_{t-1}](C^k_t)\, \mathrm{d}\mu_{t-1} \\ &= \int_{B_{t-1}} \mu_t[\mathbf{h}_{t-1}]\left(\bigcup_{k=1}^{\infty} C^k_t \right) \mathrm{d}\mu_{t-1} \\ &= \int_{B_{t-1}} \mu_t[\mathbf{h}_{t-1}](B_t)\, \mathrm{d}\mu_{t-1} \\ &= \hat{\mu}_t(B_{t-1} \times B_t). \end{aligned}$$

On the other hand, since $\phi_k(\mathbf{z})$ vanishes outside of B^k_{t-1},

$$\begin{aligned}\int_{B_{t-1}} \phi_k(\mathbf{z})\, d\mu_{t-1} &= \int_{B^k_{t-1}} \phi_k(\mathbf{z})\, d\mu_{t-1} \\ &= \int_{B^k_{t-1}} \mu_t[\mathbf{h}_{t-1}](C^k_t)\, d\mu_{t-1} \\ &= \hat{\mu}_t(B^k_{t-1} \times C^k_t).\end{aligned}$$

Since $B^k_{t-1} \times C^k_t \subseteq B^k_{t-1} \times B^k_t$, we have $\hat{\mu}_t(B^k_{t-1} \times C^k_t) \leq \hat{\mu}_t(B^k_{t-1} \times B^k_t)$ and, *a fortiori*, $\sum_{k=1}^{\infty} \hat{\mu}_t(B^k_{t-1} \times C^k_t) \leq \sum_{k=1}^{\infty} \hat{\mu}_t(B^k_{t-1} \times B^k_t)$. Therefore,

$$\begin{aligned}\hat{\mu}_t(B_{t-1} \times B_t) &= \sum_{k=1}^{\infty} \int_{B_{t-1}} \phi_k(\mathbf{z})\, d\mu_{t-1} \\ &= \sum_{k=1}^{\infty} \hat{\mu}_t(B^k_{t-1} \times C^k_t) \\ &\leq \sum_{k=1}^{\infty} \hat{\mu}_t(B^k_{t-1} \times B^k_t).\end{aligned}$$

This, together with (∗), establishes that

$$\sum_{k=1}^{\infty} \hat{\mu}_t(B^k_{t-1} \times B^k_t) = \hat{\mu}_t(B_{t-1} \times B_t). \square$$

8.5.4 *Theorem*

The measure $\hat{\mu}_t\colon \hat{\mathcal{H}}_t \to \mathbb{R}$ can be extended to a measure $\mu_t\colon \mathcal{H}_t \to [0, 1]$ that assigns measure 1 to H_t.

PROOF: We have shown that, being $\hat{\mathcal{H}}_t$ a semiring with unit H_t, $\hat{\mu}_t$ is a σ-additive measure that assigns 1 to H_t. These conditions guarantee that $\hat{\mu}_t$ can be extended to a measure μ_t over the σ-algebra generated by the rectangles in $\hat{\mathcal{H}}_t$. But this σ-algebra is none other than $\mathcal{H}_t$. □

We define recursivley the measure μ: $\mathcal{H}_\tau \to \mathbb{R}$ in the following way: μ_1 is the already known measure of space $\langle X_1, \mathcal{F}_t, \mu_1\rangle$. If μ_{t-1} is the measure over $\mathfrak{H}_{t-1} = \langle H_{t-1}, \mathcal{H}_{t-1}\rangle$, μ_t is the measure determined by the integral

$$\int_{B_{t-1}} f[B_t](\mathbf{h}_{t-1})\, d\mu_{t-1}$$

and μ is in particular μ_τ. This μ is the general measure we were looking for over the set of all possible histories of the game It is left to the reader to show that $\mu(F) = 1$.

8.6 The equilibrium concept

We have seen that each profile **b** of behavioral strategies determines a probability measure $\mu[\mathbf{b}]$ over the set of all feasible histories of a game. The rational agents playing the game always try to choose those strategies that maximize their expected utility. Our immediate task is to define this last concept.

The assumption underlying the assignment of expected utilities to the profiles of behavioral strategies is that each personal player i has a suitable preference ordering over the set F all the possible histories of the game. This ordering is representable by means of a utility function $u_i: F \to \mathbb{R}$ which is integrable with respect to $\mu[\mathbf{b}]$. The expected utility associated to strategy $\mathbf{b}$ is defined by an integral of the form

$$\int_F u_i(\mathbf{h})\,\mathrm{d}\mu[\mathbf{b}].$$

Since $\mu[\mathbf{b}]$ is a well-defined probability measure, it is enough for the function u_i to be bounded over F in order to guarantee the existence of the integral. In other words, it is sufficient the existence of a real positive number α such that $|u_i(\mathbf{h})| < \alpha$ for every feasible history $\mathbf{h} \in F$.

In order to facilitate the definition of the equilibrium concept, let us adopt the next convention: if $\mathbf{b} = (\{b_{0t}\}_{t=1}^{\tau}, \ldots, \{b_{it}\}_{t=1}^{\tau}, \ldots, \{b_{\imath t}\}_{t=1}^{\tau})$ is a profile of behavioral strategies, we denote by means of '$(\mathbf{b}; \{b'_{it}\}_{t=1}^{\tau})$' the result of replacing $\mathbf{b}$ in the system of behavioral strategies $\{b_{it}\}_{t=1}^{\tau}$ with the system $\{b'_{it}\}_{t=1}^{\tau}$ ($i = 1,\ldots, \imath$); i.e.

$$(\mathbf{b}; \{b'_{it}\}_{t=1}^{\tau}) = (\{b_{0t}\}_{t=1}^{\tau}, \cdots, \{b'_{it}\}_{t=1}^{\tau}, \cdots, \{b_{\imath t}\}_{t=1}^{\tau}).$$

8.6.1 Definition

A profile of behavioral strategies

$$\mathbf{b}^* = (\{b^*_{0t}\}_{t=1}^{\tau}, \cdots, \{b^*_{\imath t}\}_{t=1}^{\tau})$$

is an *equilibrium* of the game iff, $\forall i \in \boldsymbol{\imath} \setminus \{0\}$,

$$U_i(\mathbf{b}^*) \geq U_i(\mathbf{b}^*; \{b_{it}\}_{t=1}^{\tau}) \quad \text{for any system } \{b_{it}\}_{t=1}^{\tau}.$$

If $\tau = 1$, the equilibrium is called a *Nash equilibrium*.

This concept of equilibrium is more general than the concept of a Nash equilibrium, because it covers several stages and requires for the players to act as independent agents in each stage.

Let us call *adequate* any set of profiles of behavioral strategies for which there exists an equilibrium. On the ground of rather restrictive assumptions, Chakrabarti (1992) has shown that there exists at least one adequate set, which is a very important result, because it establishes that the equilibrium concept is not vacuous. Nevertheless, it would be mistaken to hope that it be possible to find in advance necessary and sufficient conditions guaranteeing the existence of equilibria for all the intended applications of the theory. The theory expresses the hope that such applications will satisfy the fundamental law, which is a guiding principle leading to search, for each intended application, certain factors to explain the observed phenomena. In the case of game theory such factors are profiles of behavioral strategies which must induce equilibria that explain the observed behavior. How must the theory represent such phenomena? What is the form of the guiding principle, the fundamental law of the theory? These questions call for a synthetic reformulation of what has been exposed to this point.

8.7 The game concept

The aim of this section is to introduce an axiomatic definition of the concept of dynamic game with finite horizon and discrete time. The leading thread of the discussion toward that definition is the question of the empirical content of the theory when its typical models are seen not as policy recommendations (in the normative mode), but as explanations of effectively observed behaviors (in the positive mode).

Needless to say, these modes are interrelated, and that in a very deep and interesting way: roughly, the empirical claim of the theory is that certain observed behaviors are in fact the result of 'normed', i.e. rational decisions. The first problem that this approach has to face is that of the representation of observed behaviors as conceptually different from the normed ones, in order, precisely, to be able to compare the former with the latter.

Let us start with a relatively easy case: a game of one stage with two players. Let us consider competition through the fixation of prices among two firms selling the same good, let us say kegs of beer. The production cost is constant and equal to $c = \$30$. There is a demand function $D(p) = 130 - p$ and each firm can fix the price of its product, but the consumers will buy only the product with the lowest price. Thus, if $p_i < p_j$ ($i, j = 1, 2, i \neq j$), firm i will supply the whole market, $q_1 = D(p_1)$, and j will not be able to sell anything. If both fix the same price, each one will sell half of the whole demand: $q_1 = q_2 = D(p)/2$. The benefit of price p for firm i ($i = 1, 2$) is $\pi_i = (p - c)q_i$. There are four possible prices for the firms: $p_1 = \$60$, $p_2 = \$50$, $p_3 = \$40$ and $p_4 = \$30$, with the sixteen possible results shown in Table 8.1.

For this game, $\tau = 1$, $\iota = \{1,2\}$, $X_1 = X_2 = \{p_1, p_2, p_3, p_4\}$ and $F = X_{11} \times X_{21}$. The pure strategies of i are functions s_i of $\mathfrak{a}_0(F) = \{\mathbf{o}\}$ into X_i. Since the player that sets the highest price cannot sell, both players will try to fix the lowest one, which eventually leads both to set the price of \$30, with earnings of \$0 for both. The profile of strategies (s_1^*, s_2^*) with $s_1^*(\mathbf{o}) = p_4 = s_2^*(\mathbf{o})$ is what is known as a Bertrand equilibrium.

Let us imagine now that the players are rational and carry out a deliberation process – each one separately – by which they reach the practical conclusion that the most rational thing to do is to adopt move p_4. The point is that an 'external' observer which is not aware of the thinking of the players will be able only to take note of the given manifest behavior of the players, to wit, that each one chose p_4, giving rise to history $\mathbf{h}^{16}$. In other words, $\mathbf{h}^{16}$ is observable ('empirical') but the process that led the players to choose the strategy profile (s_1^*, s_2^*) is not. The *quid* of the theory is to explain the observed history as the result of a rational choice by the players.

In a first approach, the promise of the guiding principle of the theory is that it is possible to find preference structures $\langle F, \succsim_1\rangle$ and $\langle F, \succsim_2\rangle$, one for each player, and utility functions u_1, u_2 that represent respectively such structures, such that

$$U_1(s_1^*, s_2^*) = \max_{s_1 \in S_1} U_i(s_1, s_2^*).$$

and

$$U_2(s_1^*, s_2^*) = \max_{s_2 \in S_2} U_i(s_1^*, s_2).$$

where U_i, the expected utility of player i in this case, satisfies equation

$$U_i(s_1^*, s_2^*) = \int_F u_i(\mathbf{h})\, \mathrm{d}\mu[\mathbf{b}] = u_i(\mathbf{h}^{16}) = 0. \tag{8.1}$$

because $\mathbf{b} = (s_1^*, s_2^*)$ is a pure strategy, which makes the probability of $\mathbf{h}^{16}$ to be 1. The reader may corroborate in Table 8.1 that (s_1^*, s_2^*) is the only saddle point and therefore the only Nash equilibrium of the game.

This example suggests that we should represent the empirical phenomenon, target of the theory, as an effectively observed history of the game, and that the notion of explanation of the theory is that the history effectively observed is derivable form an equilibrium with respect to certain utility functions.

Another paradigmatic example of this image is the theory of Walrasian demand, which proposes a two-stage game in which chance starts in the first stage imposing a system of prices-wealth $(\mathbf{p}, w)$ to the consumer, so that in the second stage the consumer will choose a consumption menu that maximizes his utility subject to the usual budget restriction imposed by $(\mathbf{p}, w)$.

Certainly, things are this way when the strategies are pure, but not when they are behavioral. For, if the utility function of the consumer determines a demand correspondence or function when it is maximized, which assigns to every chance action a set of optimum vectors for the consumer given that action, the maximization of an expected utility function typically is not going to determine a correspondence of histories that are optimal responses. Rather, we have seen that the

Table 8.1 Bertrand's game

$\mathbf{h}^1$	$\mathbf{h}^2$	$\mathbf{h}^3$	$\mathbf{h}^4$	$\mathbf{h}^5$	$\mathbf{h}^6$	$\mathbf{h}^7$	$\mathbf{h}^8$
(p_1,p_1)	(p_1,p_2)	(p_1,p_3)	(p_1,p_4)	(p_2,p_1)	(p_2,p_2)	(p_2,p_3)	(p_2,p_4)
(1050,1050)	(0,1600)	(0,900)	(0,0)	(0,1600)	(800,800)	(0,900)	(0,0)
$\mathbf{h}^9$	$\mathbf{h}^{10}$	$\mathbf{h}^{11}$	$\mathbf{h}^{12}$	$\mathbf{h}^{13}$	$\mathbf{h}^{14}$	$\mathbf{h}^{15}$	$\mathbf{h}^{16}$
(p_3,p_1)	(p_3,p_2)	(p_3,p_3)	(p_3,p_4)	(p_4,p_1)	(p_4,p_2)	(p_4,p_3)	(p_4,p_4)
(900,0)	(900,0)	(225,225)	(0,0)	(0,0)	(0,0)	(0,0)	(0,0)

choice of a profile of behavioral strategies transforms the set of feasible histories into a probability space.

It follows that – in contradistinction with what takes place in the application known as 'Walrasian demand theory' – we do not get a point (history) as a result of the choice of non-pure behavioral strategies, but rather measurable sets of histories with certain probabilities. What form adopts in this case the empirical phenomenon, target of the theory? It seems clear that the empirical phenomenon must be representable as an *histogram*. If this is so, the guiding principle promises that there are utility functions for the personal players, and expected utility functions obtained out of these, such that the space is determined by a profile of strategies that happens to be an equilibrium of the game. This suggests that we should treat the term 'utility' as game-theoretic term. Hence, the partial potential models can be described as follows. I shall use the term 'game' as an abbreviation of 'dynamic game with finite horizon and discrete time' and GT as abbreviaton of 'theory of dynamic games with finite horizon and discrete time'.

8.7.1 Definition

$\mathfrak{A}$ is a *partial potential model of* GT iff there exits ι, τ, X_{it}, $\mathcal{F}_{it}$, $\mathfrak{a}_t$ and ν such that:

(J0) $\mathfrak{A} = \langle \iota, \tau, X_{it}, \mathcal{F}_{it}, \mathfrak{a}_t, A_{it}, \nu \rangle$;
(J1) ι is either an initial segment of the set of natural numbers containing at least two elements, or an initial segment of the set of positive integers;
(J2) $\boldsymbol{\tau}$ is an initial segment of the set of positive numbers, where τ is the largest number in the set and $\tau \geq 1$;
(J3) X_{it} is a metric space for each $i \in \iota$ and $t \in \boldsymbol{\tau}$;
(J4) for each $i \in \iota$ and $t \in \boldsymbol{\tau}$, $\mathcal{F}_{it}$ is the σ-algebra over X_{it} determined by the open subsets of X_{it};
(J5) for each $t \in \boldsymbol{\tau}$, $\mathfrak{a}_t \colon H \to X_t$ is a correspondence:
(J6) for each $i \in \iota$ and $t \in \boldsymbol{\tau}$, $A_{it} \colon \mathfrak{a}_{t-1}(H) \to X_{it}$ is a correspondence such that $A_{it}[\mathfrak{a}_{t-1}(\mathbf{h})]$ is a compact subset of X_{it};
(J7) ν is a probability measure over the measurable space $\langle H, \mathcal{F} \rangle$.

Function ν is 'empirical' or 'observable' (in the particular case of consumer theory, ν is just the observed demand of the consumer); i.e. it is not GT-theoretical, and can be determined by means of statistical methods out of the observation of several plays of the game. What the fundamental law expresses is that there are utility functions u_i for the personal players, and utility functions obtained out of these, such that ν is as a matter of fact the probability measure determined by a profile of strategies that turns out to be an equilibrium of the game. More precisely, the fundamental law of GT can be formulated as follows.

(J8) There exist bounded utility functions $u_i \colon F \to \mathbb{R}$, and an equilibrium $\mathbf{b}^* = \left(\{b^*_{0t}\}^{\tau}_{t=1}, \ldots, \{b^*_{it}\}^{\tau}_{t=1}\right)$ of the game with respect to these functions, such that $\mu[\mathbf{b}^*] = \nu$.

It is important to stress that the identity $\mu[\mathbf{b}^*] = v$ is *not* a definition, but can be false or satisfied in a merely approximate way. The left side refers to the space determined by profile $\mathbf{b}^*$, whereas the right one refers to an histogram determined independently of the theory. We are now in position to define the concept of a game.

8.7.2 Definition

$\mathfrak{A}$ is a *game* iff there exits $\boldsymbol{\iota}$, $\boldsymbol{\tau}$, X_{it}, $\mathcal{F}_{it}$, $\mathfrak{a}_t$, A_{it}, v and u_i such that:

(J0) $\mathfrak{A} = \langle \boldsymbol{\iota}, \boldsymbol{\tau}, X_{it}, \mathcal{F}_{it}, \mathfrak{a}_t, A_{it}, v, u_i \rangle$;
(J1) $\langle \boldsymbol{\iota}, \boldsymbol{\tau}, X_{it}, \mathcal{F}_{it}, \mathfrak{a}_t, A_{it}, v \rangle$ is a partial potential model of GT;
(J2) for each $i \in \boldsymbol{\iota} \setminus \{0\}$, $u_i: F \to \mathbb{R}$, is a bounded function;
(J3) there exists an equilibrium $\mathbf{b}^* = \left(\{b^*_{0t}\}^{\tau}_{t=1}, \ldots, \{b^*_{it}\}^{\tau}_{t=1}\right)$ of the game, with respect to the functions u_i, such that $\mu[\mathbf{b}^*] = v$.

Kreps (1990: 97) has pointed out that one problem of the game-theoretic techniques is that

> some (important) sorts of games have many equilibria, and the theory is of no help in sorting out whether any one is the 'solution' and, if one is, which one is.

Nevertheless, in the positive mode that I have adopted here, the only thing that matters is the existence of some equilibrium 'explaining' the observed behavior with a certain degree of approximation.

In their classical book *Games and Decisions*, Luce and Raiffa (1957: 50) introduced a law of behavior for the players that they formulate as follows.

> Of two alternatives which give rise to outcomes, a player will choose the one which yields the more preferred outcome, or, more precisely, in terms of the utility function he will attempt to maximize expected utility.

The fundamental law as I have formulated it (J3) implies this law of behavior. Indeed, if some agent i did not behave according to it, the profile $\mathbf{b} = \left(\{b_{0t}\}^{\tau}_{t=1}, \ldots, \{b_{it}\}^{\tau}_{t=1}\right)$ of chosen strategies would not be optimal, and the observed behavior would not be the result of strategies in equilibrium. Luce and Raiffa oscillate between considering the law of behavior as a substantial empirical claim about the behavior of the agentes, and seeing it as a tautology that regulates the use of the word 'preference'. Under this interpretation, "the problem is not to attempt to verify the postulate but rather to devise suitable empirical techniques to determine individual preferences" (ibid.). The alternative to this interpretation is

> to accept certain experimental operations as defining "preferences" and then to attempt to verify [the] postulate .... This is basically much simpler for the experimentalist, but experience indicates that it is not always successful.
> (Ibid.)

SVT solves this paradox calling the attention to the fact that the utility (or preference) concept is GT-theoretical, and so the functions cannot be determined without presupposing the fundamental law. It is possible that it was the intuition of this fact what led the mentioned authors to say that this law is a tautology. Nevertheless, since it is not possible to guarantee a priori that for every interaction describable by means of the non-GT-theoretical conceptual apparatus there will always exist utility functions satisfying the fundamental law, this law is not a tautology. Moreover, since there are no "empirical techniques" – if by "empirical" we understand techniques that do not presuppose the validity of the fundamental law – enabling the determination of the utility functions, it is not possible to 'verify' the postulate in that manner. Actually, such postulate is irrefutable, unless someone proves that it is impossible to find such utility functions for every case. To prove that they do not exist for some cases may turn out to be a hard task indeed.

8.8 Empirical applicability of GT

By definition, a successful application of GT to a set of empirical data (an histogram v) consists of finding utility functions u_i and an equilibrium $\mathbf{b}^*$ of the game with respect to such functions, that explain (rationalize) the empirical data.

For the sake of the example, let us return again to classical demand theory, which is a specialization of GT that we can describe as follows. It is a family of two-stage games. In the first stage, $t = 1$, chance (0) throws a pair $(\mathbf{p}, w)$, that consists of a system of prices $\mathbf{p}$ and some amount of money w, in $P \times W$, where P is a subset of the nonnegative orthant Ω of $\mathbb{R}^L$ and W is a set of positive real numbers. Since at this stage agent 1 – the consumer – is just waiting, he chooses to do nothing ($\mathbf{n}$). In the second stage, having the information of what pair $(\mathbf{p}, w)$ was thrown by chance, the agent chooses a point $x_{12}(\mathbf{p}, w)$ in the set $X_{12} \subseteq \mathbb{R}^L$ of possible consumption menus that satisfies restriction $\mathbf{p}x \leq \mathrm{w}$, while chance rests. Hence, a typical 'play' of this game is a sequence of the form $((\mathbf{p}, w), \mathbf{n}), (\mathbf{n}, x_{12}(\mathbf{p}, w))$.

The sequence $((\mathbf{p}, w), \mathbf{n}), (\mathbf{n}, x_{12}(\mathbf{p}, w))$ satisfies the fundamental law if there exists a profile $\left(\{b^*_{0t}\}^2_{t=1}, \{b^*_{1t}\}^2_{t=1}\right)$ such that $b^*_{01}(\mathbf{p}, w) = 1, b^*_{02}(\mathbf{n}) = 1, b^*_{11}(\mathbf{n}) = 1$ and $b^*_{12}(x_{12}(\mathbf{p}, w)) = 1$; and a utility function u_1 such that $\mathrm{x}_{12}(\mathbf{p}, w)$ maximizes u_1 subject to restriction $\mathbf{p}x \leq \mathrm{w}$. A set of empirical data $\hat{x}_{12}(\mathbf{p}^1, w^1) \ldots, \hat{x}_{12}(\mathbf{p}^n, w^n)$ is rationalizable (explicable by the theory) if there exists a utility function u_1 and profiles $\left(\{b^k_{0t}\}^2_{t=1}, \{b^k_{1t}\}^2_{t=1}\right)$ $(k = 1, \ldots, n)$ such that $b^k_{01}(\mathbf{p}, w) = 1$, $b^k_{02}(\mathbf{n}) = 1$, $b^k_{11}(\mathbf{n}) = 1$, $b^k_{12}(x_{12}(\mathbf{p}^k, w^k)) = 1$ and, for every k, $x_{12}(\mathbf{p}^k, w^k)$ maximizes u_1 subject to $\mathbf{p}^k\mathbf{h} \leq w^k$ with $\hat{x}_{12}(\mathbf{p}^k, w^k) = x_{12}(\mathbf{p}^k, w^k)$.

Notice that the data $\hat{x}_{12}(\mathbf{p}^1, w^1),\ldots, \hat{x}_{12}(\mathbf{p}^n, w^n)$, obtained in a theory-independent way, are in strict canonical terms histograms $v^1,\ldots, v^n$ with $v^k((\mathbf{p}^k, w^k),\mathbf{n}),(\mathbf{n}, \hat{x}_{12}(\mathbf{p}^k, w^k)) = 1$. The Walrasian demand function is a mapping assigning to each random event $(\mathbf{p}, w)$ the optimum choice $x_{12}(\mathbf{p}, w))$ with respect to one and the same utility function u_1. This means that the actions of the same consumer are represented by a family of models that satisfy the constraint consisting of sharing the same utility function. Only in this form makes sense to use a family of such models in order to determine the utility function of one and the same agent.

The determination of a utility function out of empirical data in consumer theory departs from the notion of revealed preference. Recall that x is revealed as *directly preferred* to y in $\mathcal{E}$ ($xR^{\circ}y$) iff there exists a pair $(\mathbf{p}, w)$ such that $x_{12}(\mathbf{p}, w)$ is in $\mathcal{E}$, $y \leq \mathbf{p}w$ and $x = x_{12}(\mathbf{p}, w)$; if, moreover, $y \neq x$, we say that x is revealed as directly strictly preferred ($xP^{\circ}y$) to y. We say that x is revealed prefered to y in $\mathcal{E}$ ($xR^{\bullet}y$) iff there exists a sequence $z_1,\ldots, z_n$ such that $z_1 = x$, $z_n = y$ ($n \geq 2$) with $z_1R^{\circ}z_2$, γ $z_{k-1}R^{\circ}z_k$ for $1 < k \leq n$. $\mathcal{E}$ satisfies the *weak axiom of revealed preference* iff relations R° and P° satisfy the following condition of every $x, y \in X_{12}$:

$$xR^{\circ}y \rightarrow \neg yP^{\circ}x.$$

$\mathcal{E}$ satisfies the *strong axiom of revealed preference* iff relations $R^{\bullet}$ and P° satisfy the following condition for every $x, y \in X_{12}$:

$$xR^{\bullet}y \rightarrow \neg yP^{\circ}x.$$

Houthakker (1950) proved that if a set of empirical data $\mathcal{E}$ satisfies the strong axiom of revealed preference then there exists a utility function that rationalizes them. Out of this result an extensive literature developed, that includes the treatment of methods for the obtention of utility functions by means of diverse procedures.[1] It is clear, however, that these methods are applicable only in the particular case of classical demand theory, and cannot be generalized in order to solve at once the problem of the application of GT to different phenomena.

There is a general condition that must be satisfied by any collection of models purporting to represent the behavior of a set of agents. This is a constraint that can be formulated as follows.

Constraint. *Whenever a collection of models of GT is deemed applicable to the same set of agents, the utility function of any of them must be assumed identical in all these models.*

It is easy to see that this condition implies the strong axiom of revealed preference in the particular case of classical demand theory. At any rate, it is a condition necessary for a consistent application of GT to empirical phenomena. The main task of normal science within this scientific paradigm consists of determining the utility functions of the agents out of their observed behavior. The empirical claim of GT is that this task can be successfully pursued for the observed behavior of agents in strategic situations.

Note

1 A review of this literature, since the publication of Samuelson's seminal article (1938) until 2005, is found in Varian (2006).

9 Abstract labor and labor-value

9.1 Introduction

Just as utility is the measure of preference, (labor) value is the measure of abstract labor. The concept of abstract labor is linked with the law of value. We defined in Chapter 6 the concept of a reproducible social choice. An unquestionable presupposition of economic theory is that social human groups struggle to preserve their existence. This makes of the tendency to make reproducible social choices an iron law of economics. As explained thereby, it is clear that the economic process of a society cannot be sustained, reproduced or transformed, unless goods are distributed among the households, individuals and productive units in a certain way. It is also evident that labor must be distributed in such a way that all branches of the economy receive the necessary amount of labor in order to operate the production processes required to deliver the goods needed to reproduce the economy and sustain the members of the society (at least the labor-power). Marx (1868) formulated this law in the following, rather forceful way:

> It is *self-evident* that this *necessity* of the *distribution* of social labor in specific proportions is certainly not abolished by the *specific form* of social production; it can only change *its form of manifestation*. Natural laws cannot be abolished at all. The only thing that can change, under historically differing conditions, is the *form* in which those laws assert themselves. And the form in which this proportional distribution of labor asserts itself in a state of society in which the interconnection of social labor expresses itself as the *private exchange* of the individual products of labor, is precisely the *exchange value* of these products.

What this means is that the society, be it through a central organ, or through independent production units, must allocate labor-power in such a way that the economic process may take place and reproduce the economy. This law imposes itself in every production mode. For instance, the form of manifestation of this law in primitive societies, in which a consistent division of labor has been established, is the operation of a central organ (person, council) in charge of allocating labor on the basis of a more or less conscious accounting of labor-time. According to Ernest Mandel (1968: 60):

> So long as primitive society, co-operatively organised, does not know any division of labour other than that between the sexes, the rhythm of labour is fixed by custom and religious rites. When a more consistent division of labour has been established, the contribution to the community made by each producer has to be measurable by a common yardstick. Otherwise, labour co-operation would tend to break up through the emergence of privileged and unprivileged groups. This common measure of organisation cannot be other than *economy of labour-time.*

According to this same author,

> The village can be regarded as a big family. Its total annual production has to correspond more or less to its needs in means of subsistence, clothing, housing and tools. To avoid any imbalance between these different forms of production, to ensure that the peasants do not devote an excessive share of their time to producing pots or leather articles, while leaving part of their land uncultivated, it is necessary that the community compile a record of the amount of labour-time available and allot this labour-time first and foremost among the essential sectors of production, indispensable for the well-being of the community, while leaving everyone free to employ the rest of his time as he pleases.
>
> (Ibid.)

In differentiated societies labor may still be clearly social, insofar as there is a conscious accounting of labor. For instance, in the Japanese peasant economy,

> the principle of exchange is people and days. Thus, if household A has two people at work on household B's field for two days, household B is expected to provide its equivalent on A's fields – this may be three people one day and one person another day or any other combination to equal two people working two days … When four or five families work together in one *kattari* group [team for transplanting rice], the figuring is on the same basis. This requires a book to check days and workers.
>
> (Embree 1939: 100–1; quoted by Mandel 1968: 61)

Many other concrete historical examples of societies with a conscious accounting of labor are provided by Mandel (1968: 59ff). In all these societies there exist central organs through which the law of value imposes itself.

In contradistinction to simpler societies, modern societies are characterized by an increasing social division of labor, resulting in more complex systems of needs and the decentralization of choices. From barter to the introduction of money a long time elapsed but the net result is that, what in primitive undifferentiated societies was a direct social relationship, in modern differentiated societies became a monetary relationship or one among commodities (this is what Marx called "the fetishism of the commodity").

9.2 Abstract labor

In a capitalist economy, the equalization of labors is not carried out by a conscious accounting, but takes place through the exchange process. The exchange process equates the profiles of labor inputs through the equating of their respective products. A profile of labor inputs is a vector associated to a classification of tasks. Each position of the vector represents a certain amount of labor applied to a specific task. The convention is that entry n of labor input profile $\mathbf{y}$, real number y_n, represents a certain amount of time applied to a certain task. For instance, y_n may represent y_n hours of a mechanic applied to install the brakes of a certain model of car, or y_n hours of a mechanic applied to assemble the engine. We shall convene that, even though both tasks are performed by a mechanic, they are different types of tasks. Hence, a mechanic applied to install brakes will be represented by an entry y_n different from the entry $y_{n'}$ representing the mechanic assembling engines ($n \neq n'$).

The time required to perform a task is socially necessary labor-time. According to Marx, this has various consequences, one of them being that

> all wasteful consumption of raw material or instruments of labor is strictly forbidden, because what is wasted in this way represents a superfluous expenditure of quantities of objectified labour, labour that does not count in the product or enter into its value.
>
> (Marx 1976: 303)

Another consequence is that

> the labour-power itself must be of normal effectiveness. In the trade in which it is being employed, it must possess the average skill, dexterity and speed prevalent in that trade …[and] …it must be expended with the average amount of exertion and the usual degree of intensity.
>
> (Ibid.)

Normal labor-power expends prime materials, and employs tools and machines, in an efficient way. Therefore, the use of more labor-power in a process of the same type (a scaling of the former) should increase proportionally the use of the means of production, as well as the amount of final products. This means not only that more means of production are employed, but also that to small increases in the amount of labor-power there correspond small increases in the amount of the production means and the corresponding products. It is only natural to formulate this as a continuity condition: to an infinitesimal increase in labor-power there corresponds an infinitesimal increase in the net product. This narrative motivates the following definition.

9.2.1 *Definition*

Let $\tilde{Y}$ be a set of production processes. We say that the labor-power expended in a set of production processes is *normal* iff the following conditions are satisfied:

(1) For any nonnull processes $\tilde{\mathbf{y}}$ and $\tilde{\mathbf{y}}'$ in the set, it is the case that $\mathbf{y} \geq \mathbf{y}'$ implies $\underline{\mathbf{y}} \geqq \underline{\mathbf{y}}'$, and $\mathbf{y} \geq \mathbf{y}'$ implies $\underline{\mathbf{y}} \geq \underline{\mathbf{y}}'$;

(2) For any production process $[\mathbf{y}, \underline{\mathbf{y}}, \bar{\mathbf{y}}] \in \tilde{Y}$, if $(\mathbf{y}^k)$ is a sequence of labor expenditures in $\tilde{Y}$ converging to $\mathbf{y}$, then there are production processes $\tilde{\mathbf{y}}^k = [\mathbf{y}^k, \underline{\mathbf{y}}^k, \bar{\mathbf{y}}^k] \in \tilde{Y}$ such that $(\underline{\mathbf{y}}^k)$ converges to $\underline{\mathbf{y}}$, and $(\bar{\mathbf{y}}^k)$ converges to $\bar{\mathbf{y}}$.

Let $\tilde{Y}$ be the (normal) set of all production processes available to society at a given point in time and Y the set $\{\mathbf{y} | [\mathbf{y}, \underline{\mathbf{y}}, \bar{\mathbf{y}}] \in \tilde{Y}\}$ of all the corresponding profiles of labor inputs employed in the processes in $\tilde{Y}$. If the net products of processes $[\mathbf{y}, \underline{\mathbf{y}}, \bar{\mathbf{y}}]$ and $[\mathbf{y}', \underline{\mathbf{y}}', \bar{\mathbf{y}}']$ are equated by the market (i.e. their joint bulks have the same price), we say that the exchange process has in fact equated their respective profiles $\mathbf{y}$, $\mathbf{y}'$ of labor inputs, and write $\mathbf{y} \sim \mathbf{y}'$. If the market signals that the price of the net product of the first process is greater than that of the second, we write $\mathbf{y} \succ \mathbf{y}'$, meaning that the exchange process has estimated that $\mathbf{y}$ is yielding more value than $\mathbf{y}'$. These relations are the symmetric and asymmetric parts of a relation $\gtrsim$ that I shall call 'abstract labor'.

Not every relation of this type, however, counts as abstract labor. The first condition that abstract labor must satisfy is that the labor expenditures of all the production processes whose products compete in the same market must be comparable. This means that $\gtrsim$ must be connected over Y. The second one is that if $\mathbf{y}$ represents more abstract labor than $\mathbf{y}'$, and $\mathbf{y}'$ represents more abstract labor than $\mathbf{y}''$, then $\mathbf{y} \gtrsim \mathbf{y}''$; i.e. $\gtrsim$ is transitive. These two conditions imply that $\gtrsim$ is a weak ordering of Y (recall that every weak ordering is reflexive).

Another condition is monotonicity. This means that two production processes yielding the same (respectively more) product must represent the same (respectively a greater) amount of abstract labor; i.e. $\hat{\mathbf{y}} = \hat{\mathbf{y}}'$ must yield $\mathbf{y} \sim \mathbf{y}'$, and $\hat{\mathbf{y}} \geq \hat{\mathbf{y}}'$ must yield $\mathbf{y} \succ \mathbf{y}'$. Since $\mathbf{y} + \mathbf{y}' \geqq \mathbf{y}$, by monotonicity the abstract labor relation is semipositive: $\mathbf{y} + \mathbf{y}' \gtrsim \mathbf{y}$, with $\mathbf{y} + \mathbf{y}' > \mathbf{y}$ if $\mathbf{y} \geq \mathbf{0}$.

The third condition is the homogeneity law, also called cancellation. This law expresses that if profile $\mathbf{y}$ represents more abstract labor than $\mathbf{y}'$, the addition (or subtraction) of the same amount of labor expenditures to both processes must preserve the inequality:

$$\mathbf{y} \succsim \mathbf{y}' \quad \text{iff} \quad \mathbf{y} + \mathbf{y}'' \succsim \mathbf{y}' + \mathbf{y}''.$$

Notice that this law implies

$$\mathbf{y} \sim \mathbf{y}' \quad \text{iff} \quad \mathbf{y} + \mathbf{y}'' \sim \mathbf{y}' + \mathbf{y}''$$

(the easy proof is left to the reader).

The fourth condition is homotheticity. That $\succsim$ is homothetic means that whenever two profiles of labor inputs that represent the same amount of labor are scaled in the same magnitude, the resulting profiles will also represent equivalent expenditures of labor; i.e.

$$\text{if} \quad \mathbf{y} \sim \mathbf{y}' \quad \text{then} \quad \alpha\mathbf{y} \sim \alpha\mathbf{y}'$$

for any real $\alpha \geq 0$.

A very important condition is continuity. Continuity means that infinitesimal changes in the amounts of concrete labors expended in a process must yield an infinitesimal increase in the amount of abstract labor that it represents. I will formulate this condition in terms of the usual topological condition, namely, that the sets $\{\mathbf{y} \in Y \mid \mathbf{y} \succsim \mathbf{y}^*\}$ and $\{\mathbf{y} \in Y \mid \mathbf{y}^* \succsim \mathbf{y}\}$ are closed with respect to the usual topology of $\mathbb{R}^v$.

I will summarize the previous discussion in the definition of what I shall call an abstract labor structure.

9.2.2 *Definition*

$\mathfrak{A}$ is an *abstract labor structure* iff there exist Y and $\succsim$ such that, for all $\mathbf{y}, \mathbf{y}', \mathbf{y}'' \in Y$,

(0) $\mathfrak{A} = \langle Y, \succsim \rangle$
(1) Y is a convex polyhedral cone within the nonnegative orthant of space $\mathbb{R}^v$;
(2) $\mathfrak{A}$ is a weak order;
(3) Monotonicity: $\mathbf{y} \geq \mathbf{y}'$ implies $\mathbf{y} \succ \mathbf{y}'$;
(4) Cancellation: $\mathbf{y}' \succsim \mathbf{y}''$ iff $\mathbf{y} + \mathbf{y}' \succsim \mathbf{y} + \mathbf{y}''$;
(5) Homotheticity: if $\mathbf{y} \sim \mathbf{y}'$ then $\alpha\mathbf{y} \sim \alpha\mathbf{y}'$ for any real $\alpha \geq 0$.
(6) Continuity: the sets $\{\mathbf{y} \in Y \mid \mathbf{y} \succsim \mathbf{y}^*\}$ and $\{\mathbf{y} \in Y \mid \mathbf{y}^* \succsim \mathbf{y}\}$ are closed, with respect to the usual topology of $\mathbb{R}^v$, for any fixed, albeit arbitrary $\mathbf{y}^* \in Y$.

Axioms (1)–(6) are enough to prove the existence of the desired representation. This is the content of the following theorem.

9.2.3 Theorem

$\langle Y, \succsim \rangle$ is an abstract labor structure iff there exists a positive vector $\mathbf{r} \in \mathbb{R}^{v}$ *such that, for all* $\mathbf{y}, \mathbf{y}' \in Y$,

$$\mathbf{y} \succsim \mathbf{y}' \quad \textit{iff} \quad \mathbf{ry} \geq \mathbf{ry}'.$$

Another vector $\mathbf{r}'$ *satisfies this condition iff there exists* $\alpha > 0$ *such that* $\mathbf{r}' = \alpha\mathbf{r}$.

PROOF: Let L be any ray within Y and $\mathbf{y}_0 \neq \mathbf{0}$ a given point. Clearly, $\alpha y_0 \in L$ for every positive real number α. Notice that for every $\mathbf{y} \in Y$, since $\mathbf{y} \geq \mathbf{0}$, monotonicity implies $\mathbf{y} \succsim \mathbf{0}$. Moreover, monotonicity also implies that $\alpha \mathbf{y}_0 \succsim \mathbf{y}$ whenever $\alpha y_0 \geq \mathbf{y}$. I will show that for every $\mathbf{y} \in Y$ there is a unique $\alpha \in \mathbb{R}^0_+ = [0, \infty)$ such that $\alpha y_0 \sim \mathbf{y}$.

Let $\mathbf{y}$ be any element of Y and notice that, for sufficiently large α, $\alpha y_0 \geq \mathbf{y}$, and so $\alpha \mathbf{y}_0 \succsim \mathbf{y}$. Since $L_+ = \{\mathbf{y}' \in Y | \mathbf{y}' \succsim \mathbf{y}\}$ is closed, the set $A_+ = \{\alpha \in \mathbb{R}^0_+ | \alpha \mathbf{y}_0 \succsim \mathbf{y}\}$ is also closed because the limit of any sequence $(\alpha_k \mathbf{y}_0)$ of points of L_+, where (α_k) converges to α, is $\alpha y_0 \in L_+$. An analogous reasoning establishes that $A_- = \{\alpha \in \mathbb{R}^0_+ | \mathbf{y} \succsim \alpha \mathbf{y}_0\}$ is also closed. Moreover, for any $\alpha \in \mathbb{R}^0_+$, since $\alpha y_0 \in Y$ and $\succsim$ is connected, either $\alpha \mathbf{y}_0 \succsim \mathbf{y}$ or $\mathbf{y} \succsim \alpha \mathbf{y}_0$, which implies that $A^+ \cup A_- = \mathbb{R}^0_+$. Given that $\mathbb{R}^0_+$ is connected and both A^+ and A_- are closed, $A^+ \cap A_- \neq \emptyset$; that is to say, there exists $\alpha \in \mathbb{R}^0_+$ with $\alpha y_0 \sim \mathbf{y}$. Monotonicity implies that this number, denoted $\alpha(\mathbf{y})$, is unique. Clearly, by monotonicity,

$$\begin{aligned} \mathbf{y} \succsim \mathbf{y}' \quad & \text{iff} \quad \alpha(\mathbf{y}) y_0 \succsim \alpha(\mathbf{y}')\mathbf{y}_0 \\ & \text{iff} \quad \alpha(\mathbf{y}) \geq \alpha(\mathbf{y}') \end{aligned}$$

From now on, it will be convenient to denote the number $\alpha(\mathbf{y})$ by means of $\varphi(\mathbf{y})$. Hence, we have defined a homomorphism φ from Y into $\mathbb{R}$ that maps $\succsim$ into $\geq$.

By definition of φ, for any $\mathbf{y} \in Y$ and $\alpha > 0$, we have $\mathbf{y} \sim \varphi(\mathbf{y})\mathbf{y}_0$ and so, by homotheticity, $\alpha y \sim \alpha\varphi(\mathbf{y})\mathbf{y}_0$. On the other hand we have, also by definition of φ, $\alpha \mathbf{y} \sim \varphi(\alpha\mathbf{y})\mathbf{y}_0$. Hence, by transitivity we get $\varphi(\alpha\mathbf{y})\mathbf{y}_0 \sim \alpha\varphi(\mathbf{y})\mathbf{y}_0$ and so $\varphi(\alpha \mathbf{y}) = \alpha\varphi(\mathbf{y})$. In other words, φ is homogeneous of degree 1.

Let $\mathbf{y}, \mathbf{y}' \in Y$ and $\alpha, \alpha' \in \mathbb{R}^0_+$ be such that $\mathbf{y} \sim \alpha\mathbf{y}_0$ and $\mathbf{y}' \sim \alpha'\mathbf{y}_0$. Then we have

$$\begin{aligned} \varphi(\mathbf{y} + \mathbf{y}') &= \varphi(\alpha\mathbf{y}_0 + \alpha'\mathbf{y}_0) \\ &= \varphi((\alpha + \alpha')\mathbf{y}_0) \\ &= (\alpha + \alpha')\varphi(\mathbf{y}_0) \\ &= \alpha\varphi(\mathbf{y}_0) + \alpha'\varphi(\mathbf{y}_0) \\ &= \varphi(\alpha\mathbf{y}_0) + \varphi(\alpha'\mathbf{y}_0) \\ &= \varphi(\mathbf{y}) + \varphi(\mathbf{y}'). \end{aligned}$$

Since we already had homogeneity of degree 1, this implies that φ is actually a linear transformation from Y into $\mathbb{R}$ that preserves $\succsim$. Notice that, by monotonicity, $\varphi(\mathbf{y}) > 0$ for any $\mathbf{y} \in Y$ other than $\mathbf{0}$.

In order to show that to transformation φ there corresponds a positive matrix (vector) $\mathbf{r}$ such that $\varphi(y) = \mathbf{r}\mathbf{y}$, notice that the dimensionality μ of Y may be less than ν. Let $\mathbf{y}_1,\ldots, \mathbf{y}_\mu \in Y$ be a set of linearly independent vectors spanning Y (notice that they also form a basis for a linear space of dimension μ) chosen in such a way that $\varphi(\mathbf{y}_i) = c$ for every $i = 1,\ldots, \mu$. Keep in mind that this implies the existence of a positive α with $\mathbf{y}_i \sim \alpha\mathbf{y}_0$ for all i. Let

$$\mathbf{A} = \begin{bmatrix} \mathbf{y}_{11} & \mathbf{y}_{21} & \cdots & \mathbf{y}_{\nu 1} & -c \\ \mathbf{y}_{12} & \mathbf{y}_{22} & \cdots & \mathbf{y}_{\nu 2} & -c \\ \vdots & \vdots & \ddots & \vdots & -c \\ \mathbf{y}_{1\mu} & \mathbf{y}_{2\mu} & \cdots & \mathbf{y}_{\nu\mu} & -c \end{bmatrix}$$

and notice that the first ν components of each row of $\mathbf{A}$ are the coordinates of the basis vectors (i.e. the coordinates of row i $(1 \leq i \leq \mu)$ are the labor inputs of production process i). According to Stiemke's theorem (cf. Kemp and Kimura 1978: 3), the system of linear equations $\mathbf{Ab} = \mathbf{0}$ has a positive solution $\mathbf{b}$ iff the system of linear inequalities ${}^t\mathbf{Ab} \geq \mathbf{0}$ (where ${}^t\mathbf{A}$ denotes the transpose of $\mathbf{A}$) has no solution.

In order to show that

$${}^t\mathbf{Ab} = \begin{bmatrix} \mathbf{y}_{11} & \mathbf{y}_{12} & \cdots & \mathbf{y}_{1\mu} \\ \mathbf{y}_{21} & \mathbf{y}_{22} & \cdots & \mathbf{y}_{2\mu} \\ \vdots & \vdots & \ddots & \vdots \\ \mathbf{y}_{\nu 1} & \mathbf{y}_{\nu 2} & \cdots & \mathbf{y}_{\nu\mu} \\ -c & -c & \cdots & -c \end{bmatrix} \mathbf{b} \geq 0$$

has no solution, assume, per absurdum, that there exists a solution $\mathbf{b} = {}^t[b_1 \ldots b_\mu]$ of the system. This implies that $[-c \ldots - c]\mathbf{b} \geq 0$ and so not all the nonzero coordinates of $\mathbf{b}$ are positive. Analogously, since the remaining rows of ${}^t\mathbf{A}$ are semipositive, and no column of the $\mathbf{y}$'s is the null vector, not all nonzero coordinates of $\mathbf{b}$ are negative. After column permutations and renumbering, without loss of generality we can let $b_1,\ldots, b_k$ be the nonnegative coordinates, and $b_{k+1},\ldots, b_\mu$ the negative coordinates of **b**. Hence, there are elements **y** and $\mathbf{y}' \in Y$ such that $\mathbf{y} = \Sigma_{i=1}^{k} b_i \mathbf{y}_i \sim \Sigma_{i=1}^{k} (\alpha b_i)\mathbf{y}_0$ and $\mathbf{y}' = \Sigma_{i=k+1}^{\nu} (-b_i)\mathbf{y}_i \sim \Sigma_{i=k+1}^{\mu} (-\alpha b_i)\mathbf{y}_0$. We have,

$$\begin{aligned}
0 &\leq [-c \cdots, -c]b] \\
&= -c\left(\sum_{i=1}^{k} b_i + \sum_{i=k+1}^{\mu} b_i\right) \\
&= -c\left(\sum_{i=1}^{k} b_i\right) - c\sum_{i=k+1}^{\mu} b_i \\
&= c\left(\sum_{i=k+1}^{\mu} - b_i\right) - c\sum_{i=1}^{\mu} b_i
\end{aligned}$$

Since $c > 0$, $\Sigma_{i=k+1}^{\mu} - b_i \geq \Sigma_{i=1}^{k} b_i$, and so $\mathbf{y}' = \Sigma_{i=k+1}^{\mu}(-\alpha b_i)\mathbf{y}_0 \geq \Sigma_{i=1}^{k}(\alpha b_i)\mathbf{y}_0 = \mathbf{y}$, which in turn implies $\mathbf{y}' \succ \mathbf{y}$.

On the other hand, since ${}^{t}\mathbf{A}b \geq \mathbf{0}$,

$$b_1\mathbf{y}_1 + b_2\mathbf{y}_2 + \cdots + b_\mu \mathbf{y}_\mu = \begin{bmatrix} \mathbf{y}_{11} & \mathbf{y}_{12} & \cdots & \mathbf{y}_{1\mu} \\ \mathbf{y}_{21} & \mathbf{y}_{22} & \cdots & \mathbf{y}_{2\mu} \\ \vdots & \vdots & \ddots & \vdots \\ \mathbf{y}_{\nu 1} & \mathbf{y}_{\nu 2} & \cdots & y_{\nu\mu} \end{bmatrix} \mathbf{b} \geq \mathbf{0}$$

and so

$$\begin{aligned}
\mathbf{y} &= b_1\mathbf{y}_1 + b_2\mathbf{y}_2 + \cdots + b_k\mathbf{y}_k \\
&\geq (-b_{k+1})\mathbf{y}_{k+1} + (-b_{k+2})\mathbf{y}_{k+2} + \cdots + (b\mu)\mathbf{y}_\mu \\
&= \mathbf{y}_\mu
\end{aligned}$$

which implies that $\mathbf{y} \succ \mathbf{y}'$. Hence we have both $\mathbf{y} \succ \mathbf{y}'$ and $\mathbf{y}' \succ \mathbf{y}$. This contradiction shows that ${}^{t}\mathbf{A}\mathbf{b} \geq \mathbf{0}$ has no solution and therefore, by Stiemke's theorem, there exists a positive vector **t** such that $\mathbf{A}\mathbf{t} = \mathbf{0}$; i.e. such that

$$\begin{aligned}
& t_1 y_{11} + t_2 y_{21} + \cdots + t_\nu y_{\nu 1} - t_{\nu+1} c = 0 \\
& t_1 y_{12} + t_2 y_{22} + \cdots + t_\nu y_{\nu 2} - t_{\nu+1} c = 0 \\
& \qquad \vdots \\
& t_1 y_{1\nu} + t_2 y_{2\nu} + \cdots + t_\nu y_{\mu\nu} - t_{\nu+1} c = 0
\end{aligned}$$

Setting $r_i = t_i/t_{v+1}$, we get

$$\mathbf{Yr} = \begin{bmatrix} \mathbf{y}_{11} & \mathbf{y}_{21} & \cdots & \mathbf{y}_{v1} \\ \mathbf{y}_{12} & \mathbf{y}_{22} & \cdots & \mathbf{y}_{v2} \\ \vdots & \vdots & \ddots & \vdots \\ \mathbf{y}_{1\mu} & \mathbf{y}_{2\mu} & \cdots & \mathbf{y}_{v\mu} \end{bmatrix} \begin{bmatrix} r_1 \\ r_2 \\ \vdots \\ r_v \end{bmatrix} = \mathbf{c} = \begin{bmatrix} c \\ c \\ \vdots \\ c \end{bmatrix} = \begin{bmatrix} \varphi(\mathbf{y}_1) \\ \varphi(\mathbf{y}_2) \\ \vdots \\ \varphi(\mathbf{y}_\mu) \end{bmatrix}$$

If $\mathbf{y} \neq \mathbf{0}$ is any profile of labor inputs, since $\mathbf{y}_1,\ldots, \mathbf{y}_\mu$ span Y, there are unique numbers $\alpha_1,\ldots, \alpha_\mu$, some of them positive, with $\mathbf{y} = \alpha_1\mathbf{y}_1 + \ldots + \alpha\mathbf{y}_\mu$. Thus,

$$\begin{aligned} \mathbf{ry} &= \mathbf{r}(\alpha_1\mathbf{y}_1 + \cdots + \alpha_\mu\mathbf{y}_\mu) \\ &= \alpha_1\mathbf{ry}_1 + \cdots + \alpha_v\mathbf{ry}_\mu \\ &= \alpha_1\varphi(\alpha\mathbf{y}_0) + \cdots + \alpha_v\varphi(\alpha\mathbf{y}_0) \\ &= \alpha_1\varphi(\mathbf{y}_1) + \cdots + \alpha_v\varphi(\mathbf{y}_\mu) \\ &= \varphi(\mathbf{y}). \end{aligned}$$

Vector $\mathbf{r}$ is thus seen to be the required reduction.

According to Theorem 1 in KLST (1971: 74), the existence of such a representation entails that $\langle Y, \succsim, + \rangle$ is a closed extensive structure. Hence, if φ' is any other representation of $\succsim$, then there exists $\alpha > 0$ such that $\varphi' = \alpha\varphi$. Thus,

$$\begin{aligned} \varphi'(\mathbf{y}) &= \alpha\varphi(\mathbf{y}) \\ &= \alpha(\mathbf{ry}) \\ &= (\alpha\mathbf{r})\mathbf{y}. \ \square \end{aligned}$$

9.3 Market-determination of abstract labor

The typical narrative in volume 1 of *Das Kapital* (DK) is that labor in a capitalist economy (or in any economy, for that matter) is homogeneous, and so the value of the goods it produces can be measured in terms of the mean or minimal labor-time employed in their production. This presupposes that value is the result of a process that takes place entirely within the pure sphere of production, "independently of its form of manifestation" in the sphere of exchange:

> It becomes plain that it is not the exchange of commodities which regulates the magnitude of their values, but rather the reverse, the magnitude of the value of commodities which regulates the proportion in which they exchange.
>
> (Marx 1976: 156)

This same narrative seems to be reinforced at the beginning of his *Contribution to a Critique of Political Economy* where he appears defending the market-independent view of value:

> As exchange-values of different magnitudes they [i.e. commodities of different types] represent larger or smaller portions, larger or smaller amounts of simple, homogeneous, abstract general labour, which is the substance of exchange value.
>
> (Marx 1970: 29)

Nevertheless, seemingly contradicting the typical narrative, also in DK Marx intimated that market-exchange, a social process "that goes behind the back of the producers", is the one that actually reduces the heterogeneous labors to a common unit. And in *Contribution* he ends up asserting this same view:

> the labor of different persons is equated and treated as universal labour only by bringing one use-value into relation with another one in the guise of exchange-value.
>
> (Ibid.: 34)

This is the view that in the exchange process universal

> social labor is … *not a ready-made prerequisite but an emerging result.* (Ibid.: 45; emphasis added)

Naturally, putting together these quotations a perplexity cannot but arise:

> … a new difficulty arises: on the one hand, commodities must enter the exchange process as materialised universal labour-time, on the other hand, the labour-time of individuals becomes materialised universal labour-time only as the result of the exchange process.
>
> (Ibid.)

It is pretty clear to me that the content of this last quotation is the manifestation of an ambiguity which is present both in DK and in *Contribution*. In both works Marx starts by describing the "substance" of value as homogeneous labor, which in addition he seems to identify with abstract labor and simple or unskilled labor. The impression that one gets reading the first sections of such books is that the "substance" of value can be defined almost in purely technological terms that can be applied to any type of economy. Nevertheless, this view is actually incorrect, since it does not take into account that labor is not homogenous but rather quite diversified.

In contradistinction to the simplistic view just described, my aim in the present section is to develop the view that

> it is only the expression of equivalence between different sorts of commodities which brings to view the specific character of value creating labour, *by actually reducing the different kinds of labour embedded in the different kinds of commodity to their common quality of being human labour in general.*
>
> (Marx 1973: 142; emphasis added)

I will show in what follows that a uniform rate of profit actually induces an abstract labor relation among the expenditures of labor required to produce the commodities. In order to do this, I need to introduce additional conceptual apparatus, including the definition of production price.

First of all, let us discuss how prices shall be represented here. I shall assume that all produced goods are desirable, and so that prices are positive. This means that to each type of good l $(1 \leq l \leq \lambda)$ there corresponds a positive number p_l representing its price relative to the other goods at a given moment of the exchange process (I shall assume that we are considering an interval in which prices are fixed). Hence, a *price system* is nothing but a positive vector $\mathbf{p}$ in the simplex of the linear space $\mathbb{R}^{\lambda}$. A *wage system* is a positive vector $\mathbf{w}$ that specifies the hourly wages to be paid to the different tasks. Coordinate n represents the wage per hour for performing a task of kind n $(1 \leq n \leq \nu)$.

I will assume that the economy can be represented by a convex polyhedral cone $\tilde{Y}$ spanned by the production processes actually used in the economy. I assume, naturally, that $\tilde{Y}$ is normal. Given price and wage systems $\mathbf{p}$ and $\mathbf{w}$, the profit rate of process $\tilde{\mathbf{y}}$ is defined as

$$\pi(\tilde{\mathbf{y}}) = \frac{\mathbf{p}\hat{\mathbf{y}} - \mathbf{w}\mathbf{y}}{\mathbf{p}\underline{\mathbf{y}} + \mathbf{w}\mathbf{y}}.$$

System $\mathbf{p}$ is called a system of *production prices* whenever $\pi(\tilde{\mathbf{y}})$ is uniform; that is to say, it is the same for every process in Y. Production prices reflect the expenditures of labor assigning a higher price to those processes that employ more labor. This assertion is made more precise in the following lemma.

9.3.1 Lemma

If $\mathbf{p}$ *is a production price then* $\mathbf{y} = \mathbf{y}'$ *implies* $\mathbf{p}\hat{\mathbf{y}} = \mathbf{p}\hat{\mathbf{y}}'$, *and* $\mathbf{y} \leq \mathbf{y}'$ *implies* $\mathbf{p}\hat{\mathbf{y}} = \mathbf{p}\hat{\mathbf{y}}'$.

PROOF: Let π be the common rate of profit of all processes in the economy. I will show, in the first place, that the monetary value of the net output $\mathbf{p}\hat{\mathbf{y}}$ of process $\tilde{\mathbf{y}}$ is equal to (less than) the monetary value of net output $\mathbf{p}\hat{\mathbf{y}}'$ of process $\tilde{\mathbf{y}}'$ whenever the labor input $\mathbf{y}$ of process $\tilde{\mathbf{y}}$ is equal to (less than) the labor input $\mathbf{y}'$ of process $\tilde{\mathbf{y}}'$.

The normality of $\tilde{Y}$ implies that $\underline{\mathbf{y}} = \underline{\mathbf{y}}'$ whenever $\mathbf{y} = \mathbf{y}'$; and that $\underline{\mathbf{y}} \leq \underline{\mathbf{y}}'$ whenever $\mathbf{y} \leq \mathbf{y}'$. Thus, if $\mathbf{y} = \mathbf{y}'$, since both $\mathbf{p}$ and $\mathbf{w}$ are positive, $\mathbf{wy} = \mathbf{wy}'$ and $\mathbf{p}\underline{\mathbf{y}} = \mathbf{p}\underline{\mathbf{y}}'$. Therefore,

$$\mathbf{p}\hat{\mathbf{y}} - \mathbf{wy} = \pi(\mathbf{wy} + \mathbf{p}\underline{\mathbf{y}}) = \pi(\mathbf{wy}' + \mathbf{p}\underline{\mathbf{y}}') = \mathbf{p}\hat{\mathbf{y}}' - \mathbf{wy}'.$$

It follows that $\mathbf{p}\hat{\mathbf{y}} = \mathbf{p}\hat{\mathbf{y}}'$.

If $\mathbf{y} \leq \mathbf{y}'$, $\mathbf{wy} < \mathbf{wy}'$ and $\mathbf{p}\underline{\mathbf{y}} < \mathbf{p}\underline{\mathbf{y}}'$. Hence,

$$\mathbf{p}\hat{\mathbf{y}} - \mathbf{wy} = \pi(\mathbf{wy} + \mathbf{p}\underline{\mathbf{y}}) < \pi(\mathbf{wy}' + \mathbf{p}\underline{\mathbf{y}}') = \mathbf{p}\hat{\mathbf{y}}' - \mathbf{wy}'.$$

Adding $\mathbf{wy}$ at both sides of the extreme expressions, we get $\mathbf{p}\hat{\mathbf{y}} < \mathbf{p}\hat{\mathbf{y}}' + (\mathbf{wy} - \mathbf{wy}') < \mathbf{p}\hat{\mathbf{y}}'$, because $\mathbf{wy} - \mathbf{wy}'$ is negative. □

We have just shown that there exists a function $\varphi: K \to \mathbb{R}$ such that $\varphi(\mathbf{y}) = \mathbf{p}\hat{\mathbf{y}}$, for every process $\tilde{\mathbf{y}} = [\mathbf{y}, \underline{\mathbf{y}}, \bar{\mathbf{y}}] \in Y$. With the help of this function we may define a relation $\gtrsim$ among elements of Y as follows: $\mathbf{y} \sim \mathbf{y}'$ iff $\varphi(\mathbf{y}) = \varphi(\mathbf{y}')$ and $\mathbf{y} \succ \mathbf{y}'$ iff $\varphi(\mathbf{y}) > \varphi(\mathbf{y}')$. Let us call this relation the *reduction induced by the price system* $\mathbf{p}$. I will prove that $\gtrsim$ is actually an abstract labor relation over Y.

9.3.2 Theorem

Let $\gtrsim$ be the reduction induced by production price $\mathbf{p}$. *Actually, $\gtrsim$ is an abstract labor relation over Y.*

PROOF: (1) In order to show that Y is a convex polyhedral cone, notice that $\mathbf{y} \in Y$ iff there is a process $\tilde{\mathbf{y}} = [\mathbf{y}, \underline{\mathbf{y}}, \bar{\mathbf{y}}] \in \tilde{Y}$. It is clear that $\tilde{Y}$ is a convex polyhedral cone and so $\alpha\tilde{\mathbf{y}} = [\alpha\mathbf{y}, \alpha\underline{\mathbf{y}}, \alpha\bar{\mathbf{y}}]$ whenever $\alpha > 0$. Hence, $\alpha\mathbf{y} \in Y$. Moreover, if $\mathbf{y}$, $\mathbf{y}' \in Y$, there exist processes $[\mathbf{y}, \underline{\mathbf{y}}, \bar{\mathbf{y}}]$ and $[\mathbf{y}', \underline{\mathbf{y}}', \bar{\mathbf{y}}']$ in $\tilde{\mathbf{Y}}$ and so $[\mathbf{y} + \mathbf{y}', \underline{\mathbf{y}} + \underline{\mathbf{y}}', \bar{\mathbf{y}} + \bar{\mathbf{y}}'] \in \tilde{Y}$. Thus $\mathbf{y} + \mathbf{y}' \in Y$. It follows that Y is also a convex polyhedral cone because Y is spanned by the labor expenditures of the production process that span $\tilde{Y}$. Notice that both Y and $\tilde{Y}$ are closed with respect to the usual topologies (cf. Hestenes 1966: 15).

(2) In order to show that $\gtrsim$ is a weak ordering, notice that $\tilde{Y}$ is an economy ruled by a common system of prices. This means that any pair $\mathbf{y}$, $\mathbf{y}'$ is compared through φ:

$$\varphi(\mathbf{y}) \geq \varphi(\mathbf{y}') \quad \text{or} \quad \varphi(\mathbf{y}') \geq \varphi(\mathbf{y}').$$

Clearly,

$$\begin{aligned} \mathbf{y} \gtrsim \mathbf{y}' \quad \text{and} \quad \mathbf{y}' \gtrsim \mathbf{y}'' &\Rightarrow \varphi(\mathbf{y}) \geq \varphi(\mathbf{y}') \text{ and } \varphi(\mathbf{y}') \geq \varphi(\mathbf{y}'') \\ &\Rightarrow \varphi(\mathbf{y}) \geq \varphi(\mathbf{y}'') \\ &\Rightarrow \mathbf{y} \gtrsim \mathbf{y}''. \end{aligned}$$

(3) Relation $\gtrsim$ is monotonic because

$$\begin{aligned}\mathbf{y} \geq \mathbf{y}' &\Leftrightarrow \varphi(\mathbf{y}) \geq \varphi(\mathbf{y}')\\ &\Leftrightarrow \mathbf{y} \succ \mathbf{y}'.\end{aligned}$$

(4) That $\gtrsim$ satisfies the homogeneity law (cancellation) is established as follows. In the first place, since

$$\tilde{\mathbf{y}} + \tilde{\mathbf{y}}' = [\mathbf{y} + \mathbf{y}', \underline{\mathbf{y}} + \underline{\mathbf{y}}', \bar{\mathbf{y}} + \bar{\mathbf{y}}'],$$

$\widehat{\mathbf{y} + \mathbf{y}'} = \hat{\mathbf{y}} + \hat{\mathbf{y}}'$. Thus, for any $\mathbf{y}$, $\mathbf{y}'$, $\mathbf{y}'' \in Y$,

$$\begin{aligned}\mathbf{y} \gtrsim \mathbf{y}' &\Leftrightarrow \varphi(\mathbf{y}) \geq \varphi(\mathbf{y}')\\ &\Leftrightarrow \varphi(\mathbf{y}) + \varphi(\mathbf{y}'') \geq \varphi(\mathbf{y}') + \varphi(\mathbf{y}'')\\ &\Leftrightarrow \mathbf{p}\hat{\mathbf{y}} + \mathbf{p}\hat{\mathbf{y}}'' \geq \mathbf{p}\hat{\mathbf{y}}' + \mathbf{p}\hat{\mathbf{y}}''\\ &\Leftrightarrow \mathbf{p}(\hat{\mathbf{y}} + \hat{\mathbf{y}}'') \geq \mathbf{p}(\hat{\mathbf{y}}' + \hat{\mathbf{y}}'')\\ &\Leftrightarrow \mathbf{p}(\widehat{\mathbf{y} + \mathbf{y}''}) \geq \mathbf{p}(\widehat{\mathbf{y}' + \mathbf{y}''})\\ &\Leftrightarrow \varphi(\mathbf{y} + \mathbf{y}'') \geq \varphi(\mathbf{y}' + \mathbf{y}'')\\ &\Leftrightarrow \mathbf{y} + \mathbf{y}'' \gtrsim \mathbf{y}' + \mathbf{y}''.\end{aligned}$$

(5) The homotheticity of $\gtrsim$ is established as follows:

$$\begin{aligned}\mathbf{y} \sim \mathbf{y}' &\Leftrightarrow \varphi(\mathbf{y}) = \varphi(\mathbf{y}')\\ &\Leftrightarrow \mathbf{p}\hat{\mathbf{y}} = \mathbf{p}\hat{\mathbf{y}}'\\ &\Leftrightarrow \alpha\mathbf{p}\hat{\mathbf{y}} = \alpha\mathbf{p}\hat{\mathbf{y}}'\\ &\Leftrightarrow \mathbf{p}(\alpha\hat{\mathbf{y}}) = \mathbf{p}(\alpha\hat{\mathbf{y}}')\\ &\Leftrightarrow \varphi(\alpha\mathbf{y}) = \varphi(\alpha\mathbf{y}')\\ &\Leftrightarrow \alpha\mathbf{y} \sim \alpha\mathbf{y}'.\end{aligned}$$

(6) Finally, in order to show that the sets $\{\mathbf{y} \in Y | \mathbf{y} \gtrsim \mathbf{y}^*\}$ and $\{\mathbf{y} \in Y | \mathbf{y}^* \gtrsim \mathbf{y}\}$ are closed, let $(\mathbf{y}^k)$ be a sequence of elements of $\{\mathbf{y} \in \mathbf{Y} | \mathbf{y} \gtrsim \mathbf{y}^*\}$ converging to limit $\mathbf{y}^0$. It will be enough to prove that $\mathbf{y}^0 \gtrsim \mathbf{y}^*$.

Since Y is closed, $\mathbf{y}^0 \in Y$ and so there is in $\tilde{Y}$ a process of the form $\tilde{\mathbf{y}}^0 = [\mathbf{y}^0, \underline{\mathbf{y}}^0, \bar{\mathbf{y}}^0]$. Let $\varepsilon > 0$ be a number as small as you wish. Then there is a positive number N such that, for $k > N$, processes $[\mathbf{y}^k, \underline{\mathbf{y}}^k, \bar{\mathbf{y}}^k]$ are in the open sphere centered in $\tilde{\mathbf{y}}^0$ with radius $\varepsilon/2$. Thus, $|\underline{\mathbf{y}}^0 - \underline{\mathbf{y}}^k| < \varepsilon/2$ and $|\bar{\mathbf{y}}^0 - \bar{\mathbf{y}}^k| < \varepsilon/2$. Since

$$\begin{aligned}\hat{\mathbf{y}}^0 - \hat{\mathbf{y}}^k &= \bar{\mathbf{y}}^0 - \underline{\mathbf{y}}^0 - (\bar{\mathbf{y}}^k - \underline{\mathbf{y}}^k)\\ &= \bar{\mathbf{y}}^0 - \underline{\mathbf{y}}^0 - \bar{\mathbf{y}}^k + \underline{\mathbf{y}}^k\\ &= (\bar{\mathbf{y}}^0 - \bar{\mathbf{y}}^k) + (\underline{\mathbf{y}}^k - \underline{\mathbf{y}}^0),\end{aligned}$$

it follows that

$$\begin{aligned}\| \hat{\mathbf{y}}^0 - \hat{\mathbf{y}}^k \| &= \| (\bar{\mathbf{y}}^0 - \bar{\mathbf{y}}^k) + (\underline{\mathbf{y}}^k - \underline{\mathbf{y}}^0) \| \\ &\leq \| (\bar{\mathbf{y}}^0 - \bar{\mathbf{y}}^k) \| + \| (\underline{\mathbf{y}}^0 - \underline{\mathbf{y}}^k) \| \\ &< \varepsilon/2 + \varepsilon/2 \\ &= \varepsilon.\end{aligned}$$

We have $(\bar{\mathbf{y}}^k) \to \hat{\mathbf{y}}^0$, and so $(\varphi(\mathbf{y}^k)) \to \varphi(\mathbf{y}^0)$. Since, by hypothesis, $\varphi(\mathbf{y}^k) \geq \varphi(\mathbf{y}^*)$ for every k, it follows that $\varphi(\mathbf{y}^0) \geq \varphi(\mathbf{y}^*)$. It is concluded that $\mathbf{y}^0 \gtrsim \mathbf{y}^*$. An analogous argument shows that $\{\mathbf{y} \in Y | \mathbf{y}^* \gtrsim \mathbf{y}\}$ is also closed. □

The former theorem means that a tendency toward a uniform rate of profit involves a tendency toward a specific reduction of the expenditures of heterogeneous labors to a common unit – it leads to abstract labor. Reductions induced by production prices are called *standard reductions*.

9.4 Labor-value

Closing the circle, just as the production price induces a reduction of concrete heterogeneous labors to abstract labor, abstract labor induces a system of prices for the produced goods. In order to prove this proposition, we need to define the concept of a productive structure, and prove a more general version of the substitution theorem. Let us start with a precise definition of efficiency. Intuitively, an efficient process is characterized by producing the same or more amount of net product using less or the same amount of labor than other processes.

9.4.1 Definition

Let $\tilde{\mathbf{y}}, \tilde{\mathbf{y}}'$ be elements of the set of production processes Y. Process $\tilde{y}$ is *more efficient* than process $\tilde{\mathbf{y}}'$ iff $\check{\mathbf{y}} \geq \check{\mathbf{y}}'$. It is *strictly* more efficient iff $\check{\mathbf{y}} \geq \check{\mathbf{y}}'$. Process $\tilde{\mathbf{y}} \in Y$ is *efficient* iff there is no process in Y strictly more efficient than $\tilde{\mathbf{y}}$.

It is usual in economic theory to represent the technological possibilities of a given producer as a certain set of production processes, and the choice of the producer as a point in that set. I shall assume that there are χ producers but producers with the same technology will be treated as the same producer. I admit the possibility of alternative techniques, and so the same kind of output can be produced by different technologies. This implies that there may be more types of production processes operating than kinds of outputs; i.e. $\lambda \leq \chi$. I shall assume also that the positive net outputs of producer j are ocassionally more than one, which means that there is joint production (like leather together with beef in the cattle industry). Nevertheless, it seems that joint production is not enough to revert the inequality $\lambda \leq \chi$. Also, since the same tasks repeat in different production processes, I shall assume that there are more producers than tasks, so that $\nu \leq \chi$. Finally, I will take for granted that no process in $\tilde{Y}_j$ can be obtained technologically adding up processes from other producers. This will bring the consequence that labor inputs as well as the netputs of the processes chosen by the different producers are a linearly independent set. I shall assume that $\tilde{Y}_j$ is a convex cone for each producer j. Since the elements of $\tilde{Y}_j$ are possible for producer j, the total production set $\tilde{Y} = \sum_{j=1}^{m} \tilde{Y}_j$ is defined. I will suppose as well that in the production processes represented by the $\tilde{Y}_j$ labor is indispensable and that both labor and the whole system is productive. These concepts are made precise in the following definition.

9.4.2 Definition

$\mathfrak{B}$ is a *production structure* iff there exist positive integers χ, λ, v such that, for each $j = 1, \ldots, \chi$,

(0) $\mathfrak{B} = \langle \tilde{Y}_1, \ldots, \tilde{Y}_\chi \rangle$;
(1) $\tilde{Y}_j$ is a closed convex cone in the linear space $\mathbb{R}^{2\lambda+v}$;
(2) each element of $\tilde{Y}_j$ is a production process;
(3) there are at most as many netputs as producers ($\lambda \leq \chi$) and no more tasks than producers ($v \leq \chi$);
(4) no positive net product in $\tilde{Y}_j$ can be technologically obtained by adding processes from other producers, and no expenditure of labor can be obtained combining labor expenditures from other technologies; i.e. any family $\{\mathbf{y}_1, \ldots, \mathbf{y}_\chi\}$ of labor inputs corresponding to technologies of different producers, as well as any collection $\{\hat{\mathbf{y}}_1, \cdots, \hat{\mathbf{y}}_x\}$ of netputs, is linearly independent;
(5) Labor is indispensable; i.e. $\mathbf{y} = \mathbf{0}$ implies $\underline{\mathbf{y}} = \underline{\mathbf{0}}$ and $\bar{\mathbf{y}} = \bar{\mathbf{0}}$ for any process $[\mathbf{y}\ \underline{\mathbf{y}}\ \bar{\mathbf{y}}] \in Y_j$;
(6) Labor is productive; i.e. $\underline{\mathbf{y}} = \underline{\mathbf{0}}$ or $\bar{\mathbf{y}} = \bar{\mathbf{0}}$ implies $\mathbf{y} = \mathbf{0}$ for any process $[\mathbf{y}, \underline{\mathbf{y}}, \bar{\mathbf{y}}] \in Y_j$;
(7) $\mathfrak{B}$ is productive; that is, $\sum_{j=1}^{\chi} \tilde{Y}_j$ contains a least one process $\tilde{\mathbf{y}}$ with positive net output: $\hat{\mathbf{y}} > \hat{\mathbf{0}}$;
(8) Labor is normal.

A determined technology for producer j can be represented by the ray generated by a certain process $\tilde{\mathbf{y}}_j \in Y_j : \{\alpha\tilde{\mathbf{y}}_j | \alpha \geq 0\}$. This ray includes all the production process that are scalings of $\tilde{\mathbf{y}}_j$. By a chosen production structure we understand the convex polyhedric cone $\tilde{Y}$ generated by the technologies chosen by the producers; that is to say, the convex hull of the rays $\{\alpha\tilde{\mathbf{y}}_j | \alpha \geq 0\}$. It is possible to show, upon the basis of Definition 9.4.2, that each producer can choose an efficient production process, but the proof of this assertion requires a previous lemma.

9.4.3 *Lemma*

Let $\tilde{Y}^{+} \subset \sum_{j=1}^{\chi} \tilde{Y}_j$ be the set of aggregated processes with nonnegative netputs of production structure $\mathfrak{B}$. For any process $\tilde{\mathbf{y}} \in \tilde{Y}^{+}$ there is an efficient process $\tilde{\mathbf{y}}^{*} \in \tilde{Y}^{+}$ such that $\hat{\mathbf{y}}^{*} \geqq \hat{\mathbf{y}}$ and $\mathbf{y}^{*} \leqq \mathbf{y}$.

PROOF: I will show, first, that set

$$E(\tilde{\mathbf{y}}) = \{\tilde{\mathbf{y}}' | \hat{\mathbf{y}}' \geqq \hat{\mathbf{y}} \text{ and } y' \leqq y\}$$

is compact, and I will use the fact that the function $\psi : E(\tilde{\mathbf{y}}) \to \mathbb{R}$, that maps each vector $\tilde{\mathbf{y}}' \in E(\tilde{\mathbf{y}})$ into the number

$$(\hat{y}'_1 + \cdots + \hat{y}'_\lambda) - (y'_1 + \cdots + y'_\nu),$$

is continuous. It will follow (by Weierstrass theorem) that ψ reaches a maximum $\tilde{\mathbf{y}}^{*} \in E(\tilde{\mathbf{y}})$. It will be easy to see that $\tilde{\mathbf{y}}^{*}$ is an efficient point in $\tilde{Y}^{+}$.

Since $\tilde{\mathbf{0}} \in E(\tilde{Y}^{+})$, in order to show that $E(\tilde{\mathbf{y}})$ is bounded notice that the set

$$F = \{\mathbf{y}' | [\mathbf{y}' \mathbf{y}' \bar{\mathbf{y}}'] \in E(\tilde{\mathbf{y}})\}$$

is bounded, because $\mathbf{0} \leq \mathbf{y}' \leq \mathbf{y}$ for every $[\mathbf{y}' \mathbf{y}' \bar{\mathbf{y}}'] \in E(\tilde{\mathbf{y}})$.

Now, if $E(\tilde{\mathbf{y}})$ were not bounded, there would be a sequence $(\tilde{\mathbf{y}}'_k)$ in $E(\tilde{\mathbf{y}})$ such that the sequence of norms $(\|\tilde{\mathbf{y}}'_k\|)$ is increasing and unbounded. Nevertheless, it can be seen that the sequence of labor expenditures $(\mathbf{y}'_k)$ converges to a limit $\mathbf{y}' \geq \mathbf{0}$ (not necessarily in F) because F is bounded. Let

$$\tilde{\mathbf{y}}''_k = (\| \tilde{\mathbf{y}}'_k \|)^{-1} \tilde{\mathbf{y}}'_k.$$

Since $\tilde{Y}^{+}$ is a cone, $\tilde{\mathbf{y}}''_k \in \tilde{\mathbf{y}}^{+}$. Furthermore, $(\tilde{\mathbf{y}}''_k)$ is bounded because $\|\tilde{\mathbf{y}}''_k\| \leq 1$ for every k. Therefore, we can claim that (a subsequence of) $(\tilde{\mathbf{y}}''_k)$ converges to a point that must be in $\tilde{Y}^{+}$ because $\tilde{Y}^{+}$ is closed. Since $(\|\tilde{\mathbf{y}}''_k\|) \to 1$, $\tilde{\mathbf{y}}'' \neq \tilde{0}$ and so, due to the productivity of Y and labor indispensability, $\bar{\mathbf{y}}'' \geq \bar{\mathbf{0}}$. On the other hand, since $(\mathbf{y}'_k) \to \mathbf{y}'$ as $k \to \infty$,

$$\begin{aligned}
\mathbf{y}'' &= \lim_{k \to \infty} y''_k \\
&= \lim_{k \to \infty} (\| \mathbf{y}'_k \| + 1)^{-1} \cdot \lim_{k \to \infty} \mathbf{y}'_k \\
&= 0 \cdot \mathbf{y}' \\
&= 0.
\end{aligned}$$

Hence, given that labor is indispensable, $\bar{\mathbf{y}}'' = \bar{\mathbf{0}}$. This contradiction shows that $E(\tilde{\mathbf{y}})$ is bounded.

On the other hand, it is easy to see that $E(\tilde{\mathbf{y}})$ is closed, because the limit of any convergent sequence of points of $E(\tilde{\mathbf{y}})$ is in $\tilde{Y}^{+}$ – which is closed – and also satisfies the condition for belonging to $E(\tilde{\mathbf{y}})$.

Clearly, since ψ is continuous, it reaches a global maximum at a point $\tilde{\mathbf{y}}^*$ in $E(\tilde{\mathbf{y}})$. I claim that this point is efficient in $\tilde{Y}^+$. For suppose, per contra, that there is a $\tilde{\mathbf{y}}^{**}$ strictly more efficient than $\tilde{\mathbf{y}}^*$. Then $\psi(\tilde{\mathbf{y}}^{**}) > \psi(\tilde{\mathbf{y}}^*)$, but this is impossible because ψ had reached a maximum in $\tilde{y}^*$. □

A non-substitution theorem asserts, essentially, that rational producers cannot help but choosing a certain technology because that technology is the only efficient one. The non-substitution theorem for a static Leontief economy was proven independently for the first time by Samuelson (1951, 1961) and Georgescu Roegen (1967), by means of calculus techniques. Using more general techniques, the theorem was proven by Koopmans (1951) for the case of three industries, but the most perspicuous formulation and proof of this result is due to Arrow (1951). Levhari (1965) provides another proof of the theorem showing that, even though a producer may shift from one activity to another, and back to the first, as the interest rate changes in the same direction, that is not possible for the productive system as a whole. Mirrles (1969) proved the theorem for a dynamic economy which excludes joint production. Stiglitz (1970) admits durable goods within a dynamic economy in balanced growth.

The meaning of the following theorem is that processes from all production branches can be chosen in such a way that any nonnegative linear combination of these processes is efficient (i.e. the convex cone $\tilde{Y}$ generated by these processes is a subset of the set E of all efficient processes). In contradistinction, the import of the non-substitution theorems is, essentially, that there is a finite number of activities such that each efficient aggregated process can be expressed as linear combination of these processes (i.e. the set of all efficient process E is a subset of $\tilde{Y}$). Even though the propositions are expressed together in the usual statements of the theorem, they must be carefully distinguished.

In order to facilitate the proof of the following theorem, it will be useful at this point to introduce the following matrices. Assuming that the producers have chosen processes $\tilde{\mathbf{y}}_1, \cdots, \tilde{\mathbf{y}}_\chi$, the labor inputs of the processes can be seen as the columns of matrix

$$\mathbf{Y} = \begin{bmatrix} y_{11} & \cdots & y_{1\chi} \\ \vdots & \ddots & \vdots \\ y_{\nu 1} & \cdots & y_{\nu\chi} \end{bmatrix} \tag{9.1}$$

where vector ${}^t[y_{1j} \ldots y_{\nu j}]$ represents the labor inputs of process $\tilde{\mathbf{y}}_j$. Analogously, the material inputs can be seen as the columns of

$$\underline{\mathbf{Y}} = \begin{bmatrix} \underline{y}_{11} & \cdots & \underline{y}_{1\chi} \\ \vdots & \ddots & \vdots \\ \underline{y}_{\lambda 1} & \cdots & \underline{y}_{\lambda\chi} \end{bmatrix} \tag{9.2}$$

and the outputs as the columns of

$$\bar{\mathbf{Y}} = \begin{bmatrix} \bar{y}_{11} & \cdots & \bar{y}_{1\chi} \\ \vdots & \ddots & \vdots \\ \bar{y}_{\lambda 1} & \cdots & \bar{y}_{\lambda\chi} \end{bmatrix} \tag{9.3}$$

therefore, the matrix of netputs is

$$\hat{\mathbf{Y}} = \bar{\mathbf{Y}} - \underline{\mathbf{Y}} = \begin{bmatrix} \hat{y}_{11} & \cdots & \hat{y}_{1\chi} \\ \vdots & \ddots & \vdots \\ \hat{y}_{\lambda 1} & \cdots & \hat{y}_{\lambda\chi} \end{bmatrix} \tag{9.4}$$

Any level of simultaneous operation of the processes can be expressed in stock version as process

$$\begin{aligned} \tilde{\mathbf{y}} &= [\mathbf{y}\ \underline{\mathbf{y}}\ \bar{\mathbf{y}}] \\ &= \left[\sum_{j=1}^{\chi} a_j \mathbf{y}_j\ \sum_{j=1}^{\chi} a_j \underline{\mathbf{y}}_j\ \sum_{j=1}^{\chi} a_j \bar{\mathbf{y}}_j\right] \\ &= [\mathbf{Ya}\ \underline{\mathbf{Y}}\mathbf{a}\ \bar{\mathbf{Y}}\mathbf{a}]. \end{aligned} \tag{9.5}$$

In flow version as process

$$\begin{aligned} \check{\mathbf{y}} &= [-\mathbf{y}\ \hat{\mathbf{y}}] \\ &= \left[-\sum_{j=1}^{\chi} a_j \mathbf{y}_j\ \sum_{j=1}^{\chi} a_j \hat{\mathbf{y}}_j\right] \\ &= [-\mathbf{Ya}\ \hat{\mathbf{Y}}\mathbf{a}], \end{aligned} \tag{9.6}$$

where $\mathbf{a} = [a_1 \dots a_\chi] \geqq \mathbf{0}$ is a 'state' or 'activation' of the chosen technologies. The set $\{\mathbf{Ya} | \mathbf{a} \geqq \mathbf{0}\} = \{\mathbf{y} | [\mathbf{y}\ \underline{\mathbf{y}}\ \bar{\mathbf{y}}] \in \tilde{Y}\}$ of labor inputs of $\tilde{Y}$ will be denoted as Y; that of netputs as $\{\hat{\mathbf{Y}}\mathbf{a} | \mathbf{a} \geqq \mathbf{0}\} = \{\hat{\mathbf{x}} | [\mathbf{y}\ \underline{\mathbf{y}}\ \bar{\mathbf{y}}] \in \tilde{Y}\}$ as $\hat{Y}$. Using this terminology we can proceed.

9.4.4 Theorem

There exists, in any production structure $\mathfrak{B}$, *a finite number of activities* $\tilde{\mathbf{y}}_1, \cdots, \tilde{\mathbf{y}}_\chi$, *one for each producer, such that every linear combination of these activities is efficient.*

PROOF: Let $\tilde{\mathbf{y}}$ be an efficient aggregated process whose netput is positive, $\hat{\mathbf{y}} > \hat{0}$, and let $\{\tilde{\mathbf{y}}_1, \cdots, \tilde{\mathbf{y}}_x\}$ a family of processes such that $\tilde{\mathbf{y}}_1 = \sum_{k=1}^{x} \tilde{\mathbf{y}}_j$. I will show that the convex cone $\tilde{Y}$ generated by these processes is a a set of efficient activities.

If $\mathbf{Y}$ is the matrix of labor expenditures corresponding to processes $\tilde{\mathbf{y}}_1, \cdots, \tilde{\mathbf{y}}_x$, and $\hat{Y}$ that corresponding to the netputs, process $\tilde{\mathbf{y}}$ can be written, in flow version, as $\check{\mathbf{y}} = [-\mathbf{Ya}, \hat{\mathbf{Y}}\mathbf{a}]$ for a certain activation $\mathbf{a} > \mathbf{0}$.

Suppose that there exists an inefficient element $\tilde{\mathbf{y}}'$ in $\tilde{Y}$, so that $\check{\mathbf{y}}' = [-\mathbf{Ya}', \hat{\mathbf{Y}}\mathbf{a}']$ for some activation $\mathbf{a}' \geq \mathbf{0}$. By Lemma 9.4.3, there exists an efficient process $\check{\mathbf{y}}^*$ such that $\hat{\mathbf{y}}^* \geqq \hat{\mathbf{y}}'$ and $\mathbf{y}^* \leqq \mathbf{y}'$, where at least one of these inequalities is strict; i.e. $\hat{\mathbf{y}}^* \geq \hat{\mathbf{y}}'$ or $\mathbf{y}^* \leq \mathbf{y}'$.

Let $\mathbf{y}'' = (1-\alpha)\mathbf{Ya} + \alpha\mathbf{Ya}'$, $\mathbf{y}'' = (1-\alpha)\underline{\mathbf{Y}}\mathbf{a} + \alpha\underline{\mathbf{Y}}\mathbf{a}'$, and $\bar{\mathbf{y}}'' = (1-\alpha)\bar{\mathbf{Y}}\mathbf{a} + \alpha\bar{\mathbf{Y}}\mathbf{a}'$ for $\alpha < 0$. If α is sufficiently small, $\mathbf{a}'' = (1-\alpha)\mathbf{a} + \alpha\mathbf{a}' \geq \mathbf{0}$ is an activation, so that

$$\begin{aligned}
\tilde{\mathbf{y}}'' &= [\mathbf{y}'', \underline{\mathbf{y}}'', x''] \\
&= [\mathbf{Y}((1-\alpha)\mathbf{a} + \alpha\mathbf{a}'), \underline{\mathbf{Y}}((1-\alpha)\mathbf{a} + \alpha\mathbf{a}'), \bar{\mathbf{Y}}((1-\alpha)\mathbf{a} + \alpha\mathbf{a}')] \\
&= [\mathbf{Ya}'', \underline{\mathbf{Y}}\mathbf{a}'', \bar{\mathbf{Y}}\mathbf{a}'']
\end{aligned}$$

is a process in $\tilde{Y}$. Let $\beta = -(\alpha/(1-\alpha))$. Then $0 < \beta < 1$ and

$$(1-\beta)[-\mathbf{y}'', \hat{\mathbf{y}}''] + \beta[-\mathbf{y}^*, \hat{\mathbf{y}}^*]$$

is an aggregated process. But

$$(1-\beta)\mathbf{y}'' + \beta\mathbf{y}^* = Y\mathbf{a} - \beta(\mathbf{y}' - \mathbf{y}^*) \leqq \mathbf{Ya}$$

because $\mathbf{y}' \geqq \mathbf{y}^*$.

On the other hand,

$$\begin{aligned}
(1-\beta)\hat{\mathbf{y}}'' + \beta\hat{\mathbf{y}}^* &= \frac{1}{1-\alpha}((1-\alpha)\hat{\mathbf{Y}}\mathbf{a} + \alpha\hat{\mathbf{Y}}\mathbf{a}') + \beta\hat{\mathbf{y}}^* \\
&= \hat{\mathbf{Y}}\mathbf{a} + \frac{\alpha}{1-\alpha}\hat{\mathbf{y}}\mathbf{a}' + \beta\hat{\mathbf{y}}^* \\
&= \hat{\mathbf{Y}}\mathbf{a} - \beta\hat{\mathbf{Y}}\mathbf{a}' + \beta\hat{\mathbf{y}}^* \\
&= \hat{\mathbf{Y}}\mathbf{a} + \beta(\hat{\mathbf{y}}^* - \hat{\mathbf{Y}}\mathbf{a}') \\
&= \hat{\mathbf{Y}}\mathbf{a} + \beta(\hat{\mathbf{y}}^* - \hat{\mathbf{y}}') \\
&\geqq \hat{\mathbf{Y}}\mathbf{a}
\end{aligned}$$

because $\hat{\mathbf{y}}^* \geqq \hat{\mathbf{y}}'$.

Since

$$\begin{bmatrix} -(\mathbf{Ya} - \beta(\mathbf{y}' - \mathbf{y}^*)) \\ \hat{\mathbf{Y}}\mathbf{a} + \beta(\hat{\mathbf{y}}^* - \hat{\mathbf{y}}') \end{bmatrix} \geqq \begin{bmatrix} -\mathbf{Ya} \\ \hat{\mathbf{Y}}\mathbf{a} \end{bmatrix},$$

the assumption that $\tilde{\mathbf{y}}'$ is strictly less efficient than $\tilde{\mathbf{y}}^*$ implies that

$$\begin{bmatrix} -(\mathbf{Ya} - \beta(\mathbf{y}' - \mathbf{y}^*)) \\ \hat{\mathbf{Y}}\mathbf{a} + \beta(\hat{\mathbf{y}}^* - \hat{\mathbf{y}}') \end{bmatrix} \geq \begin{bmatrix} -\mathbf{Ya} \\ \hat{\mathbf{Y}}\mathbf{a} \end{bmatrix}$$

But this contradicts the assumption that $\tilde{\mathbf{y}}$ is efficient. □

Hence, we can assume that the producers choose to operate a family of efficient processes whose aggregated netput $\hat{\mathbf{y}}$ is positive. Notice that this does not require to assume that the entrepreneurs are 'competitive' (price-takers).

Notice that, just as production prices induce an abstract labor relation among labor expenditures, reductions induce a value relation among netputs, in the sense of the following definition.

9.4.5 *Definition*

If $\tilde{\mathbf{y}} = [\mathbf{y}, \underline{\mathbf{y}}, \bar{\mathbf{y}}]$ and $\tilde{\mathbf{y}}' = [\mathbf{y}', \underline{\mathbf{y}}', \bar{\mathbf{y}}']$ are any elements of $\tilde{Y}$, say that the netput of $\tilde{\mathbf{y}}$ is *strictly more valuable* than the netput of $\tilde{\mathbf{y}}'$ (written $\hat{\mathbf{y}} \gtrdot \hat{\mathbf{y}}'$) iff $\mathbf{ry} > \mathbf{ry}'$. If $\mathbf{ry} \geq \mathbf{ry}'$ we say that $\tilde{\mathbf{y}}$ is *at least as valuable* as the netput of $\tilde{\mathbf{y}}'$ (written $\hat{\mathbf{y}} \geqslant \hat{\mathbf{y}}'$).

Making use of Theorem 9.4.4, it is possible to prove that any abstract labor relation over the set Y of labor expenditures induces a system of prices for the corresponding outputs; that is to say, a numerical representation of $\geqslant$.

9.4.6 *Theorem*

Let $\tilde{\mathbf{y}}_1, \cdots, \tilde{\mathbf{y}}_x$ be nonzero efficient production processes within a productive structure $\langle \mathbf{Y}_j \rangle$, with $\tilde{\mathbf{y}}_j \in Y_j$ for $j = 1, \cdots, \chi$, $\sum_j \hat{\mathbf{y}}_j > \hat{\mathbf{0}}$, and $\tilde{Y}$ the convex hull of $\{\tilde{\mathbf{y}}_1, \cdots, \tilde{\mathbf{y}}_x\}$. Let $Y\{\mathbf{y} | [\mathbf{y}, \underline{\mathbf{y}}', \bar{\mathbf{y}}] \in \tilde{Y}\}$, and suppose that $\langle Y, \succsim \rangle$ is an abstract labor structure. Then there exists a price system $\mathbf{p} > \mathbf{0}$ such that, for every $\tilde{\mathbf{y}}, \tilde{\mathbf{y}}' \in \tilde{Y}$, $\mathbf{p}\hat{\mathbf{y}} \geq \mathbf{p}\hat{\mathbf{y}}'$ iff $\mathbf{y} \succsim \mathbf{y}'$. This system is unique up to similarity transformations.

PROOF: Since the processes in $\tilde{Y}$ are normal and efficient, it is impossible to have either $\hat{\mathbf{y}} = \hat{\mathbf{y}}'$ and $\mathbf{y} \leq \mathbf{y}'$ (for in this case $\tilde{\mathbf{y}}$ would be more efficient than $\tilde{\mathbf{y}}'$), or $\hat{\mathbf{y}} \geq \hat{\mathbf{y}}'$ and $\mathbf{y} \leqq \mathbf{y}'$ (for in this case $\tilde{\mathbf{y}}$ would be, again, more efficient than $\tilde{\mathbf{y}}'$). Therefore, $\hat{\mathbf{y}} \geqq (\geq)\hat{\mathbf{y}}'$ implies $\mathbf{y} \geqq (\geq)\mathbf{y}'$ for every $\tilde{\mathbf{y}}, \tilde{\mathbf{y}}' \in Y$. It follows that $\hat{\mathbf{y}} \geqq (\geq)\hat{\mathbf{y}}'$ implies $\mathbf{ry} \geq (>)\mathbf{ry}'$.

Let $\mathbf{t} = [\mathbf{ry}_1 \cdots \mathbf{ry}_\chi]$ and $\mathbf{A}$ be the matrix

$$\mathbf{A} = \begin{bmatrix} \hat{y}_{11} \cdot & \cdots & \hat{y}_{1\chi} \\ \vdots & \ddots & \vdots \\ \hat{y}_{\lambda 1} & \cdots & \hat{y}_{\lambda\chi} \\ -\mathbf{ry}_1 & \cdots & -\mathbf{ry}_\chi \end{bmatrix}$$

If the inequality

$$\mathbf{Aa} \geq \mathbf{0} \tag{9.7}$$

has no solution, then $\mathbf{bA} = \mathbf{0}$ has a positive solution $\mathbf{b}$ (cf. Gale 1960: 49, Corollary 2)).

Assume, *per contra*, that $\mathbf{Aa} \geq \mathbf{0}$ has a solution $\mathbf{a}$. Then $-\mathbf{ta} \geq 0$ and $\mathbf{a}$ cannot be null, because the product of at least some row of $\mathbf{A}$ with $\mathbf{a}$ is not null; but $\mathbf{a}$ cannot be semipositive either, and so it has to contain at least one negative entry. Let $a_1,\ldots, a_k$ be the nonnegative entries and $a_{k+1},\ldots, a_\chi$ the negative ones. Given that, by hypothesis,

$$a_1\hat{\mathbf{y}}_1 + \cdots + a_k\hat{\mathbf{y}}_k + a_{k+1}\hat{\mathbf{y}}_{k+1} + \cdots + a_\chi\hat{\mathbf{y}}_\chi = \hat{\mathbf{Y}}\mathbf{a} \geqq \mathbf{0},$$

it follows that

$$a_1\hat{\mathbf{y}}_1 + \cdots + a_k\hat{\mathbf{y}}_k \geqq (-a_{k+1})\hat{\mathbf{y}}_{k+1} + \cdots + (-a_\chi)\hat{\mathbf{y}}_\chi,$$

where $[a_1 \cdots a_k\ 0 \cdots 0]$ γ $[0 \cdots 0\ -a_{k+1},\ldots, -a_\chi]$ are activations of the system.

As all the productive processes of the system are efficient, we must have

$$a_1\mathbf{y}_1 + \cdots + a_k\mathbf{y}_k \geq (-a_{k+1})\mathbf{y}_{k+1} + \cdots + (-a_\chi)\mathbf{y}_\chi,$$

if $\hat{\mathbf{Y}}\mathbf{a} \geq \mathbf{0}$, for otherwise process $\sum_{j=1}^{k} a_j\tilde{\mathbf{y}}_j$ would be strictly more efficient than $\sum_{j=k+1}^{x}(-a_j)\tilde{\mathbf{y}}_j$.

Therefore,

$$\mathbf{r}\left(\sum_{j=1}^{k} a_j\mathbf{y}_j\right) > \mathbf{r}\left(\sum_{j=k+1}^{\chi}(-a_j)\mathbf{y}_j\right)$$

or

$$\mathbf{r}\left(\sum_{j=1}^{\chi} a_j\mathbf{y}_j\right) > 0.$$

Hence,

$$\begin{aligned} -\mathbf{ta} &= -[\mathbf{ry}_1 \ \cdots \ \mathbf{ry}_\chi]^t[a_1 \cdots a_\chi] \\ &= -\sum_{j=1}^{\chi} a_j\mathbf{ry}_j \\ &= -\mathbf{r}\left(\sum_{j=1}^{\chi} a_j\mathbf{y}_j\right) \\ &< 0. \end{aligned}$$

This contradicts the assumption that $-\mathbf{ta} \geq 0$. On the other hand, if $\hat{\mathbf{Y}}\mathbf{a} = \mathbf{0}$, then $-\mathbf{ta} > 0$,

$$a_1\hat{\mathbf{y}}_1 + \cdots + a_k\hat{\mathbf{y}}_k = (-a_{k+1})\hat{\mathbf{y}}_{k+1} + \cdots + (-a_\chi)\hat{\mathbf{y}}_\chi,$$

and so efficiency yields

$$a_1\mathbf{y}_1 + \cdots + a_k\mathbf{y}_k \geqq (-a_{k+1})\mathbf{y}_{k+1} + \cdots + (-a_\chi)\mathbf{y}_\chi.$$

By an analogous reasoning, $-\mathbf{ta} \leq 0$, which now contradicts the assumption that $-\mathbf{ta} > 0$. Thus, in any case, $\mathbf{Aa} \geq \mathbf{0}$ has no solution.

Let $[b_1 \cdots b_\lambda b_{\lambda+1}]$ be a solution of $\mathbf{bA} = \mathbf{0}$. We have, for each j,

$$b_1\mathbf{y}_{1j} + \cdots b_\lambda\mathbf{y}_{\lambda j} = b_{\lambda+1}\mathbf{r}\mathbf{y}_j.$$

For $l = 1,\ldots,\lambda$, let p_l be the number $b_l/b_{\lambda+1}$. Then $\mathbf{p} = [p_1 \cdots p_{1\lambda}]$ is the positive vector that we were looking for.

For any production processes $\tilde{\mathbf{y}}$ and $\tilde{\mathbf{y}}'$ in $\tilde{Y}$, let $\mathbf{a}$ and $\mathbf{a}'$ be activations such that $\check{\mathbf{y}} = [-\mathbf{Ya}, \hat{\mathbf{Y}}\mathbf{a}]$ and $\check{\mathbf{y}}' = [-\mathbf{Ya}', \hat{\mathbf{Y}}\mathbf{a}']$. I will show that $\mathbf{p}\hat{\mathbf{y}} \geq \mathbf{p}\hat{\mathbf{y}}'$ iff $\hat{\mathbf{y}} \succcurlyeq \hat{\mathbf{y}}'$. If $\mathbf{p} > \mathbf{0}$ is such that $\mathbf{p}\hat{\mathbf{Y}} = [\mathbf{r}\mathbf{y}_1 \cdots \mathbf{r}\mathbf{y}_\chi]$ we have, for each producer j, $\Sigma_{l=1}^{L} p_l \hat{\mathbf{y}}_{lj} = \mathbf{r}\mathbf{y}_j$. Therefore,

$$\begin{aligned}
\mathbf{p}\hat{\mathbf{y}} \geq \mathbf{p}\hat{\mathbf{y}}' &\Leftrightarrow \sum_{j=1}^{\chi} a_j \mathbf{p}\hat{\mathbf{y}}_j \geq \sum_{j=1}^{\chi} a'_j \mathbf{p}\hat{\mathbf{y}}_j \\
&\Leftrightarrow \sum_{j=1}^{\chi} a_j \mathbf{r}\mathbf{y}_j \geq \sum_{j=1}^{\chi} a'_j \mathbf{r}\mathbf{y}_j \\
&\Leftrightarrow \mathbf{r}\left(\sum_{j=1}^{\chi} a_j \mathbf{y}_j\right) \geq \mathbf{r}\left(\sum_{j=1}^{\chi} a'_j \mathbf{y}_j\right) \\
&\Leftrightarrow \mathbf{r}\mathbf{y} \geq \mathbf{r}\mathbf{y}' \\
&\Leftrightarrow \hat{\mathbf{y}} \succcurlyeq \hat{\mathbf{y}}'.
\end{aligned}$$

In order to show that $\mathbf{p}$ is unique up to similarity transformations, it will be enough to see that $\langle \hat{Y}, \succcurlyeq, + \rangle$ is a closed extensive structure. But this is easily seen to follow from the fact that

$$\begin{aligned}
\psi(\hat{\mathbf{y}} + \hat{\mathbf{y}}') &= \mathbf{r}(\mathbf{y} + \mathbf{y}') \\
&= \mathbf{r}\mathbf{y} + \mathbf{r}\mathbf{y}' \\
&= \psi(\hat{\mathbf{y}}) + \psi(\hat{\mathbf{y}}')
\end{aligned}$$

Hence, if $\mathbf{p}'$ is another price system representing $\succcurlyeq$ there is a positive number α such that $\mathbf{p}' = \alpha\mathbf{p}$. □

9.5 The meaning and relevance of abstract labor

It is a requirement of methodological individualism[1] that explanations in the social or 'behavioral' sciences be grounded upon individual choices. What this means is that the reductions must be the result of conscious individual choices.

This does not necessarily mean that there must be a great elector choosing the reductions. What it means is that the process ending in a reduction must be produced by individual choices, even if the result was not the goal of any individual: It can be an *unintended consequence* of a lot of individual choices. But, at any rate, What is the empirical reality of a reduction? How can it be empirically detected in an economic process? Is there an entity or process that could be identified as a reduction? Moreover, assuming that such an entity or process can be identified, the question arises whether is is relevant in the explanation of some economic process within capitalism.

Reductions can be seen as equilibrium wage systems established by a fictitious "market participant" (cf. Arrow and Debreu 1954: 274) through the establishment of a system of equilibrium production prices. Just as equilibrium price systems are not necessarily the price systems observed in the actual state of the market, reductions are not necessarily the profiles of wages actually paid by the firms. The market participant in Marxian economics has enough information to compute an equilibrium production price system which allows the reproduction of the economic process by means of its associated reduction. In the next chapter I shall proceed to define with precision the concept of a Marxian equilibrium, and then to prove its existence.

Note

1 The concept of methodological individualism that I presuppose here is explained in García de la Sienra (2010).

10 Classical economics

10.1 Introduction

My aim in this chapter is to re-intepret Marxian economics from the vantage point of the theory of labor-value developed in Chapter 9, which I consider a reformation of Marx's own theory by means of logical tools that were not available in Marx's time. The result is a full integration of neoclassical and Marxian economics – of "bourgeois subjectivist" and "Marxist" economics. I guess the resulting theory is sort of reformulation of "classical economics".

Classical economics is a sophisticated dynamic theory of capitalism that analyzes the motions of the different factors and their causal relationships. This analysis is carried out against the background of a system of production prices taken as fixed until the forces of the economy generate a new system of production prices. The prevailing system of production prices is not necessarily the system of market prices as observed in the public square, but rather a sort of 'theoretical' structure around which the market prices 'oscillate'. These production prices are constituents of what I shall call a classical equilibrium, namely a reproducible state of the economy. Clearly, the theory does not claim that the economy is ever found in such a state, but only that it "moves around" *that* equilibrium, which is subject to constant strain. The equilibrium price is analogous to what dynamic theory calls a "sink".

In developed capitalism, the action of the investors in the financial markets seeking the highest returns for their capitals – this process is called 'arbitrage' – unleashes a tendency to the establishment of a uniform rate of profit. The level of this rate depends upon many factors like the strength of the trade unions, the scarcity of labor for certain industries, the political risks, and so on: it is the unintended consequence of the actions of many agents, and also of natural forces.

As Theorem 9.3.2 suggests, once a technology and uniform rate of profit (a system of production prices) is established, and acquires certain stability, it induces an abstract labor relation among the different expenditures of labor inputs, and a corresponding reduction of the heterogeneous labors, giving certain weights to the different tasks. These weights or ponderations determine the equilibrium wages up to some positive scaling. This scaling is not arbitrary but has a maximum, as well as a minimum level determined by the reduction: the abstract labor relation sets the range within which the level of the salaries can move in equilibrium. What this means is that, keeping the technology, as well as the relative prices unchanged, the profit rate can move only within a certain range. In order to prove this, which is nothing but the fundamental Marxian theorem, we need some previous definitions.

10.2 The fundamental Marxian theorem

Suppose that a given technology $\tilde{Y}$ is established, let $\mathbf{p}$ be the price system induced by reduction $\mathbf{r}$ ($\mathbf{p}$ is not necessarily a production price), and $\mathbf{w} = [w_1 \cdots w_v]$ the established system of wages, where w_n is the salary for one hour of laboring in task n ($1 \leq n \leq v$).

Since ponderations $\mathbf{r}$ are relative, it is necessary to find a numeraire in terms of whose ponderation the other ponderations are expressed. In order to do that, consider a fixed vector of labor inputs $\mathbf{y}_0 = [y_{10} \cdots y_{v0}] \in Y$. The amount of social labor represented by $\mathbf{y}_0$ is $\mathbf{ry}_0$. If y_{n0} is positive, $r_n y_{n0}$ is the weight that the amount of labor y_{n0} of task n has in the corresponding production process. The amount of abstract labor contained in any other vector of labor inputs $\mathbf{y}$ can be expressed as a multiple of $\mathbf{y}_0$. Clearly, since

$$\mathbf{ry} = \mathbf{r}\left(\frac{\mathbf{ry}}{\mathbf{ry}_0}\mathbf{y}_0\right),$$

$\mathbf{y} \sim (\mathbf{ry}/\mathbf{ry}_0)\mathbf{y}_0$, and so vector $\mathbf{y}$ is equivalent to $\mathbf{ry}/\mathbf{ry}_0$ units of complex $\mathbf{y}_0$. Since $(1/\mathbf{ry}_0)\mathbf{r}$ is also an admissible reduction, we can assume from now on that $\mathbf{r}$ has been relativized to $\mathbf{y}_0$ in this way. Hence, $\mathbf{ry}$ is the amount of labor associated to $\mathbf{y}$ in terms of $\mathbf{y}_0$. Notice that, in particular, if $\mathbf{y}_0$ contains only simple unskilled labor, then $\mathbf{r}$ reduces all the types of trades to simple unskilled labor, in which case the concrete heterogeneous trades in labor input vector $\mathbf{y}$ are all made equivalent to a certain number of hours of simple unskilled labor. Even though the existence of such a vector is not necessary, it is very usual to find such vectors in any economy, and so I will suppose from now on, in order to fix ideas, that $\mathbf{ry}$ represents a certain amount of simple unskilled labor.

If $[\mathbf{y}_0, \underline{\mathbf{y}}_0, \bar{\mathbf{y}}_0]$ is a production process in which precisely one hour of simple unskilled labor is employed, $w_0 = \mathbf{p}\hat{\mathbf{y}}_0 = \mathbf{ry}_0$ is an amount of money that represents one hour of such type of labor. Thus, if $\tilde{\mathbf{y}} = [\mathbf{y}, \underline{\mathbf{y}}, \bar{\mathbf{y}}]$ is any production process, we may represent the labor-value of $\hat{\mathbf{y}}$ by means of $\mathbf{p}\hat{\mathbf{y}}/w_0$. If the reduction-*cum*-price system is normalized, $w_0 = 1$ and so $\mathbf{p}\hat{\mathbf{y}}$ is a good representation of labor-value indeed. Having this in mind, and dealing only with production processes $\hat{\mathbf{y}} \geq \hat{\mathbf{0}}$, we may proceed to define a host of concepts typical of the theory of value.

10.2.1 Definition

If **a** is any activation of the production system,

(1) The *variable capital* v is the monetary value of the labor force operated with intensity **a**: $v = \mathbf{wYa}$.
(2) The *constant capital* c is the monetary value of the inputs operated with intensity $\mathbf{a} : c = \mathbf{p\underline{Y}a}$.
(3) The *monetary value of the net product* is $p = \mathbf{p\hat{Y}a}$.
(4) Thc *total profit or benefit* b is the difference between the monetary value of the net product and that of the variable capital: $b = p - v$.
(5) the average rate of profit π is the ratio between total profit b and the costs of capital: $c + v$: $\pi = b/(c + v)$.
(6) The *maximum rate of profit* π^* is $\pi^* = p/c$.

Notice that the maximum rate of profit prevails whenever the value of variable capital is $v = 0$.

Let ${}^t[b_{1n} \cdots b_{\lambda n}]$ be the subsistence consumption menu of workers performing task n under the price and wage system **p, w**. Then matrix

$$\mathbf{B} = \begin{bmatrix} b_{11} & \cdots & b_{1v} \\ \vdots & \ddots & \vdots \\ b_{\lambda 1} & \cdots & b_{\lambda v} \end{bmatrix}$$

is the worker's consumption system. Hence, assuming (as we shall do) that the worker's do not save their salaries, $w_i = \sum_{i=1}^{n} p_i b_{ij}$. For activation **a** we have $v = \mathbf{pBYa}$, and so in this case the necessary labor-time to operate system $\tilde{Y}$ with intensity **a** (which should not be confused with the socially necessary labor-time required to perform task n) is precisely v. If v is below the value of the minimum subsistence basket, the process is not feasible, because the labor-power cannot be reproduced. The minimum wage for trade n is $\underline{w}_n = \mathbf{pb}_n$; we shall assume that $v \geq \underline{w}$.

Since the value added by the labor-power to the net product under activation **a** is nothing but p, we are entitled to introduce the following definition.

10.2.2 Definition

The *surplus rate* or *rate of exploitation* under activation **a** is

$$\varsigma = \frac{\text{added value} - \text{necessary labor time}}{\text{necessary labor time}} = \frac{p - v}{v}.$$

The following proposition is known as the fundamental Marxian theorem. It was rigorously proven for the first time, for specific models of LTV, by Morishima and Seton (1961), and later by Okishio (1963). The following one is the most general version thus far.

10.2.3 Theorem (fundamental marxian theorem)

If the value v of the wages paid by the firm operating nonnull process $\tilde{\mathbf{y}}$ *is less than or equal to the value created by the firm,* $p = \mathbf{p}\hat{\mathbf{y}} > 0$, *then the profit rate* π *is positive iff the surplus rate* ς *is positive. Moreover, the surplus rate is an increasing function of the average profit rate.*

PROOF: Since $p > 0$, the minimum value that ς can adopt is 0, namely, when the value v of the salaries v equals the value p added by the workers. On the other hand, the relationship between the average rate of profit π and the surplus rate ς, is determined in the following way:

$$\begin{aligned}\pi &= \frac{p-v}{c+v}\\ &= \frac{p(p-v)}{p(c+v)}\\ &= \frac{p(p-v)}{vc+pc-vc+pv}\\ &= \frac{(p-v)p}{vc+(p-v)c+vp}\\ &= \frac{(p-v)p}{vc}\cdot\frac{vc}{vc+(p-v)c+vp}\\ &= \frac{\varsigma\pi^*}{1+\varsigma+\pi^*}\end{aligned}$$

Since $1 + \varsigma + \pi^*$ and π^* are always positive, $\varsigma\pi^*$ is positive iff $\varsigma > 0$, in which case

$$\frac{\varsigma\pi^*}{1+\varsigma+\pi^*} > 0.$$

Thus, π is positive iff ς is positive. Moreover, π is an increasing function $\pi{:}S \to \mathbb{R}$ of ς, where $S = [0, (p - w)/w]$; i.e. ς ranges from 0 to the maximum exploitation rate. □

Until now, the level of the average profit rate has depended upon activation **a**. It would not depend on any particular activation if π were uniform, in which case **p** would assume the form of production price; that is to say,

$$\mathbf{p}\bar{\mathbf{Y}} = (1+\pi)[\mathbf{wY} + \mathbf{p}\underline{\mathbf{Y}}].$$

As a matter of fact, we have the following equivalences.

10.2.4 Theorem

If π is uniform, then the following assertions are equivalent for every activation $\mathbf{a}$:

(1) *π^* is independent of* $\mathbf{a}$.
(2) *ς is independent of* $\mathbf{a}$.
(3) $\mathbf{wY} \propto \pi\mathbf{Y}$.

PROOF: Assume that π is uniform. We have:

(1) $\Rightarrow$ (2). Suppose that π^* is independent of $\mathbf{a}$. Since

$$\pi = \frac{\varsigma r^*}{1+\varsigma+r^*},$$

it follows that

$$\varsigma = \frac{\pi(1+\pi^*)}{\pi^*-\pi}.$$

Given that the right side of this equation is independent of activation $\mathbf{a}$, the left one must also be so.

(2) $\Rightarrow$ (3). Suppose that ς is independent of any activation. This means that ς is a constant such that

$$\frac{\mathbf{p}\hat{\mathbf{y}}-\mathbf{wy}}{\mathbf{wy}} = \varsigma$$

for any process $\tilde{\mathbf{y}} \in \tilde{Y}$. Since $\mathbf{ry} = \mathbf{p}\hat{\mathbf{y}}$, it follows that

$$\mathbf{wy} = \kappa\mathbf{ry}$$

where $\kappa = 1/(\varsigma + 1)$.

(3) $\Rightarrow$ (1). Suppose that $\mathbf{wy} = \kappa\mathbf{ry}$ for some κ and every $\tilde{\mathbf{y}} \in \tilde{Y}$. Since $\mathbf{ry} = \mathbf{p}\hat{\mathbf{y}}$ and $\mathbf{p}$ is a production price, we have

$$\frac{1}{1+r}\mathbf{p}\underline{\mathbf{y}} = \mathbf{wy} + \mathbf{p}\underline{\mathbf{y}}$$

Therefore,

$$\begin{aligned}\frac{1}{1+r}\mathbf{p}\bar{\mathbf{y}} - \mathbf{p}\underline{\mathbf{y}} &= \mathbf{wy}\\ &= \kappa\mathbf{p}\hat{\mathbf{y}}\\ &= \kappa(\mathbf{p}\bar{\mathbf{y}} - \mathbf{p}\underline{\mathbf{y}})\end{aligned}$$

from where, finally,

$$\frac{1}{1+\pi}\mathbf{p}\bar{\mathbf{y}} = \mathbf{p}\underline{\mathbf{y}}.$$

hence, if $\gamma' = 1/(1 + \pi)$,

$$\begin{aligned} \varsigma &= \frac{\mathbf{p}\bar{\mathbf{y}} - \mathbf{p}\underline{\mathbf{y}}}{\mathbf{p}\underline{\mathbf{y}}} \\ &= \frac{\mathbf{p}\bar{\mathbf{y}}}{\mathbf{p}\underline{\mathbf{y}}} - 1 \\ &= \frac{\mathbf{p}\bar{\mathbf{y}}}{\gamma'\mathbf{p}\bar{\mathbf{y}}} - 1 \\ &= \gamma. \end{aligned}$$

where $\gamma = (1/\gamma') - 1$. □

10.3 General equilibrium

The capitalist economy is a complex mechanism that has to fulfill several conditions in order to operate well and reproduce itself. In this section I will propose a formulation of a set of conditions sufficient to guarantee the existence of what I shall call a classical equilibrium.

Roughly speaking, a classical equilibrium is a state of the economy in which a production price prevails that allows the reproduction of the economy while the agents maximize their utility. Other conditions are: (1) the optimal consumption menus of the working class are enough to guarantee the subsistence of the workers, and they are also feasible, in the sense that they are affordable with their salaries; (2) the production processes chosen by the firms are feasible, in the sense that they do not demand more labor-power and material inputs than they are available in the economy, and also reproduce the economy, guaranteeing at least a return to the previous levels of social wealth (simple reproduction), or even creating more wealth than the original one at the the beginning of the cycle (augmented reproduction).

A classical economy is similar to what Debreu (1959: 78) called 'private ownership economy', but it includes the apparatus of the labor theory of value. Actually, a classical economy integrates this theory with the concepts of what Debreu calls 'theory of value'. The main novelties reside in that there is a financial capital market in which the firms can borrow or give away credits in order to operate a process, and the concept of an equilibrium price includes also a uniform rate of profit whose level depends upon the rate of surplus value.

Regarding the description of any consumer *i*, I will adopt the usual attribution of a regular, continuous, locally nonsatiated and strictly convex preference relation $\succsim_i$ over the set X_i of possible consumption menus. This set is assumed to be a closed convex cone in the nonnegative orthant of $\mathbb{R}^\lambda$; notice that this implies that $\mathbf{0} \in X_i$.

The financial market allows the firms to get more resources in order to produce more, or give away resources in order to produce less but gaining money at a certain interest rate. Clearly, in equilibrium, this rate has to be equal to the profit rate, and I will prove that this is indeed so. The initial resources of firm $j \in \chi$ are represented by vector $\boldsymbol{\omega}_j$. Given a price system $\mathbf{p} \in P = \{[p_1 \cdots p_\lambda] | \sum_{l=1}^{\lambda} p_1 = 1\}$ and wage system $\mathbf{w} = [w_{1'} \cdots w_v] \in W$ (W is the positive orthant of $\mathbb{R}^v$), firm j may decide to operate a production process $\tilde{\mathbf{y}}$ subject to $\mathbf{p\underline{y}} + \mathbf{wy} = \mathbf{p}\omega_j$, or see to transfer some of its initial resources to other firm, or try to borrow more resources from it. I shall represent the stocks acquired or given away by firm j by means of vectors of the form $\mathbf{c}_j$. Since the $\mathbf{c}_j$ are transferences from other firms, or are transferred to other firms, and the total resources vector of the firms is $\boldsymbol{\omega}_f$, it follows that firm j cannot obtain transferences above $\omega_f - \omega_j$, and give away more that ω_j. Hence, at any rate, we always have $-\omega_j \leqq \mathbf{c}_j \leqq \omega_f - \omega_j$ for every firm j and so the set of all possible transferences for firm j is the rectangle $C_j = \{\mathbf{c}_j \in \mathbb{R}^\lambda \mid -\omega_j \leqq \mathbf{c}_j \leqq \omega_f - \omega_j\}$, which is obviously compact and convex. Associated with this set is the closed interval $I_j(\mathbf{p}) = \{\mathbf{pc} | \mathbf{c} \in C_j\}$ of all credits feasible for firm j at $\mathbf{p}$. I_j is a correspondence $I_j{:}P \to \mathbb{R}$.

Each firm j will always choose a process in Y_j that maximizes its profits at $(\mathbf{p}, \mathbf{c}_j)$ subject to $\mathbf{p\underline{y}} + \mathbf{pBy} = \mathbf{p}\boldsymbol{\omega}_j + \mathbf{pc}_j$, with $\mathbf{c} \in C_j$. I will suppose that the credits c are paid at the end of the cycle.

Marx assumed that there was a subsistence basket $\mathbf{b}$ for any worker and that the salary of the workers was barely sufficient to buy this basket. I will suppose that the basket depends upon the kind of trade or task the worker is engaged in: the subsistence basket for workers of trade i will be denoted $\mathbf{b}_i$.

Given a price system $\mathbf{p}$ and a system $(\mathbf{c}_j)$ of transfers, the income of a worker is composed of various factors: the value of the minimum consumption $\mathbf{pb}_i$ plus the value of his initial endowment $\mathbf{p}\boldsymbol{\omega}_i$, plus the return of his investments in all the firms of the economy $\sum_{j=1}^{\chi} \theta_{ij} M_j(\mathbf{p}, \mathbf{c}_j)$, where $\boldsymbol{\theta}_{ij}$ is the share of agent i in firm j, and $M_j(\mathbf{p}, \mathbf{c}_j)$ is the benefit of firm j. Marx assumed that the workers had no initial endowments and no investments in the firms ($\boldsymbol{\theta}_{ij} = 0$ for each worker i). I assume here that there is no essential difference between investors and workers, and so all investors are also workers.

Since no economy can operate at all without resources, $\boldsymbol{\omega} = \omega_f + \omega_c$ is sufficient to operate production processes of all kinds feeding the workers; i.e. $\omega > \mathbf{0}$ and $\mathbf{b}_i \leq \omega_i$ for each i. Accordingly, I shall take this for granted in what follows. Notice that this implies that the sets C_j are nonempty.

There is a host of concepts that we have to define with some precision in order to proceed.

10.3.1 Definition

(1) The *feasibility set* for firm j at $\mathbf{p}$ with transference $\mathbf{c}_j \in C_j$ is given by

$$B_j(\mathbf{p}, \mathbf{c}_j) = \{\tilde{\mathbf{y}} \in \tilde{Y}_j | \mathbf{p\underline{y}} + \mathbf{pBy} \leq \mathbf{p}\boldsymbol{\omega}_j + \mathbf{pc}_j\}.$$

B_j is a correspondence $B_j{:}P \times C_j \to Y_j$.

(2) The *aggregated feasibility set* for the firms at $\mathbf{p}$ is

$$B_f(\mathbf{p}) = \{\tilde{\mathbf{y}} \in \tilde{Y} | \mathbf{p}\underline{\mathbf{y}} + \mathbf{pBy} \leq \mathbf{p}\boldsymbol{\omega}_f\}.$$

B_f is a correspondence $B_f: P \to Y_j$.

(3) The *maximum profit* for firm j at $(\mathbf{p}, \mathbf{c}_j)$ if interest rate r over the transference prevails is

$$M_j(\mathbf{p}, \mathbf{c}_j) = \max\{\mathbf{p}\hat{\mathbf{y}} - \mathbf{pBy} - r\mathbf{pc}_j | \tilde{\mathbf{y}} \in B_j(\mathbf{p}, \mathbf{c}_j)\}.$$

M_j is a function $M_j: P \times C_j \to \mathbb{R}$.

(4) The *aggregated maximum profit* for the firms at $\mathbf{p}$ is

$$M_f(\mathbf{p}) = \max\{\mathbf{p}\hat{\mathbf{y}} - \mathbf{pBy} | \tilde{\mathbf{y}} \in B_f(\mathbf{p})\}.$$

M_f is a function $M_f: P \to \mathbb{R}$.

(5) The *optimality set* for firm j at $\mathbf{p}$ with transference $\mathbf{c}_j \in C_j$ is

$$A_j(\mathbf{p}, \mathbf{c}_j) = \{\tilde{\mathbf{y}} \in B_j(\mathbf{p}, \mathbf{c}_j) | \mathbf{p}\hat{\mathbf{y}} - \mathbf{pBy} - r\mathbf{pc}_j = M_j(\mathbf{p}, \mathbf{c}_j)\}.$$

A_j is a correspondence A_j: $P \times C_j \to Y_j$.

(6) The *aggregated optimality set* for the firms at $\mathbf{p}$ is

$$A_f(\mathbf{p}) = \{\tilde{\mathbf{y}} \in B_f(\mathbf{p}) | \mathbf{p}\hat{\mathbf{y}} - \mathbf{pBy} = M_f(\mathbf{p})\}.$$

A_f is a correspondence $A_f: P \to Y$.

(7) The *feasibility set* for consumer i at $\mathbf{p}$ with transferences $\mathbf{c}_1, \cdots, \mathbf{c}_\chi$, fixed shares $\boldsymbol{\theta}_{i1}, \ldots, \boldsymbol{\theta}_{ij}, \ldots, \boldsymbol{\theta}_{i\chi}$, and initial endowment $\boldsymbol{\omega}_i$ is given by

$$B_i(\mathbf{p}, (\mathbf{c}_j)) = \left\{\mathbf{x} \in X_i | \mathbf{px} \leq \mathbf{pb}_i + \mathbf{p}\boldsymbol{\omega}_i + \sum_{j=1}^{\chi} \boldsymbol{\theta}_{ij} M_j(\mathbf{p}, \mathbf{c}_j)\right\}.$$

B_i is a correspondence $B_i: P \times C_1 \times \cdots \times C_\chi \to X_i$.

(8) The *aggregated feasibility set* for the consumers at $\mathbf{p}$ is given by

$$B_c(\mathbf{p}) = \{\mathbf{x} \in X | \mathbf{px} \leq \mathbf{pBy} + \mathbf{p}\boldsymbol{\omega}_c + M_f(\mathbf{p})\}.$$

B_c is a correspondence $B_c: P \to X$.

(9) The *optimality set* for consumer i at $\mathbf{p}$ with transferences $\mathbf{c}_1,\ldots,\mathbf{c}_\chi$, shares $\boldsymbol{\theta}_{i1},\ldots,\boldsymbol{\theta}_{ij},\ldots,\boldsymbol{\theta}_{i\chi}$, and initial endowment $\boldsymbol{\omega}_i$ is given by

$$A_i(\mathbf{p},(\mathbf{c}_j)) = \{\mathbf{x}_i \in B_i(\mathbf{p},(\mathbf{c}_j)) | \mathbf{x}_i \gtrsim_i \mathbf{x}'_i \text{ for every } \mathbf{x}'_i \in B_i(\mathbf{p},(\mathbf{c}_j))\}$$

A_i is a correspondence $A_i{:}P \times C_1 \times \cdots \times C_\chi \to X_i$.

(10) The *aggregated optimality set* for the consumers at $\mathbf{p}$ with transferences $\mathbf{c}_1,\ldots,\mathbf{c}_\chi$ is given by

$$A_c(\mathbf{p}) = \{\mathbf{x} \in B_c(\mathbf{p}) | \mathbf{x} = \sum_{i=1}^{I} \mathbf{x}_i \text{ and } \mathbf{x}_i \in A_i(\mathbf{p},(\mathbf{c}_j))$$

$$\text{for every } i \text{ and some } (\mathbf{c}_j) \in_{j=1}^{\chi} C_j\}.$$

A_c is a correspondence $A_c{:}P \times C_1 \times \cdots \times C_\chi \to X$

A less precise definition of maximum profit is due originally to Roemer (1981: 73). It is interesting to see the motivation behind the definition of M_j. Actually, if $\mathbf{c}_j \in C_j$ are the resources transferred or borrowed, the profit is

$$\max\{\mathbf{p}\,\bar{\mathbf{y}} + [\mathbf{pc}_j + \mathbf{p}\boldsymbol{\omega}_j - (\mathbf{p}\underline{\mathbf{y}} + \mathbf{wy})] - (1+r)\mathbf{pc}_j - \mathbf{p}\boldsymbol{\omega}_j | \tilde{\mathbf{y}} \in B_j(\mathbf{p},\mathbf{w},\mathbf{c}_j)\}$$

"where the terms are, respectively, income from production, the value of assets not used in production but held over to the next period, the value of borrowing repaid, and the value of today's endowments". But the expression can be simplified to obtain (3).

10.4 Equilibrium

At the beginning of the cycle, social wealth is $\boldsymbol{\omega}$, and the total amount of labor is $\boldsymbol{l}$. In order to fix ideas, I will assume that the global production process $\tilde{\mathbf{y}}$ finds enough resources in order to be operated in $\boldsymbol{\omega}$, and that $\boldsymbol{l}$ provides enough labor-power to operate it. Hence, we must have $\mathbf{y} \leq \boldsymbol{l}$ and $\underline{\mathbf{y}} + \mathbf{By} \leq \boldsymbol{\omega}$. The consumer demand can be just $\mathbf{By}$, but it can also be $\mathbf{x} \geq \mathbf{By}$. Hence, in order for $\boldsymbol{\omega}$ to provide enough resources to satisfy both the producers' and consumers' demand, it must be that $\underline{\mathbf{y}} + \mathbf{x} \leqq \boldsymbol{\omega}$.

Consuming $\underline{\mathbf{y}} + \mathbf{x}$, the economy produces output $\bar{\mathbf{y}}$, and so the new wealth of society $\boldsymbol{\omega}'$ is this output plus those goods left after chunk $\underline{\mathbf{y}} + \mathbf{x}$ is removed from $\boldsymbol{\omega}$:

$$\boldsymbol{\omega}' = \bar{\mathbf{y}} + (\boldsymbol{\omega} - \underline{\mathbf{y}} - \mathbf{x}) = \boldsymbol{\omega} + \hat{\mathbf{y}} - \mathbf{x}.$$

In order to at least replenish the material inputs consumed by process $\tilde{\mathbf{y}}$ (which I take as a condition of equilibrium), the new social wealth cannot be inferior to the original one: $\boldsymbol{\omega}' \geqq \boldsymbol{\omega} \geqq \mathbf{0}$, or $\mathbf{x} - \hat{\mathbf{y}} - \boldsymbol{\omega} \leqq \mathbf{0}$. In other words, excess demand $\mathbf{z} =$

$\mathbf{x} - \hat{\mathbf{y}} - \boldsymbol{\omega}$ must be zero or semi-negative. Taking this reflection into account, we may proceed to define the crucial notion of equilibrium.

10.4.1 Definition

An *economic equilibrium* is a tuple $((\mathbf{x}_i), (\tilde{\mathbf{y}}_j), \mathbf{p}, (\mathbf{c}_j))$ such that

(1) $\mathbf{x}_i \in A_i(\mathbf{p}, (\mathbf{c}_j))$;
(2) $\tilde{\mathbf{y}}_j \in A_j(\mathbf{p}, \mathbf{c}_j)$;
(3) the economy is reproducible; i.e. the net product, after the maintenance of the working class and its additional consumption $\mathbf{x}$ has been discounted, is at least equal to the original amount of total resources $\boldsymbol{\omega}$; i.e. excess demand $\mathbf{z} = \mathbf{x} - \hat{\mathbf{y}} - \boldsymbol{\omega}$ is zero or semi-negative;
(4) $\mathbf{p}$ is a production price; i.e. the profit rate π is uniform with $0 \leq \pi \leq (\mathbf{p}\hat{\mathbf{y}}_j - \mathbf{pBy}_j)/\mathbf{pBy}_j$;
(5) the financial capital market clears: $\sum_{j=1}^{\chi} \mathbf{c}_j = \mathbf{0}$;
(6) there exist a reduction $\mathbf{w}$ with $\mathbf{pB} = \mathbf{wy}$.

In order to prove the existence of an equilibrium, let us introduce some auxiliary concepts and lemmas. Notice that none of the sets introduced in the definition are empty.

Let $\tilde{Y}'$ be the set $\{[\mathbf{y}, \underline{\mathbf{y}}, \bar{\mathbf{y}}] \in \tilde{\mathrm{Y}} | \mathbf{y} \leqq \boldsymbol{l} \text{ and } \mathbf{y} \leqq \boldsymbol{\omega}\}$ of all production processes that satisfy the labor and material resources restriction.

Let $\hat{X}'$ be the set $\{\mathbf{x} \in X | \mathbf{x} \leq \hat{\mathbf{y}} + \boldsymbol{\omega} \text{ for some } \tilde{\mathbf{y}} \in \tilde{Y}'\}$ of consumptions feasible given the labor and material resources restriction.

Let $\hat{Y}$ be the set $\{\hat{\mathbf{y}} - \mathbf{By} | \tilde{\mathbf{y}} \in \tilde{Y}'\}$ of all net products, after basic consumptions are discounted, of processes feasible given the labor and material resources restriction.

Let Z be the set $\hat{X} - \hat{Y} - \{\boldsymbol{\omega}\}$.

Let $A{:}P \times \times C_1 \times \cdots \times C_\chi \to \hat{X} \times \hat{Y}$ be defined by condition $A(\mathbf{p}, (\mathbf{c}_j)) = A_c(\mathbf{p}, (\mathbf{c}_j)) \times A_f(\mathbf{p})$.

Let ς be the correspondence $\varsigma: P \times C_1 \times \ldots \times C_\chi \to Z$ such that

$$\varsigma(\mathbf{p}, (\mathbf{c}_j)) = \{\mathbf{x} - \hat{\mathbf{y}} - \boldsymbol{\omega} | (\mathbf{x}, \tilde{\mathbf{y}}) \in A(\mathbf{p}, (\mathbf{c}_j))\}.$$

In order to prove the existence of an equilibrium, several previous lemmas are needed.

10.4.2 Lemma

For every price vector $\mathbf{p}$ *and every transfer* $\mathbf{c}_j$, *sets* $B_j(\mathbf{p}, \mathbf{c}_j)$ *and* $B_f(\mathbf{p})$ *are non-empty, compact, and convex.*

PROOF: $\tilde{\mathbf{0}} \in B_j(\mathbf{p}, \mathbf{c}_j)$ for every $(\mathbf{p}, \mathbf{c}_j) \in P \times C_j$ and so $B_j(\mathbf{p}, \mathbf{c}_j) \neq \varnothing$. Moreover, if $(\tilde{\mathbf{y}}^k)$ is a sequence in $B_j(\mathbf{p}, \mathbf{c}_j)$ converging to limit $\tilde{\mathbf{y}}^0$, it is the case that $\mathbf{p}\underline{\mathbf{y}}^k + \mathbf{pBy}^k \leq \mathbf{p}\boldsymbol{\omega}_j + \mathbf{pc}_j$ for every k, and so

$$\mathbf{p}\underline{\mathbf{y}}^0 + \mathbf{pBy}^0 = \lim_{k\to\infty}(\mathbf{p}\underline{\mathbf{y}}^k + \mathbf{pBy}^k) \leq \mathbf{p}\boldsymbol{\omega}_j + \mathbf{pc}_j,$$

implying that $\tilde{\mathbf{y}}^0 \in B_j(\mathbf{p}, \mathbf{c}_j)$. Since $0 \leq \mathbf{pBy} \leq \mathbf{p}\boldsymbol{\omega}_j + \mathbf{pc}_j$ for every $[\mathbf{y}, \underline{\mathbf{y}}, \bar{\mathbf{y}}] \in B_j(\mathbf{p}, \mathbf{c}_j)$, set $\{\mathbf{y} | [\mathbf{y}, \underline{\mathbf{y}}, \bar{\mathbf{y}}] \in B_j(\mathbf{p}, \mathbf{c}_j)\}$ is bounded. This, together with the argument in the proof of Lemma 9.4.3, implies that $B_j(\mathbf{p}, \mathbf{c}_j)$ is bounded.

Let $\tilde{\mathbf{y}}^1$, $\tilde{\mathbf{y}}^2$ be any elements of $B_j(\mathbf{p}, \mathbf{c}_j)$, and $\alpha \in [0, 1]$. Clearly,

$$\begin{aligned}
&\mathbf{p}[\alpha\underline{\mathbf{y}}^1 + (1-\alpha)\underline{\mathbf{y}}^2] + \mathbf{pB}[\alpha\mathbf{y}^1 + (1-\alpha)\mathbf{y}^2] \\
&= \alpha(\mathbf{p}\underline{\mathbf{y}}^1 + \mathbf{pBy}^1) + (1-\alpha)(\mathbf{p}\underline{\mathbf{y}}^2 + \mathbf{pBy}^2) \\
&\leq \alpha(\mathbf{p}\boldsymbol{\omega}_j + \mathbf{pc}_j) + (1-\alpha)(\mathbf{p}\boldsymbol{\omega}_j + \mathbf{pc}_j) = \mathbf{p}\boldsymbol{\omega}_j + \mathbf{pc}_j,
\end{aligned}$$

and so $\alpha\tilde{\mathbf{y}}^1 + (1-\alpha)\tilde{\mathbf{y}}^2 \in B_j(\mathbf{p}, \mathbf{c}_j)$.

An entirely analogous argument, whose details are left to the reader, shows that $B_f(\mathbf{p})$ is nonempty, compact, and convex as well. □

10.4.3 Lemma

The correspondences B_j and B_f are continuous; that is to say, they are both lower semicontinuous (lsc) and upper semicontinuous (usc).

PROOF: Let $(\mathbf{p}^k, \mathbf{c}_j^k)$ be a sequence in $P \times C_j$ converging to point $(\mathbf{p}, \mathbf{c}_j)$, and $\tilde{\mathbf{y}}$ a point of $B_j(\mathbf{p}, \mathbf{c}_j)$. It is required to show the existence of a sequence $\tilde{\mathbf{y}}^k$ in $\tilde{Y}_j$ converging to $\tilde{\mathbf{y}}$, with $\tilde{\mathbf{y}}^k \in B_j(\mathbf{p}^k, \mathbf{c}_j^k)$ for each k.

Since $\tilde{\mathbf{y}}$ is a limit point of set $\tilde{Y}_j$, for any positive ε the set $\{\tilde{\mathbf{y}}' \in \tilde{Y}_j | |\tilde{\mathbf{y}}' - \tilde{\mathbf{y}}| < \varepsilon\}$ contains a point $\tilde{\mathbf{y}}' \neq \tilde{\mathbf{y}}$, which clearly satisfies $|\mathbf{y}' - \mathbf{y}| < \varepsilon$ and $|\underline{y}' - \underline{y}| < \varepsilon$.

Since $(\mathbf{p}^k) \to \mathbf{p}$, there exists a positive integer N such that

$$k > N \quad \text{implies} \quad |\mathbf{p}^k\underline{\mathbf{y}}' - \mathbf{p}\underline{\mathbf{y}}'| < \varepsilon/4$$

and $\mathbf{y}'$ can be chosen in such a way that

$$|\mathbf{p}\underline{\mathbf{y}}' - \mathbf{p}\underline{\mathbf{y}}| < \varepsilon/4.$$

Hence,

$$|\mathbf{p}^k\underline{\mathbf{y}}' - \mathbf{p}\underline{\mathbf{y}}| \leq |\mathbf{p}^k\underline{\mathbf{y}}' - \mathbf{p}\underline{\mathbf{y}}'| + |\mathbf{p}\underline{\mathbf{y}}' - \mathbf{p}\underline{\mathbf{y}}| < \varepsilon/2.$$

Following a similar argument, we get

$$|\mathbf{p}^k\mathbf{B}\mathbf{y}' - \mathbf{pBy}| < \varepsilon/2,$$

and so

$$\mathbf{p}^k\underline{\mathbf{y}}' - \mathbf{p}^k\mathbf{B}\mathbf{y}' < \varepsilon.$$

Choosing ε smaller than $h^k = \mathbf{p}^k\boldsymbol{\omega}_j + \mathbf{p}^k\mathbf{c}_j^k$, we obtain a process $\tilde{\mathbf{y}}^k = \tilde{\mathbf{y}}'$ in $B_j(\mathbf{p}^k, \mathbf{c}_j^k)$. Since $\tilde{\mathbf{y}}'$ can be chosen as close to $\tilde{\mathbf{y}}$ as we want, we have obtained the required sequence $(\tilde{\mathbf{y}}^k) \to \tilde{\mathbf{y}}$.

Let $(\mathbf{p}^k, c_j^k)$ be – as before – a sequence lying in $P \times C_j$ such that $(\mathbf{p}^k, c_j^k) \to (\mathbf{p}^0, c_j^0)$, and let $(\tilde{\mathbf{y}}^k)$ be a sequence converging to $\tilde{\mathbf{y}}^0$ such that $\tilde{\mathbf{y}}^k \in B_j(\mathbf{p}^k, c_j^k)$ for each k. It is required to prove that $\tilde{\mathbf{y}}^0 \in B_j(\mathbf{p}, c_j)$.

Let $h^k = \mathbf{p}^k\boldsymbol{\omega}_j + \mathbf{p}^k\mathbf{c}_j^k$. Since $(h^k) \to h = \mathbf{p}\boldsymbol{\omega}_j + \mathbf{p}\mathbf{c}_j$ and $\mathbf{p}^k\underline{\mathbf{y}}^k + \mathbf{p}^k\mathbf{B}\mathbf{y}^k \leq h^k$ for every k,

$$\begin{aligned}\mathbf{p}\underline{\mathbf{y}} + \mathbf{p}\mathbf{B}\mathbf{y} &= \lim_{k\to\infty} \mathbf{p}^k\underline{\mathbf{y}} + \mathbf{p}^k\mathbf{B}\mathbf{y}^k \\ &\leq \lim_{k\to\infty} h^k \\ &= \mathbf{p}\boldsymbol{\omega}_j + \mathbf{p}\mathbf{c}_j,\end{aligned}$$

which means that $\tilde{\mathbf{y}}^0 \in B_j(\mathbf{p}, c_j)$.

The continuity of B_f is proven in an entirely analogous way and is left to the reader. □

Since function $f(\mathbf{p}, c_j, \tilde{\mathbf{y}}) = \mathbf{p}\hat{\mathbf{y}} - \mathbf{p}\mathbf{B}\mathbf{y} - r\mathbf{p}\mathbf{c}_j$ is continuous on $P \times C_j \times \tilde{Y}_j$, it reaches a maximum $M_j(\mathbf{p}, \mathbf{c}_j)$ over $B_j(\mathbf{p}, \mathbf{c}_j)$. This establishes that M_j is well defined and that $A_j(\mathbf{p}, \mathbf{c}_j) \neq \varnothing$. $A_j(\mathbf{p}, \mathbf{c}_j)$ is clearly bounded because $A_j(\mathbf{p}, \mathbf{c}_j) \subset B_j(\mathbf{p}, \mathbf{c}_j)$.

10.4.4 Lemma (Berge's maximum theorem I)

The correspondences A_j and A_f are upper semicontinuous (usc).

PROOF: Let $(\mathbf{p}^k, c_j^k)$ be a sequence lying in $P \times C_j$ such that $(\mathbf{p}^k, c_j^k) \to (\mathbf{p}^0, c_j^0)$, and let $(\tilde{\mathbf{y}}^k)$ be a sequence converging to $\tilde{\mathbf{y}}^0$ such that $\tilde{\mathbf{y}}^k \in A_j(\mathbf{p}^k, c_j^k)$ for each k.

Since B_j is continuous, $\tilde{\mathbf{y}}^0 \in B_j(\mathbf{p}^0, c_j^0)$. Suppose, nevertheless, that $\tilde{\mathbf{y}} \notin A_j(\mathbf{p}^0, c_j^0)$. Then there must be a $\tilde{\mathbf{y}}' \notin B_j(\mathbf{p}^0, c_j^0)$ such that

$$\mathbf{p}^0\underline{\mathbf{y}}' + \mathbf{p}^0\mathbf{B}\mathbf{y}' = \alpha' > \alpha = \mathbf{p}^0\underline{\mathbf{y}}^0 + \mathbf{p}^0\mathbf{B}\mathbf{y}^0.$$

It follows that sequence $(\mathbf{p}^k\underline{\mathbf{y}}^k + \mathbf{p}^k\mathbf{B}\mathbf{y}^k)$ converges to α and, since B_j is lsc, there is a sequence $(\tilde{\mathbf{y}}'^k) \to \tilde{\mathbf{y}}'^0$ such that $\tilde{\mathbf{y}}'^k \in B_j(\mathbf{p}^k, c_j^k)$ for each k. Clearly, sequence $(\mathbf{p}^k\underline{\mathbf{y}}'^k + \mathbf{p}^k\mathbf{B}\mathbf{y}'^k)$ converges to $\mathbf{p}\underline{\mathbf{y}}'^0 + \mathbf{p}\mathbf{B}\mathbf{y}'^0$ and so, for sufficiently large k, the profits that the operation of $\tilde{\mathbf{y}}'^k$ would yield to firm j at prices $\mathbf{p}^k$ are larger than the profits that the operation of $\tilde{\mathbf{y}}^k$ would yield to j under the same prices. This contradicts the assumption that $\tilde{\mathbf{y}}^k \in A_j(\mathbf{p}^k, c_j^k)$, and so $\tilde{\mathbf{y}}^0 \in A_j(\mathbf{p}, c_j)$. The upper semicontinuity of A_f is proven in an entirely analogous way and is left to the reader. □

10.4.5 Lemma

Functions M_j and M_f are continuous.

PROOF: Since function $f(\mathbf{p}^k, c_j^k, \tilde{\mathbf{y}}) = \mathbf{p}\bar{\mathbf{y}} - \mathbf{pBy} - r\mathbf{pc}_j$ is continuous on $P \times C_j \times \tilde{Y}_j$, and B_j is continuous at $(\mathbf{p}^k, c_j^k) \in P \times C_j$, function M_j is also continuous.[1] The continuity of M is proven in an analogous way and is left to the reader. □

10.4.6 Lemma

The correspondences B_i and B_c are lsc.

PROOF: It is required to prove, in the first place, that if $(\mathbf{p}^k)$ is a sequence in P converging to $\mathbf{p}$, and $\mathbf{x}_i \in B_i(\mathbf{p}, (\mathbf{c}_j))$, then there exists a sequence $(\mathbf{x}_i^k)$ that converges to $\mathbf{x}_i$ with $\mathbf{x}_i^k \in B_i(\mathbf{p}^k, (\mathbf{c}_j))$ for every k.

Let

$$h = \mathbf{pb}_i + \mathbf{p}\boldsymbol{\omega}_i + \sum_{j=1}^{\chi} \theta_{ij} M_j(\mathbf{p}, \mathbf{c}_j)$$

and

$$h^k = \mathbf{p}^k\mathbf{b}_i + \mathbf{p}^k\boldsymbol{\omega}_i + \sum_{j=1}^{\chi} \theta_{ij} M_j(\mathbf{p}^k, \mathbf{c}_j).$$

Assume that $(\mathbf{p}^k)$ is such a sequence and $\mathbf{x}_i \in B_i(\mathbf{p}, (\mathbf{c}_j))$. Since $(\mathbf{p}^k) \to \mathbf{p}$ and M_j is continuous in $\mathbf{p}$, $(\mathbf{p}^k\mathbf{x}_i) \to \mathbf{px}_i$ and $(h^k) \to h$.

Given that $\mathbf{p} \geq 0$, some of the prices might be 0, and so at this point nothing precludes the possibility of h being 0 (because the positive items in $\mathbf{b}_i$ and $\boldsymbol{\omega}_i$ may be among those having zero price, and $\boldsymbol{\theta}_{ij}$ may be also 0 for every j). If this were the case, it would be that $\mathbf{px}_i = h = 0$, and there are two cases: $\mathbf{p}^k\mathbf{x}_i = 0$ for all but a finite number of ks, or $\mathbf{p}^k\mathbf{x}_i > 0$ for infinitely many ks.

Within the first case, we let $\mathbf{x}_i^k$ be $\mathbf{b}_i$ if $\mathbf{p}^k\mathbf{x}_i \neq 0$, and $\mathbf{x}_i^k$ be $\mathbf{x}_i$ itself if $\mathbf{p}^k\mathbf{x}_i = 0$. It follows that $\mathbf{x}_i^k \in B_i(\mathbf{p}^k, (\mathbf{c}_j))$ for every k and $(\mathbf{x}_i^k) \to \mathbf{x}_i$.

In the second case, if $\mathbf{p}^k\mathbf{x}_i > 0$, let α^k be the number such that $\alpha^k\mathbf{p}^k\mathbf{x}_i = h^k$ and set $\mathbf{x}_i^k = \alpha^k\mathbf{x}_i$. Take any sequence (α^k) converging to 1, such that $\alpha^k = h^k/\mathbf{p}^k\mathbf{x}_i$ if $\mathbf{p}^k\mathbf{x}_i > 0$, and set $\mathbf{x}_i^k = \alpha^k\mathbf{x}_i$. If $\mathbf{p}^k\mathbf{x}_i = 0$,

$$\begin{aligned}
\mathbf{p}^k\mathbf{x}_i^k &= \mathbf{p}^k(\alpha^k\mathbf{x}_i) \\
&= \alpha^k\mathbf{p}^k\mathbf{x}_i \\
&= \alpha^k \cdot 0 \\
&= 0 \\
&\leq h^k.
\end{aligned}$$

If $\mathbf{p}^k\mathbf{x}_i > 0$,

$$\begin{aligned}\mathbf{p}^k\mathbf{x}_i^k &= \mathbf{p}^k(\alpha^k\mathbf{x}_i)\\ &= \alpha^k\mathbf{p}^k\mathbf{x}_i\\ &= (h^k/\mathbf{p}^k\mathbf{x}_i)\mathbf{p}^k\mathbf{x}_i\\ &= h^k.\end{aligned}$$

Hence, at any rate, $\mathbf{x}_i^k \in B_i(\mathbf{p}^k, (\mathbf{c}_j))$ for every k, and $(\mathbf{x}_i^k) \to \mathbf{x}_i$.

If $\mathbf{p}\mathbf{x}_i < h$, it follows that there exists a positive integer N such that

$$k > N \quad \text{implies} \quad \mathbf{p}^k\mathbf{x}_i < h^k.$$

Let

$$\beta^k = \begin{cases} 1 & \text{if} \quad \mathbf{p}^k\mathbf{x}_i \leq h^k \\ h^k/\mathbf{p}^k\mathbf{x}_i & \text{if} \quad \mathbf{p}^k\mathbf{x}_i > h^k, \end{cases}$$

and set $\mathbf{x}_i^k = \beta^k\mathbf{x}_i$. Then we have

$$\mathbf{p}^k\mathbf{x}_i^k = \beta^k\mathbf{p}^k\mathbf{x}_i = h^k,$$

implying that $\mathbf{x}_i^k \in B_i(\mathbf{p}^k)$. On the other hand, the sequence $(\mathbf{x}_i^k)$ eventually converges to $\mathbf{x}_i$. □

10.4.7 Lemma (Berge's maximum theorem II)

For any given system of transfers $(\mathbf{c}_j)$, A_i *and* A_c *are upper semicontinuous.*

PROOF: Let $(\mathbf{p}^k)$ be a sequence in P converging to $\mathbf{p}^0$, and $(\mathbf{x}^k)$ a sequence in X_i such that $\mathbf{x}^k \in A_i(\mathbf{p}^k, (\mathbf{c}_j))$ for each k, converging to $\mathbf{x}^0$. In order to show that A_i is upper semicontinuous (usc), we have to show that $\mathbf{x}_i^0 \in A_i(\mathbf{p}, (\mathbf{c}_j))$.

Since $\succsim_i$ is nonsatiated for every i, any optimal choice is in the frontier of the budget set:

$$\mathbf{p}^k\mathbf{x}_i^k = \mathbf{p}^k\mathbf{b}_i + \mathbf{p}^k\boldsymbol{\omega}_i + \sum_{j=1}^{\chi}\theta_{ij}M_j(\mathbf{p}^k, \mathbf{c}_j).$$

Since M_j is continuous at $P \times C_j$, we have

$$\mathbf{p}\mathbf{x}_i^0 = \lim_{k\to\infty} M_j(\mathbf{p}^k, \mathbf{c}_j^k) = M_j(\mathbf{p}, \mathbf{c}_j).$$

Therefore,

$$\mathbf{p}\mathbf{x}_i = \lim_{k\to\infty} \mathbf{p}^k\mathbf{x}_i^k$$

$$= \mathbf{p}\mathbf{b}_i + \mathbf{p}\boldsymbol{\omega}_i + \sum_{j=1}^{\chi}\theta_{ij}M_j(\mathbf{p},\mathbf{c}_j),$$

and so $\mathbf{x}_i \in B_i(\mathbf{p},(\mathbf{c}^j))$. In order to derive a contradiction, suppose that $\mathbf{x}_i^0 \notin A_i(\mathbf{p},(\mathbf{c}_j))$ and let $\mathbf{x}_i'$ be any element of $A_i(\mathbf{p},(\mathbf{c}_j))$. Then $\mathbf{x}_i' \succ_i \mathbf{x}_i$ and, by Lemma 10.4.6, there exists a sequence $((\mathbf{x}_i^k)')$ such that $(\mathbf{x}_i^k)' \in B_i(\mathbf{p},(\mathbf{c}^j))$ and $((\mathbf{x}_i^k)') \to \mathbf{x}_i'$. Hence, $\mathbf{x}_i^k \succsim_i (\mathbf{x}_i^k)'$ for each k and $\mathbf{x}_i^0 = \lim_{k\to\infty}\mathbf{x}_i^k \succsim_i \lim_{k\to\infty}(\mathbf{x}_i')^k = \mathbf{x}_i'$ by the continuity of the preference relation. This contradiction establishes that $\mathbf{x}_i^0 \in A_i(\mathbf{p},(\mathbf{c}_j))$.

Making use of this result, the reader may prove that A_c is also usc, by means of an analogous argument. □

10.4.8 Lemma

Z is compact.

PROOF: The argument in the proof of Lemma 9.4.3 shows that $\tilde{Y}' = \{[\mathbf{y},\underline{\mathbf{y}},\bar{\mathbf{y}}] \in \tilde{Y} | \mathbf{y} \leqq \mathbf{l} \text{ and } \underline{\mathbf{y}} \leqq \boldsymbol{\omega}\}$ is bounded. Clearly, if $(\tilde{\mathbf{y}}^k)$ is a sequence in $\tilde{Y}'$ converging to $\tilde{\mathbf{y}}^0$ the sequence of coordinates (y^k) converges to $\mathbf{y}^0 \leqq \boldsymbol{l}$ and that of $(\underline{\mathbf{y}}^k)$ to $\underline{\mathbf{y}}^0 \leqq \boldsymbol{\omega}$, and so $\tilde{\mathbf{y}}^0 \in \tilde{Y}'$.

Since $\tilde{Y}'$ is bounded, the sets $\hat{X} = \{\mathbf{x} \in X | \mathbf{x} \leq \hat{\mathbf{y}} + \boldsymbol{\omega} \text{ for some } \tilde{\mathbf{y}} \in \tilde{Y}'\}$ and $\hat{Y} = \{\hat{\mathbf{y}} - \mathbf{B}\mathbf{y} | \tilde{\mathbf{y}} \in \tilde{Y}'\}$ are also bounded. In order to show that they are also closed, notice that if $(\mathbf{x}^k)$ is a sequence of elements of $\check{Y}$ converging to $\mathbf{x}^0$, there exists a sequence $(\hat{\mathbf{y}}^k)$ of elements of $\tilde{Y}'$ such that $\mathbf{x}^k \leq \hat{\mathbf{y}}^k + \boldsymbol{\omega}$. It follows that there is a convergent subsequence $(\hat{\mathbf{y}}^{k_l})$ of $(\hat{\mathbf{y}}^k)$, and so $\mathbf{x}^0 = \lim_{k\to\infty}\mathbf{x}^k = \lim_{k_l\to\infty}\mathbf{x}^{k_l} \leq \lim_{k_l\to\infty}\hat{\mathbf{y}}^{k_l} + \omega$, implying that $\mathbf{x}^0 \in \hat{X}$. In order to show that Y is also closed, let $(\hat{\mathbf{y}}^k - \mathbf{B}\mathbf{y}^k)$ be a convergent sequence of elements of $\hat{Y}$ and consider the associated sequence $(\tilde{\mathbf{y}}^k)$ of elements of $\tilde{Y}'$. The compactness of $\tilde{Y}'$ implies that there is a subsequence $(\tilde{\mathbf{y}}^{k_l})$ that converges to a limit $\tilde{\mathbf{y}}^0$ within $\tilde{Y}'$. Hence, $\lim_{k\to\infty}\hat{\mathbf{y}}^k - \mathbf{B}\mathbf{y}^k = \lim_{k_l\to\infty}\hat{\mathbf{y}}^{k_l} - \mathbf{B}\mathbf{y}^{k_l} = \hat{\mathbf{y}}^0 - \mathbf{B}\mathbf{y}^0$. Since Z is a difference $\hat{X} - \hat{Y} - \{\boldsymbol{\omega}\}$ of compact sets, it follows that Z is compact. □

10.4.9 Lemma (Berge's maximum theorem III)

Correspondence A is upper semicontinuous.

PROOF: Let $(\mathbf{p}^k,\mathbf{c}_1^k,\ldots,\mathbf{c}_\chi^k)$ be a sequence in $P \times C_1 \times \cdots \times C_\chi$ such that $(\mathbf{p}^k,\mathbf{c}_1^k,\ldots,\mathbf{c}_\chi^k) \to (\mathbf{p}^0,\mathbf{c}_1^0,\ldots,\mathbf{c}_\chi^0)$, and let $(\mathbf{x}^k,\tilde{\mathbf{y}}^k)$ be a sequence of points in

$A(\mathbf{p}^k, \mathbf{c}_1^k, \ldots, \mathbf{c}_\chi^k) = A_c(\mathbf{p}^k, (\mathbf{c}_j^k)) \times A_f(\mathbf{p}^k)$ converging to point $(\mathbf{x}^0, \tilde{\mathbf{y}}^0)$. Clearly, the upper semicontinuity of A_c and A_f imply that $\mathbf{x}^0 \in A_c(\mathbf{p}^k, (\mathbf{c}_j^k))$ and $\tilde{\mathbf{y}}^0 \in A_f(\mathbf{p})$, and so $(\mathbf{x}^0, \tilde{\mathbf{y}}^0) \in A_c(\mathbf{p}^0, (\mathbf{c}_j^0)) \times A_f(\mathbf{p}^0)$. □

10.4.10 Lemma

ς is upper semicontinuous.

PROOF: Notice, in the first place, that $\varsigma(\mathbf{p}, (\mathbf{c}_j))$ is nonempty for every system $(\mathbf{p}, (\mathbf{c}_j)) \in P \times C_1 \times \ldots \times C_\chi$ because $A(\mathbf{p}, (\mathbf{c}_j))$ is nonempty for any such system.

Let $(\mathbf{p}^k, \mathbf{c}_1^k, \ldots, \mathbf{c}_\chi^k)$ be a sequence in $P \times C_1 \times \cdots \times C_\chi$ such that $(\mathbf{p}^k, \mathbf{c}_1^k, \ldots, \mathbf{c}_\chi^k) \to (\mathbf{p}^0, \mathbf{c}_1^0, \ldots, \mathbf{c}_\chi^0)$. Let $(\mathbf{z}^k)$ be a sequence in Z converging to $\mathbf{z}^0$, such that $\mathbf{z}^k \in \varsigma(\mathbf{p}^k, (\mathbf{c}_j^k))$ for every k. Each $\mathbf{z}^k$ is of the form $\mathbf{z}^k = \mathbf{x}^k - \hat{\mathbf{y}}^k - \boldsymbol{\omega}$, where $(\mathbf{x}^k, \tilde{\mathbf{y}}^k) \in A(\mathbf{p}^k, (\mathbf{c}_j^k))$. Since A is usc, there exists $(\mathbf{x}^0, \tilde{\mathbf{y}}^0) \in A(\mathbf{p}^0, (\mathbf{c}_j^0))$ with $(\mathbf{x}^k, \tilde{\mathbf{y}}^k) \to (\mathbf{x}^0, \tilde{\mathbf{y}}^0)$. This implies that $(\mathbf{z}^k) \to \mathbf{z}^0 \in \varsigma(\mathbf{p}^0, (\mathbf{c}_j^0))$. □

10.4.11 Lemma

For any fixed system $(\mathbf{p}, (\mathbf{c}_j)) \in P \times C_1 \times \ldots \times C_\chi$, $\varsigma(\mathbf{p}, (\mathbf{c}_j))$ *is closed, convex, and* $\mathbf{p}\varsigma(\mathbf{p}, (\mathbf{c}_j)) \leq 0$.

PROOF: If $(\mathbf{z}^k)$ is a convergent sequence of points of $\varsigma(\mathbf{p}, (\mathbf{c}_j))$, let $(\mathbf{p}^k, (\mathbf{c}_j^k))$ be a constant sequence, such that $(\mathbf{p}^k, (\mathbf{c}_j^k)) = (\mathbf{p}, (\mathbf{c}_j))$ for every k. Trivially, $\mathbf{z}^k \in \varsigma(\mathbf{p}^k, (\mathbf{c}_j^k))$, but ς is usc, which implies that $\lim_{k\to\infty} \mathbf{z}^k \in \varsigma(\mathbf{p}, (\mathbf{c}_j))$. Hence, $\varsigma(\mathbf{p}, (\mathbf{c}_j))$ is closed.

Let $\mathbf{x}^1 - \hat{\mathbf{y}}^1 - \boldsymbol{\omega}^1$ and $\mathbf{x}^2 - \hat{\mathbf{y}}^2 - \boldsymbol{\omega}^2$ be any elements of $\varsigma(\mathbf{p}, (\mathbf{c}_j))$, and $\alpha \in [0, 1]$. The $\mathbf{x}^m$ ($m = 1, 2$) are of the form $\sum_{i=1}^{l} \mathbf{x}_i^m$, with $\mathbf{x}_i^m \in A_i(\mathbf{p}, (\mathbf{c}_j))$. It is immediate that

$$\begin{aligned}\alpha\mathbf{x}^1 + (1-\alpha)\mathbf{x}^2 &= \alpha\sum_{i=1}^{l}\mathbf{x}_i^1 + (1-\alpha)\sum_{i=1}^{l}\mathbf{x}_i^2 \\ &= \sum_{i=1}^{l}\alpha\mathbf{x}_i^1 + \sum_{i=1}^{l}(1-\alpha)\mathbf{x}_i^2 \\ &= \sum_{i=1}^{l}[\alpha\mathbf{x}_i^1 + (1-\alpha)\mathbf{x}_i^2].\end{aligned}$$

On the other hand, setting $h = \mathbf{pb}_i + \mathbf{p}\boldsymbol{\omega}_i + \sum_{j=1}^{\chi} \theta_{ij} M_j(\mathbf{p}, \mathbf{c}_j)$, since $\mathbf{x}_i^m \in B_i(\mathbf{p}, (\mathbf{c}_i))$, $\mathbf{p}\mathbf{x}_i^m \leq h$, and so $\mathbf{p}(\alpha\mathbf{x}^1 + (1-\alpha)\mathbf{x}^2) \leq h$. Hence, $\alpha\mathbf{x}^1 + (1-\alpha)\mathbf{x}^2 \in B_i(\mathbf{p}, (\mathbf{c}_j))$.

Moreover, for every $\mathbf{x}_i \in A_i(\mathbf{p}, (\mathbf{c}_j))$, given that $\succsim_i$ is strictly convex,

$$\begin{aligned}\mathbf{x}_i^1, \mathbf{x}_i^2 \in A_i(\mathbf{p}, (\mathbf{c}_j)) &\Rightarrow \mathbf{x}_i^1 \succsim_i \mathbf{x}_i \text{ and } \mathbf{x}_i^2 \succsim_i \mathbf{x}_i \\ &\Rightarrow \alpha\mathbf{x}_i^1 + (1-\alpha)\mathbf{x}_i^2 \succsim_i \mathbf{x}_i \\ &\Rightarrow \alpha\mathbf{x}^1 + (1-\alpha)\mathbf{x}^2 \in A_i(\mathbf{p}, (\mathbf{c}_j)).\end{aligned}$$

Both $\tilde{\mathbf{y}}^1$ and $\tilde{\mathbf{y}}^2$ are in $A_f(\mathbf{p})$, which is convex, and so $\alpha\mathbf{x}^1 + (1-\alpha)\mathbf{x}^2 \in A_f(\mathbf{p})$. Thus, $(\alpha\mathbf{x}^1 + (1-\alpha)\mathbf{x}^2, \alpha\tilde{\mathbf{y}}^1 + (1-\alpha)\tilde{\mathbf{y}}^2) \in A(\mathbf{p}^k, (\mathbf{c}_j^k))$, and

$$(\alpha\mathbf{x}^1 + (1-\alpha)\mathbf{x}^2) - (\alpha\tilde{\mathbf{y}}^1 + (1-\alpha)\tilde{\mathbf{y}}^2) - \boldsymbol{\omega} \in \varsigma(\mathbf{p}^k, (\mathbf{c}_j^k)).$$

Finally, let $\mathbf{z} = \mathbf{x} - \hat{\mathbf{y}} - \boldsymbol{\omega}$ be any element of $\varsigma(\mathbf{p}, (\mathbf{c}_j))$. Since $\mathbf{x} \in A_c(\mathbf{p}, (\mathbf{c}_j^k))$ and $\tilde{\mathbf{y}} \in A_f(\mathbf{p})$, we have

$$\begin{aligned}\mathbf{px} &\leq \mathbf{pBy} + \mathbf{p}\boldsymbol{\omega}_c + M_f(\mathbf{p}) \\ &= \mathbf{pBy} + \mathbf{p}\boldsymbol{\omega}_c + \mathbf{p}\hat{\mathbf{y}} - \mathbf{pBy} \\ &= \mathbf{p}\boldsymbol{\omega}_c + \mathbf{p}\hat{\mathbf{y}} \\ &\leq \mathbf{p}\boldsymbol{\omega} + \mathbf{p}\hat{\mathbf{y}}.\end{aligned}$$

Thus, $\mathbf{pz} = \mathbf{px} - \mathbf{p}\boldsymbol{\omega} + \mathbf{p}\hat{\mathbf{y}} \leq 0$. □

10.4.12 Theorem

There exists an economic equilibrium.

PROOF: Since Z is compact, ς is nonempty, closed and convex, and $\mathbf{p}\varsigma(\mathbf{p}, (\mathbf{c}_j)) \leq 0$, there is a system $(\mathbf{p}, (\mathbf{c}_j)) \in P \times C_1 \times \ldots \times C_\chi$ and a $\mathbf{z} \in \varsigma(\mathbf{p}, (\mathbf{c}_j))$ such that $\mathbf{z} \leqq \mathbf{0}$ (cf. Debreu 1959: 83). In other words, there exists $(\mathbf{x}, \tilde{\mathbf{y}}) \in A(\mathbf{p})$ such that $\mathbf{x} - \hat{\mathbf{y}} - \boldsymbol{\omega} \leqq \mathbf{0}$ or $\hat{\mathbf{y}} \geqq \mathbf{x} + \boldsymbol{\omega}$; i.e. the activated aggregated process $\tilde{\mathbf{y}}$ is reproducible. Obviously, since $\boldsymbol{\omega} > \mathbf{0}$ and $\mathbf{p} \geq \mathbf{0}$, $\mathbf{p}\boldsymbol{\omega} > 0$ and $\tilde{\mathbf{y}}$ is nonnull.

Let $\tilde{\mathbf{y}}_1, \ldots, \tilde{\mathbf{y}}_\chi$ be a decomposition of $\tilde{\mathbf{y}}$ with credits $c_1, \ldots, c_\chi$, such that $\tilde{\mathbf{y}}_j \in A_j(\mathbf{p}, \mathbf{c}_j)$ for every j, $\sum_{j=1}^{\chi} \mathbf{c}_j = 0$ and $c_j = \mathbf{pc}_j \in I_j(\mathbf{p})$.

In order to show that $\mathbf{p}$ is a production price, let r be the interest rate and notice that at point $c = \mathbf{pc} \in I_j(\mathbf{p}, \mathbf{w})$ M_j adopts the value

$$\begin{aligned}M_j(\mathbf{p}, \mathbf{w}, \mathbf{c}) &= \mathbf{p}\hat{\mathbf{y}} - \mathbf{wy} - r\mathbf{pc} \\ &= \pi_j(\tilde{\mathbf{y}}) \cdot (\mathbf{p}\boldsymbol{\omega}_j + c) - rc.\end{aligned}$$

As the reader can easily check, if $\tilde{\mathbf{y}}'$ maximizes π_j at $c' \in I_j(\mathbf{p}, \mathbf{w})$, then there is an $\alpha \geq 0$ such that $\alpha\hat{\mathbf{y}}$ maximizes π_j at c'. Thus, since π is homogeneous of degree zero,

$$\pi_j(\tilde{\mathbf{y}}) = \pi_j(\alpha\tilde{\mathbf{y}}) = \pi_j(\tilde{\mathbf{y}}')$$

and so the profit rate of the profit-maximizing processes is constant at all credits $c \in I_j(\mathbf{p}, \mathbf{w})$. Therefore,

$$\begin{aligned} M_j(\mathbf{p}, \mathbf{w}, \mathbf{c}) &= \pi_j \cdot (\mathbf{p}\boldsymbol{\omega}_j + c) - rc \\ &= \pi_j \mathbf{p}\boldsymbol{\omega}_j + \pi_j c - rc \\ &= \pi_j \mathbf{p}\boldsymbol{\omega}_j + (\pi_j - r)c. \end{aligned}$$

Since $I_j(\mathbf{p}, \mathbf{w})$ is a closed interval, M_j assumes a maximum at some point $c^* \in I_j$ and so, at that point,

$$\frac{dM_j}{dc} = \pi_j - r = 0.$$

This shows that the profit rate of all optimum process is constant and equal to r for every j. Hence, $\mathbf{p}$ is a production price system and so it is positive.

By Theorem 9.3.2, it follows that there exist a reduction $\mathbf{w}$ with $\mathbf{pB} = \mathbf{w}$. The equilibrium profit rate is, therefore, $r = \pi = (\mathbf{p}\hat{\mathbf{y}}_j - \mathbf{pBy}_j)/\mathbf{pBy}_j$. □

10.5 The empirical claim

In Chapter 6 we defined an economy as a structure of the form

$$\mathfrak{A} = \langle \{(X_i, \succsim_i)\}_{i \in \mathfrak{l}}, \{Y_j\}_{j \in \mathcal{X}}, \boldsymbol{t}, \boldsymbol{l}, \Omega, \boldsymbol{\omega}, \boldsymbol{\tau}, \{\eta_k\} \rangle.$$

We have specified these concepts to some extent (with the exception of τ) in order to characterize classical economies. Functions η_k describe the actually observed behavior of the agents, which is supposed to be based on a limited, imperfect knowledge of the actual prevailing equilibrium of the system, or its tendencies of change. The empirical claim is that the agents' actions, including the occasional fixation of local prices, takes place within a band determined by the equilibrium price, which in turn is determined by the social ponderation of the different trades and the structure of the industry. One of the most suggestive formulations given by Marx is that the system of prices is something like a nomic transformation of abstract labor; that it arises out of abstract labor *durch allgemeine Gesetze bestimmte Modifikationen.*[2] But it is perhaps more exact to say that the 'observed' system of prices approaches a production price system which is a nomic modification of the state of the production system together with some standard reduction determined by the social ponderation of the different tasks (a ponderation which is the result of a rather long catalactic process).

The Leontief model (in the Tarskian sense of 'model') is quite illustrative of the former ideas. It represents a technology in which every kind of good is produced by only one production process (there are no alternative techniques), there is no joint production, and the only primary factor is labor, which is supposed to be homogeneous. The matrix $\underline{\mathbf{Y}}$ of inputs is square of order λ, while the matrix of outputs $\overline{\mathbf{Y}} = \mathbf{I}$ is the identity matrix of order λ. If labor is assumed to be homogeneous, the matrix of labor inputs **Y** is a column vector of v dimensions, but here we will keep supposing that labor is heterogeneous, and so **Y** is still a matrix of order $v \times \chi$. It is assumed that the branches of the economy are interconnected, and so the matrix of inputs, $\underline{\mathbf{Y}}$, is indecomposable.[3]

Let **w**, be the prevailing equilibrium wage system, namely a standard reduction, and **p** the price system induced by **w**. Then **p** adopts the form of production price:

$$\mathbf{pI} = (1 + \pi)[\mathbf{wY} + \mathbf{p\underline{Y}}].$$

Since $\pi \geq \pi^* \geq 0$, $\rho = 1/(1 + \pi)$ is defined and we have

$$\mathbf{p}[\rho\mathbf{I} - \underline{\mathbf{Y}}] = \mathbf{wY}.$$

Hence (by theorem 9.4.6) $\mathbf{p} > \mathbf{0}$, $\rho > \boldsymbol{\theta}^*$, where $\boldsymbol{\theta}^*$ is the Frobenius root of $\underline{\mathbf{Y}}$.[4] Therefore, $\rho\mathbf{I} - \underline{\mathbf{Y}}$ is nonsingular and $[\rho\mathbf{I} - \underline{\mathbf{Y}}]^{-1}$ is a semipositive matrix. This is how price system **p** is obtained as a function of the production structure and a reduction **w**:

$$\mathbf{p} = [\rho\mathbf{I} - \underline{\mathbf{Y}}]^{-1} \cdot \mathbf{wY}.$$

This is the specific form that the law of value adopts in Leontief economies.

In general, the analysis starts taking as given both the structure of the industry and the social ponderations **w**. Out of this it can determine the corresponding system of production prices **p**, the profit rate, and the Walrasian demand function. The empirical claim is, roughly, that the actually observed prices "move around" **p**, and that the observed demand is "close" to the Walrasian demand function.

Notes

1 Cf. Debreu (1959: 19), Proposition 4. φ is our B_j and g is our M_j.
2 Quoted by Hamminga (1990: 92).
3 For a precise definition of this concept, cf. Takayama (1985: 370).
4 By theorem 4.D.2 in Takayama (1985: 392).

11 The logical structure of Sraffian economic theory

11.1 Introduction

The aim of the present chapter is to identify the logical structure of the Sraffian theory of value. Perhaps the most interesting and relevant methodological considerations in economics are related to the production of empirical claims within a given disciplinary matrix – to use Kuhn's term. Each paradigm has its own "methodology of economics", as each school has its own principles and methods, which cannot be described philosophically without probing deeply into the logical structure of its defining theory.

Following Sraffa's *Production of Commodities by Means of Commodities* (PCC; Sraffa 1960), I intend to identify its basic theory-element through its fundamental law(s), and the general form of its empirical claim. The main problems that such a reconstruction must solve are those of figuring out the fundamental laws of the theory and the general form of its empirical claim and domain of intended applications.

11.2 The conceptual framework

Two outstanding concepts of PCC are those of method of production and standard commodity. Roughly, a method of production is a system of interconnected production processes operating during a whole year. The simplest example Sraffa provides is that of a couple of processes producing wheat and iron for subsistence:

$$\begin{array}{llllll} 280 \text{ qtr. wheat} & + & 12 \text{ t. iron} & \rightarrow & 400 \text{ qtr. wheat} \\ 120 \text{ qtr. wheat} & + & 8 \text{ t. iron} & \rightarrow & 20 \text{ t. iron} \end{array}$$

The concepts of reproduction, private property and social wealth (not the words) suggest themselves immediately: At the beginning of the cycle (the year), "the society" has an endowment $\boldsymbol{\omega} = (400, 20)$ consisting of 400 qtr. of wheat and 20 t. of iron. The farmer has at his disposal (owns) 280 qtr. of wheat and 12 t. of iron, $\boldsymbol{\omega}_1 = (280, 12)$; the ironmaker has (owns) 120 qtr. of wheat and 8 t. of iron to start his production process, $\boldsymbol{\omega}_2 = (120, 8)$. There is no hint of rational choice (profit maximizing) or alternative production processes here: the producers just replicate the cycle as if they were doomed to do so. At the end of the cycle "the society" returns to the original state, but the wheat and the iron are allocated in a different way. This time, the farmer has all the wheat, $\omega_1' = (0, 20)$, and the ironmaker all the iron, $\omega_2' = (400, 0)$. Thus, the cycle cannot be repeated if the producers do not find a way of reallocating the commodities in order to replicate the situation at the beginning of the cycle. Sraffa never says that they will coordinate, or how a coordination can be reached. He only points out that the cycle cannot be replicated unless trade takes place among the producers according to certain proportions.

Actually, in the example the exchange-value required is 10 qtr. of wheat for 1 t. of iron. These values can be represented by means of a price vector (1, 10), where wheat is clearly performing as a numeraire. The wealth of the farmer at these values (relative prices) is (1, 10)·(400, 0) = 400, and that of the ironmaker is (1, 10)·(0, 200) = 2000. In order to start over the process, the farmer demands 12 t. of iron with a cost of (1, 10) · (0, 12) = 120; the ironmaker demands 120 qtr. of wheat with a cost of (1, 10) · (120, 0) = 120. Thus, at these prices, the required trade is balanced and the process can be reproduced.

In general terms, the method of production and exchange-values under conditions of simple reproduction can be represented by means of a set of equations like

$$\begin{array}{lllll} A_a p_a & + \; B_a p_b & + \cdots + & K_a p_k & = A p_a \\ A_b p_a & + \; B_b p_b & + \cdots + & K_b p_k & = B p_b \\ & & \vdots & & \\ A_k p_a & + \; B_k p_b & + \cdots + & K_k p_k & = K p_k \end{array} \tag{11.1}$$

where the types of commodities are $a, b, \ldots, k$, the amounts of the same used up in production are $A, B, \ldots, K$, and the system of relative prices or exchange-values is $(p_a, \ldots, p_k)$. Since the system is self-replacing, $A_a + A_b + \cdots A_k = A$; $B_a + B_b + \cdots + B_k = B$; …; $K_a + K_b + \cdots + K_k = K$.

In order to describe in general productive systems, in more commonly used terminology, let the index n ($n = 1, \ldots, \nu$) run over the types of trades, j ($j = 1, \ldots, \chi$) run over the producers (entrepreneurs or firms), and l ($l = 1, \ldots, \lambda$) run over the types of commodities. Assuming that the firms have chosen χ production processes, the labor inputs can be seen as the columns of

$$\mathbf{Y} = \begin{bmatrix} y_{11} & \cdots & y_{1\chi} \\ \vdots & \ddots & \vdots \\ y_{\nu 1} & \cdots & y_{\nu\chi} \end{bmatrix} \tag{11.2}$$

where vector ${}^{t}[y_{1j} \cdots y_{vj}]$ represents the labor inputs of production process j. Analogously, the material inputs can be seen as the columns of

$$\underline{\mathbf{Y}} = \begin{bmatrix} \underline{y}_{11} & \cdots & \underline{y}_{1\chi} \\ \vdots & \ddots & \vdots \\ \underline{y}_{\lambda 1} & \cdots & \underline{y}_{\lambda\chi} \end{bmatrix} \tag{11.3}$$

and the outputs as the columns of

$$\bar{\mathbf{Y}} = \begin{bmatrix} \bar{y}_{11} & \cdots & \bar{y}_{1\chi} \\ \vdots & \ddots & \vdots \\ \bar{y}_{\lambda 1} & \cdots & \bar{y}_{\lambda\chi} \end{bmatrix}. \tag{11.4}$$

Within this conceptual framework, a standard way of representing the system of equations (11.1) is the following.

$${}^{t}\underline{\mathbf{Y}}_{p} = {}^{t}\bar{\mathbf{Y}}_{\mathrm{p}} \tag{11.5}$$

where $\chi = \lambda$ and ${}^{t}\bar{\mathbf{Y}}$ is a matrix that has zeros everywhere except in the main diagonal, because Sraffa is assuming at this point that there is no joint production. The positive column vector $\mathbf{p}={}^{t}[p_1 \cdots p\lambda]$ of commodity prices is called the *price-distribution system*. Notice that, since Sraffa does not consider variation in production, but takes matrices $\underline{\mathbf{Y}}$ and $\bar{\mathbf{Y}}$ as fixed, he does not make any assumptions about production possibility sets. Another reason for this is that he does not introduce any consideration of choice by entrepreneurs, who might decide which production processes operate. In particular, he does not assume explicitly constant returns of scale, although he actually scales the production processes, the rows of matrix $\underline{\mathbf{Y}}$, when he defines the standard commodity.

Since Sraffa considers the commodities required to maintain the labor-power as inputs in the production process, and system (11.1) represents the case of mere subsistence without any surplus, it is not necessary to consider matrix $\mathbf{Y}$ of labor inputs. In this case it is sufficient the introduction of the set $\mathcal{B}$ of all possible aggregate consumption bundles ("baskets") that allow laborers to provide one unit of labor. $\mathcal{B}$ is a subset of the nonnegative orthant of $\mathbb{R}^n$.

In order to account for production with surplus and joint production, it is necessary to consider the matrix of labor inputs. Sraffa introduces the concept of labor input vector, represented by a $\chi \times 1$ positive matrix $\mathbf{y}$, since he assumes that labor is homogeneous. Nevertheless, since the restriction of homogeneous labor is not necessary in the general case (it is in order to determine the standard commodity for non-joint production systems), it is more convenient to use matrix $\mathbf{Y}$ as defined above. At any rate, in the case of homogeneous labor, all entries are 0, excepting those in the first column. With such proviso, in the case of homogeneous labor (the only case considered by Sraffa), **Y** is assumed normalized, so that the sum of the entries in the first column is 1 (i.e. total labor, which is supposed homogeneous, is made equal to 1).

Other terms introduced by Sraffa are rate of profit $\pi \geq 0$ and wage rate $w \geq 0$. Nevertheless, when heterogeneous labor is considered, it is required to introduce a $v \times 1$ matrix (vector) **w** of wage rates, one for each trade. In the case of homogenous labor, all entries of **w** are equal.

By a *method of production* or *production structure* we understand a triple $(\mathbf{Y}, \underline{\mathbf{Y}}, \bar{\mathbf{Y}})$ such that **Y** is a labor input vector, $\underline{\mathbf{Y}}$ is a matrix of fixed gross commodity inputs, and $\bar{\mathbf{Y}}$ is a matrix of fixed gross outputs. A method of production $(\mathbf{Y}, \underline{\mathbf{Y}}, \bar{\mathbf{Y}})$ is *self-replacing* if the output of each commodity in each period is at least as large as the amount of the commodity used as an input. This condition can be expressed as

$$\mathbf{1}(\bar{\mathbf{Y}} - \underline{\mathbf{Y}}) \geqq \mathbf{0}, \tag{11.6}$$

where 1 denotes the row vector with all entries equal to 1. The method is called of *subsistence* if $\mathbf{1}(\bar{\mathbf{Y}} - \underline{\mathbf{Y}}) = \mathbf{0}$ and of *surplus* if $\mathbf{1}(\bar{\mathbf{Y}} - \underline{\mathbf{Y}}) \geq \mathbf{0}$. It is required that the inputs used to feed the workers in the productive structure be no less than the basket **b** required to reproduce the labor power (this condition can be formulated with precision but I shall no longer consider it here).

11.3 The basic theory-element

By means of the previous conceptual framework, it is possible to introduce the concept of a Sraffian economy.

11.3.1 Definition

$\mathfrak{S}$ is a *Sraffian economy* iff there exist Y, $\underline{\mathbf{Y}}$, $\bar{\mathbf{Y}}$, $\mathcal{B}$, π, **w** and **p**, such that

(0) $\mathfrak{S} = \langle \underline{\mathbf{Y}}, \bar{\mathbf{Y}}, \mathbf{y}, \mathcal{B}, \pi, \mathbf{w}, \mathbf{p} \rangle$;
(1) $(\mathbf{Y}, \underline{\mathbf{Y}}, \bar{\mathbf{Y}})$ is a self-replacing production structure;
(2) $\mathcal{B}$ is monotone; i.e. $\mathbf{b} \in \mathcal{B}$ and $\mathbf{b}' \geqq \mathbf{b}$ imply $\mathbf{b}' \in \mathcal{B}$;
(3) **w** is a $v \times 1$ matrix;
(4) π is a nonnegative real number;
(5) **p** is a positive λ-dimensional vector;
(6) $(1 + \pi)\underline{\mathbf{Y}}^{\mathrm{t}}\mathbf{p} + \mathbf{Y}^{\mathrm{t}}\mathbf{w} = \bar{\mathbf{Y}}^{\mathrm{t}}\mathbf{p}$.

Axiom (6) of Definition 11.3.1 is one of the the fundamental laws of Sraffa's theory. It asserts that, for every self-replacing production structure, there exists a system (π,**w**,**p**) under which the production process is reproducible.

If non-joint production and other natural regularity conditions are assumed on the matrices $\underline{\mathbf{Y}}$ and $\bar{\mathbf{Y}}$, it is possible to prove the existence of a family of systems (π,**w**,**p**) that satisfy the fundamental law, and a whole bunch of general structural theorems follow from the definition of Sraffian economy (cf. Ballesteros, Beato, Jerison, and Oliu 1976).

But there are no analogous general conditions in the case of joint production. All known conditions, like the system's being all-engaging, are too strong and hold only exceptionally (cf. Schefold 2005: 545). This is typical of *T*-theoretical terms: the existence of the corresponding magnitudes must be established in every case, depending on the empirical conditions presented by the case, and they cannot be determined without presupposing the validity of the fundamental law. Clearly, terms $\mathbf{w}$, π and $\mathbf{p}$ are Sraffian-theoretical and, so, finding a general sufficient condition implying the existence of the corresponding required magnitudes, satisfied by all intended applications, is out of the question.

As I have pointed out elsewhere (García de la Sienra 2009), in spite of the use of familiar economic terms (in the present case, terms like 'commodity input' or 'subsistence'), the structural axioms of an economic theory, and even the laws, do not make or imply any empirical claim.

> In order to produce an empirical claim by means of them, you need to stipulate a particular empirical interpretation of the terms and not only that, but also apply somehow the axioms to a real agent [or structure].
>
> (García de la Sienra 2009: 357)

The application of the conceptual framework of an economic theory *T* to a real phenomenon, agent or structure requires the fleshing out of the terms, by means of empirical information. There is hardly a better generic description of the domain of intended applications of the Sraffian theory than that given by the astronaut arriving from the moon:

> The significance of the equations is simply this: that if a man fell from the moon on the earth, and noted the amount of things consumed in each factory and the amount produced by each factory during a year, he could deduce at which values the commodities must be sold, if the rate of interest must be uniform and the process of production repeated. In short, the equations show that the conditions of exchange are entirely determined by the conditions of production.
>
> (D3/ 12/ 7: 87; quoted by Kurz and Salvadori 2004: 1546)[1]

Yet, in the first place, it is not clear whether the description of the production structure should include each factory on planet Earth, in the European Union, or in a single country like the United States. Or centrally planned economies as well as capitalist: the specification of the domain of intended applications of the theory requires an empirical, appropriate description of the real production structures to which the members of the school intend to apply the theory. Once this is done, in relation to any of these structures, the phrase "he could deduce…" is too optimistic. Even aliens with extraordinary powers might have trouble figuring out what are the values at which "commodities must be sold, if the rate of interest must be uniform and the process of production repeated". The determination of these values is the substance of the Sraffian "normal science", which of course does not consist of proposing abstract assumptions in order to mathematically derive existence theorems.

Perhaps something like this is what Schefold has in mind when he asks whether joint production leads to a triumph of economic over mathematical logic. But there is no such a triumph. A correct logical reconstruction of a scientific theory must show the form that the normal science problems adopt in the discipline. In the present case, the conditions leading to the system of prices must be determined empirically. Whether the system under scrutiny is all-engaging, or satisfies other condition out of which prices can be computed, is an entirely empirical matter.

11.4 The standard commodity

The standard commodity, which is taken by Sraffa as an invariable measure of value, is not defined for joint production systems. As Schefold puts it:

> The decisive defining property of the standard commodity (constant proportion between indirect means of production and indirect labour) cannot meaningfully be applied to joint production systems, however. The prices of several jointly produced commodities in a 'capital-intensive' process may move in different directions relatively to those of other commodities jointly produced by a 'labour-intensive process'. Hence, the thought-experiment underlying the construction of the 'invariable measure of value' cannot be extended to multiple-product industries. Insofar it was … a mistake of Sraffa's to postulate a standard commodity in his theory of joint production.
>
> (Schefold 2005: 535)

What this means is that the concept of standard commodity is not a general concept in Sraffa's theory. The focus of normal science, therefore, cannot be on the determination of a standard commodity, but rather on systems (π, $\mathbf{w}$, $\mathbf{p}$) satisfying at least the fundamental law, Axiom (6) of Definition 11.3.1.

Hence, Vela Velupillai's (2008: 326) contention that Sraffa's mathematics in PCC did "bypass the fixed point approach and attack the equations directly to give existence of solutions, with a simpler kind of mathematics', one with 'algorithmic overtones'", even if true, does not address in general the relevant issues of normal science, since it does not apply to the joint-production case. But the claim is not true even in the case of simple systems. Punzo (1986) had already proposed to interpret Sraffa's mathematics "as constructivist; therefore, closer to mathematical intuitionism than to mathematical formalism". But

> Punzo is not correct in asserting that Sraffa does not go beyond elementary algebra. There are mathematical proofs involving problems of convergence, even if they are only sketched. Sraffa left his proofs incomplete, perhaps in

> part because he lacked the training of a mathematician. But he used economic intuition as a complement and created an employment for mathematically oriented economists.
>
> (Ibid.: 357)

At any rate, what matters is not the use of this or that mathematical method in normal science: Any method can be used if it promises to work in the endeavor to find the solution to the problems. The demand for economic theory to use only constructive methods is far-fetched: normal science is by itself sufficiently hard as to require further restrictions springing from an intuitionistic philosophical program that dislikes the axiom of choice or the law of excluded middle.

11.5 The empirical claim

Let me finish with a comment on the form of the empirical claims that Sraffian theory calls for. First of all, the nomological sentence

$$(1+\pi)\underline{\mathbf{Y}}^{t}\mathbf{p} + \mathbf{Y}^{t}\mathbf{w} = \bar{\mathbf{Y}}^{t}\mathbf{p} \tag{6}$$

is far from being an empirical claim and not only that: It does not allow the formulation of any such claim because it does not connect the theoretical terms with non-theoretical ones. Unlike Marx, who connects his concept of labor-value with observed prices through his Law of Value, Sraffa does not specify any such connection. Price system **p**, as determined by law (6), need not coincide with the system of prices actually observed in the marketplace. Marx claimed that the prices actually observed in the marketplace were a nomic modification of labor-values, but nobody seems to know if Sraffa was interested in connecting his systems of prices, wages and profit rates with any non-theoretic magnitudes, and which ones might these be. In particular, Sraffian prices, even if it were possible to determine them for a particular real-concrete productive system, are not connected by Sraffa to any 'observable' magnitude.

An example of an empirical claim that might be made with Sraffa's conceptual apparatus is something like this: that the actual prices of the productive structure under investigation 'orbitate' around the Sraffian prices. Indeed, according to Nicholas (2011: 158),

> the implication of Sraffa's analysis is that reproduction or equilibrium prices are centres of gravity for the movement of actual prices rather than, as for Marx, averages of actual prices.

But then Sraffa's theory would have to introduce an additional sentence (law) specifying such a nomic connection between Sraffian and observed or actual prices.

Sraffa thought that, given an empirical description of a productive structure $\langle \underline{\mathbf{Y}}, \bar{\mathbf{Y}}, \mathbf{Y}, \mathcal{B} \rangle$, it was possible to find a system $(\pi, \mathbf{w}, \mathbf{p})$ (at least one) that satisfies fundamental law (6). The task of normal science is, precisely, to find such a system. If there are several such systems, the task is to find them all. Sraffa never said this but, if the production structure is observably reproducing itself, one of those systems must be actually operating under the observable motion of prices, wages and profit rates; the problem is then to determine that one. Another possibility is the normative use of such systems. But this requires something like a central planner choosing the system that is more convenient according to an exogenous criterion. And both uses require connecting the theoretical magnitudes with non-theoretic ones (relative to Sraffa's theory).

Hence, what is missing in Sraffa's theory is a theoretical systematization, a nomological sentence relating systems $(\pi, \mathbf{w}, \mathbf{p})$ with empirically observed magnitudes (like observed prices, wage and benefit rates, or what have you). Sraffa never introduced such a sentence and so, up to this point, his theory is not quite yet an empirical scientific theory. If Sraffian prices could be determined for a given real-concrete productive system, these prices would be hovering above the economic process, without any declared connection to it. It is clear that no empirical claims can be made with the theory as it stands now.

11.6 What can/ought be done?

It is impossible to know what Sraffa would have replied to these comments. Supposing that he accepted the need of another nomological sentence relating his theoretic terms to non-theoretic ones, we will never know which would be his candidates for this last role. Yet, the prominence of prices, profit rates and wages suggests that we are before a sort of theory of value. If we follow this route, the theory could be completed as a theory of these magnitudes. If that is done, the missing law would be one relating Sraffa's theoretical systems $(\pi, \mathbf{w}, \mathbf{p})$ to empirical systems $(\pi^*, \mathbf{w}^*, \mathbf{p}^*)$.

There are many possible ways in which this law can be formulated, but the basic idea is that the observed systems $(\pi^*, \mathbf{w}^*, \mathbf{p}^*)$ 'orbitate' around the theoretical ones. Even a stochastic version of this law can be given, for instance postulating a normal distribution on the sample space of observable feasible systems $(\pi^*, \mathbf{w}^*, \mathbf{p}^*)$, with $(\pi, \mathbf{w}, \mathbf{p})$ in the mean.

Note

1 The notation exemplified by 'D3/ 12/ 7' is a canonical way of referring to Sraffa's documents in the Wren Library.

12 The logical structure of econometrics

12.1 Motivation

My aim in this final chapter is to formalize in a detailed way Spanos' (1986) econometric methodological doctrine from the point of view of SVT. As we shall see, SVT provides a very natural reconstruction of the doctrine, one that integrates the doctrine in a general methodological and philosophical framework. Hence, this chapter purports to fill a gap that was noted a long time ago by Bruce J. Caldwell:

> One approach which to my knowledge has been completely ignored is the integration of economic methodology and philosophy with econometrics. Methodologists have generally skirted the issue of methodological foundations of econometric theory, and the few econometricians who have addressed the philosophical issues have seldom gone beyond gratuitous references to such figures as Feigel and Carnap.
>
> (Caldwell 1984: 216)

In a paper published in 2000, George C. Davis points out that

> Since 1982, the interest in economic methodology has increased but most methodologists have focused on the larger methodological issues, such as the scientific status or realism of economics, rather than the 'methodological foundations' of econometrics. Similarly, most econometricians addressing 'the philosophical issues' have developed their own methodologies and just updated the 'gratuitous references' to now be Popper (1968), Lakatos (1973), or Kuhn (1970) (e.g., Darnell and Evans, 1990; Hendry, 1993, 1995; Spanos, 1986). Consequently, it appears Caldwell's observation is still applicable to a significant degree and worthy of consideration.

In the aforementioned paper, Davis presents an interesting reconstruction of Haavelmo's methodological foundations of econometrics from the point of view of Suppe's semantic view of theories (cf. Suppe 1989), which should not be confused with SVT. My aim is to apply this last metatheory to Spanos' doctrine, which is a systematic and detailed development of Haavelmo's view, formulated in a more contemporary language.

12.2 Real concrete DGPS

What econometricians call 'data generation process' is nothing less than a system or phenomenon taken as a target of scientific research, out of which empirical data in a numerical form are expected to flow, or be painstakingly obtained. From an ontological point of view, it is a real and concrete economic system or phenomenon that behaves in a random way. Spanos' working definition of DGP is "the mechanism underlying the observable phenomena of interest" (Spanos 1986: 20). The term is also

> used to designate the phenomenon of interest which a theory purports to explain. The concept is used in order to emphasise the intended scope of the theory as well as the source of the observable data. Defined this way, the concept of the actual DGP might be a real observable phenomenon or an experimental-like situation depending on the intended scope of the theory.
>
> For example, in the case of the demand schedule discussed in Chapter 1, if the intended scope of the theory is to determine a relationship between a hypothetical range of prices and the corresponding intentions to buy by a group of economic agents, at some particular point in time, the actual DGP might be used to designate the experimental-like situation where such data could be generated. On the other hand, if the intended scope of the theory is to explain observed quantity or/and price changes over time, then the actual DGP should refer to the actual market process giving rise to the observed data. It should be noted that the intended scope of the theory is used to determine the choice of the observable data to be used.
>
> (Spanos 1986: 661–2)

In the language of Chapter 4, the DGP is a real concrete *subjekt* that remains outside the head, independent of it and of any theory; it is a "chance mechanism" giving rise to observable data. Pretheoretical thought can grasp its existence and some of its properties and effects, providing the starting point for a description of the same in a language that contains general but not idealized terms. This description is sufficient in order to *refer* to the DGP and start probing into it. Hence, the rather strange (idealistic) doctrine of the "theory dependence" of observation is rejected as unnecessary and confusing. This is not to deny that theories can lead to discover new aspects of the process or entity; only that its existence does not depend of any conceptualization. It is just not true that we do not have access to the world independently of our theoretical systematizations; if that were the case we would never be able to notice that the axioms of an idealized theory are actually false or inaccurate.

For econometrics the DGP is a random 'mechanism' but randomness must be taken as an objetive property of real things and not as a subjective measure of certainty. As Patrick Suppes (1984: 10) puts it: "the fundamental laws of natural phenomena are essentially probabilistic rather than deterministic in character". This same proposition can be extended to include social, and not only natural phenomena. In adopting the frequency interpretation of probability, Spanos actually accepts this proposition, that I will take also here for granted.

Spanos' uses 'theory' in order to refer to a certain interpretation of probability theory that purports to explain a certain phenomenon of interest. In the jargon of SVT, a theory is far more than that. It is the general description of a class of set-theoretical structures, plus a family of intended applications including qualitative descriptions of their structure. In Spanos' use, it is the application of the concept of a probability space to a particular target system, together with several estimation methods intended to determine *T*-theoretic parameters. Hence, it seems only natural to propose a definition of econometrics as probability theory together with a (rather large) class of random target systems of an economic nature, with corresponding methods to estimate the parameters that characterize them.

The former view implies that the basic theory-element of econometrics is given by Kolmogorov's axioms for probability, but there is far more to econometrics than such axioms. In the final section I will present a detailed, albeit compact characterization of econometric theory.

12.3 Random experiments

The starting point of Spanos' econometric doctrine is the concept of a random experiment $\mathcal{E}$, which he characterizes as an idealized representation of the DGP that satisfies the three conditions of the following definition.

12.3.1 Definition

A *random experiment* is an experiment $\mathcal{E}$ that satisfies the following conditions:

(1) all possible distinct outcomes are known a priori;
(2) in any particular trial the outcome is not known a priori;
(3) it can be repeated under identical conditions.

Examples of a random experiment are: the throwing of fair coin, or a lottery repeated under similar circumstances. The former definition of random experiment – nay, the very word 'experiment' – suggests that the mechanism producing the outcomes is under the control of the observer. For, otherwise, it would be impossible to repeat the process "under identical conditions". That is why some authors prefer to characterize a random experiment as a process by which something uncertain is observed. Sometimes the observer is only a passive observer of a process that behaves in a random way, without being able to influence in the least the outcome of the process. Accordingly, I will introduce the more general concept of a random process modifying clause (3) as follows: it repeats itself under analogous conditions. When these conditions are under the control of the observer the process is an experiment.

On the other hand, the random process (or its description) does not have to be idealized. For instance, the set of outcomes of throwing a fair coin is exactly described as consisting of two elements, namely head and tail. Thus, the sample space usually is not an idealized construct, especially when it is finite. The set-theoretical operations are not idealized either, as they have a very clear and intuitive meaning.

Actually, Definition 12.3.1 is suited for the relative-frequency interpretation of probability, which requires the repetition of the same experiment. The problem is that it is not uncommon to find in economics that probabilities have to be obtained out of single-case occurrences of singular events, without any possibility of repetition. The reason why philosophers like Karl Popper and Patrick Suppes moved away from the relative-frequency to consider the propensity interpretation of the probability of singular events as fundamental or primary is the single-case problem.

Since we find in the economic realm many random phenomena occurring only once, the propensity interpretation seems more appropriate for econometrics. The conditional probability structures are more appropriate for propensity representations of probability, and more fundamental than the usual probability spaces defined by the Kolmogorov axioms. Nevertheless, it will be convenient to begin by recalling the definition of these spaces.

12.4 Probability spaces

A probability space represents the possible results of a random experiment or process, called *events*, each one of which may happen with a certain probability. For example, the result of throwing two dice may be the event "seven turns out" or "a pair number turns out". The event "seven turns out" is composed of the elementary events (1,6), (2,5), (3,4), (4,3), (5,2), (6,1), and it is represented by the set

$$\{(1,6),(2,5),(3,4),(4,3),(5,2),(6,1)\}.$$

Hence, it can be seen that the events of a probability space may be elementary or composed out of elementary events. An elementary event, in the former example, is "(2,5) turns out"; this event is a constituent of the complex event "seven turns out". In general, each complex event is identified with the set of all the elementary events that constitute it, the occurrence of any of these being sufficient for the occurrence of the complex event. Elementary events are called *sample points* and the set of all the sample points is called *sample space*.

From a logical point of view, 'sample space' is a primitive term which is characterized axiomatically merely as a nonempty set *S*, and 'sample point' is defined just as any element of the sample space. The space of events, which is the family of complex events, is also introduced as a primitive term and characterized as an algebra of sets over *S*. The third primitive is 'probability measure', axiomatically characterized as a measure over the algebra of events. The canonical definition of 'probability space' is the following.

12.4.1 Definition

$\mathfrak{S}$ is a *probability space* iff there exist S, $\mathcal{F}$ and P such that

(0) $\mathfrak{S} = \langle S, \mathcal{F}, P \rangle$.
(1) S is a nonempty set.
(2) $\mathcal{F}$ is a σ-algebra of sets over S.
(3) P is a function $P: \mathcal{F} \rightarrow [0, 1]$ which is additive; that is to say, for every $A \in \mathcal{F}$ and for any finite decomposition $A_1, \ldots, A_n \in \mathcal{F}$ of A:

$$P(A) = \sum_{k=1}^{n} P(A_k).$$

(4) $P(S) = 1$.

Recall that a σ-algebra of sets over S is a ring of sets, with S as unit, closed under countable unions. A compact way of formulating axiom 3 consists of saying that P is a measure over $\mathcal{F}$. As we said above, set S is called *sample space*, its elements *elementary events*, and $\mathcal{F}$ is the set of events. P is called a *probability measure* over $\mathcal{F}$. The set-theoretical terms admit an interesting probabilistic interpretation (see Table 12.1).

The following are elementary identities that hold in every probability space. Their proof is easy and is left to the reader.

12.4.2 Theorem

Let $\langle S, \mathcal{F}, P \rangle$ be a probability space. Then:

(1) *For every $A \in \mathcal{F}$: $P(S \setminus A) = 1 - P(A)$.*
(2) $P(\varnothing) = 0$.
(3) *For every $A, B \in \mathcal{F}$, if $A \subseteq B$ then*

$$P(B \setminus A) = P(B) - P(A).$$

(4) *For every $A, B \in \mathcal{F}$, if $A \subseteq B$ then $P(A) \leq P(B)$.*
(5) *For every $A \in \mathcal{F}$: $0 \leq P(A) \leq 1$.*
(6) *For every $A, B \in \mathcal{F}$,*

$$P(A \cup B) = P(A) + P(B) - P(A \cap B).$$

The sample space of a probability space may be finite, countably infinite, or continuous. If S is at most countable, at least some elementary events must get positive probabilities. This is done through a function called 'probability distribution'.

Table 12.1 Correlations between set-theoretic and probabilistic notions

Set Theory	***Probability Theory***
$A \in \mathcal{F}$	A is an event.
$A \cap B = \emptyset$	Events A and B are incompatible.
$A_i \cap A_j = \emptyset$	Events $A_1,\ldots,A_n$ with $i \neq j$ and $1 \leq i, j \leq n$ are pairwise incompatible.
$\bigcap_{i=1}^{n} A_i = B$	B is the event that all events $A_1,\ldots,A_n$ occur together.
$\bigcup_{i=1}^{n} A_i = B$	B is the event that occurs if at least one of the events $A_1,\ldots,A_n$ occur.
$A' = S \setminus A$	The event that occurs when A does not occur.
$A = \emptyset$	Event A is impossible.
$A = S$	Event A is inevitable or certain.
$B \subseteq A$	The occurrence of event B brings about the occurrence of event A.

12.4.3 *Definition*

Let S be an at most countable set. A *probability distribution* over S is a function $p{:}S \rightarrow [0, 1]$ such that

$$\sum_{x \in S} p(x) = 1.$$

A probability distribution assigns positive probabilities at least to some elementary events. If it assigns positive probabilities to all of them it is called a *simple distribution*.

It is easy to see that a probability distribution over a set S generates in a natural way a probability space if, for each subset A of S, $P(A)$ is defined by means of equality

$$P(A) = \sum_{x \in A} p(x).$$

As space of events it is usual to take the power set of S.

A σ-algebra particularly important in probability theory is the minimum set containing all the intervals of $\mathbb{R}$ which is closed under countable unions. This algebra is called *Borel algebra*, denoted by $\mathcal{B}$, and its elements are called *Borel sets*. These notions are essential for the definition of the concept of a random variable.

12.4.4 *Definition*

$\mathfrak{S} = \langle S, \mathcal{F}, P \rangle$ is a *countably additive probability space* iff $\mathfrak{S}$ is a probability space such that

$$P\left(\bigcup_{n=1}^{\infty} A_n\right) = \sum_{n=1}^{\infty} P(A_n).$$

The probability measures of countable additive probability spaces have the continuity properties expressed in the following theorem.

12.4.5 Theorem

Let $\langle S, \mathcal{F}, P\rangle$ be a probability space. The following assertions are equivalent

(1) *$\langle S, \mathcal{F}, P\rangle$ is countably additive;*
(2) If *$\{A_n\}_{n\in\omega}$ is an increasing sequence of elements of $\mathcal{F}$:*

$$A_1 \subset A_2 \subset \cdots \subset A_n \subset \cdots,$$

such that $\cup_{n\in\omega} A_n = S$, then $\lim_{n\to\infty} P(A_n) = 1$;
(3) If *$\{A_n\}_{n\in\omega}$ is a decreasing sequence of elements of $\mathcal{F}$:*

$$A_1 \supset A_2 \supset \cdots \supset A_n \supset \cdots,$$

such that $\cap_{n\in\omega} A_n = \varnothing$, then $\lim_{n\to\infty} P(A_n) = 0$.

PROOF: Suppose that $\langle S, \mathcal{F}, P\rangle$ is a countably additive probability space, let $\{A_n\}_{n\in\omega}$ be an increasing sequence of elements of $\mathcal{F}$ such that $\cup_{n\in\omega} A_n = S$, and define the sequence of events $\{B_n\}_{n\in\omega}$ as follows:

$$B_1 = A_1; \quad B_n = A_n \setminus \bigcup_{k<n} A_k.$$

Clearly, for each $n \in \omega$, $A_n = \cup_{k=1}^{n} B_n$, and so $\cup_{n\in\omega} B_n = \cup_{n\in\omega} A_n = S$. Since the sets B_n are pairwise disjoint, $P(\cup_{n\in\omega} B_n) = \sum_{n\in\omega} P(B_n) = 1$ and the sequence

$$P(B_1), \sum_{k=1}^{2} P(B_k), \cdots, \sum_{k=1}^{n} P(B_k), \cdots$$

converges to 1. But

$$P(A_n) = P(\bigcup_{k=1}^{n} B_k) = \sum_{k=1}^{n} P(B_k)$$

for each $n \in \omega$, and therefore $\lim_{n\to\infty} P(A_n) = 1$.

Assume now that any increasing sequence of elements of $\mathcal{F}$ satisfies condition 12.4.5 (2), and let $\{B_n\}_{n\in\omega}$ be a decreasing sequence of elements of $\mathcal{F}$:

$$B_1 \supset B_2 \supset \cdots \supset B_n \supset \cdots,$$

such that $\bigcap_{n\in\omega} A_n = \varnothing$, and define the sequence of events $\{C_n\}_{n\in\omega}$ by means of condition "$C_n = S\backslash A_n$". Clearly, $S\backslash A_n \subseteq S\backslash A_{n+1}$, and so $\{B_n\}_{n\in\omega}$ is a decreasing sequence of events with

$$\bigcup_{n\in\omega} C_n = \bigcup_{n\in\omega}(S\backslash A_n) = S\backslash \bigcap_{n\in\omega} A_n = S.$$

Finally, suppose that any decreasing sequence of elements of $\mathcal{F}$ satisfies condition 12.4.5 (3), and let $\{A_n\}_{n\in\omega}$ be a collection of pairwise disjoint elements of $\mathcal{F}$. For each $n \in \omega$, set

$$B_n = \bigcup_{n=1}^{\infty} A_n \backslash \bigcup_{k=1}^{n} A_k.$$

Then $\{B_n\}_{n\in\omega}$ is a decreasing sequence of elements of $\mathcal{F}$ such that $\bigcap_{n=1}^{\infty} B_n = \varnothing$. Hence,

$$\begin{aligned} 0 &= \lim_{n\to\infty} P(B_n) \\ &= P(\bigcup_{n=1}^{\infty} A_n \backslash \bigcup_{k=1}^{n} A_k) \\ &= P(\bigcup_{n=1}^{\infty} A_n) - \lim_{n\to\infty} P(\bigcup_{k=1}^{n} A_k) \\ &= P(\bigcup_{n=1}^{\infty} A_n) - \lim_{n\to\infty} \sum_{k=1}^{n} P(A_k). \end{aligned}$$

Therefore,

$$\begin{aligned} P(\bigcup_{n=1}^{\infty} A_n) &= \lim_{n\to\infty} \sum_{k=1}^{n} P(A_k) \\ &= \sum_{n=1}^{\infty} P(A_n). \ \square \end{aligned}$$

A probability space whose sample space S is at most countable is called *discrete*. It is called *continuous* if the probability of any elementary event is zero.

12.5 Random variables

A random variable over a probability space is a function that associates to every elementary event of the space a certain numerical result. If S is the set of all the possible outcomes of throwing simultaneously two dice, an example of a random variable would be the function that assigns to each elementary event the payoff that turns out for the player if that event happens (provided that the function assigns the same payoff to all the different ways in which the event happens). For instance, as we saw above, the event "seven turns out" is represented as

$$A = \{(1,6),(2,5),(3,4),(4,3),(5,2),(6,1)\}.$$

But the casino must pay the same amount to the player no matter how the event comes up, and so a random variable X representing the rule of paying an established amount m to seven must map every element of A into a number representing that amount of money: $X(x) = m$ for every $x \in A$. In general, in economic situations in which utility depends upon chance, it will turn out that the utility function is a random variable. This motivates the relevance of the following definition.

12.5.1 Definition

Let $\mathfrak{S} = \langle S, \mathcal{F}, P\rangle$ be a probability space. A (real) *random variable* (r.v.) over S is a function X that maps each elementary event into the measurable space $\langle \mathbb{R}, \mathcal{B}\rangle$, where $\mathcal{B}$ is the σ-algebra of Borel sets, and X is measurable, i.e. $X^{-1}(B) = \{x \in S | X(x) \in B\}$ is an event in $\mathcal{F}$ for every $B \in \mathcal{B}$.

The measurability of the r.v. allows the induction of a probability measure in the space of values of the variable, in the sense of the following proposition.

12.5.2 Theorem

Let $\mathfrak{S} = \langle S, \mathcal{F}, P\rangle$ be a probability space, and X a r.v. over S. The function $P_X : \mathcal{B} \to \mathbb{R}$, defined by condition

$$P_X(B) = P[X^{-1}(B)],$$

is a probability measure over $\mathcal{B}$. If P is σ-additive, so is P_X.

PROOF: Clearly, the codomain of P_X is [0, 1], and so it will suffice to show that P_X is additive. Let $B_1, \ldots, B_n \in \mathcal{B}$ be a finite decomposition of any Borel set $B \in \mathcal{B}$. It is easy to see that

$$X^{-1}\left(\bigcup_{k=1}^{n} B_k\right) = \bigcup_{k=1}^{n} X^{-1}(B_k),$$

and so

$$P_X\left(\bigcup_{k=1}^{n} B_k\right) = P\left[X^{-1}\left(\bigcup_{k=1}^{n} B_k\right)\right]$$
$$= P\left(\bigcup_{k=1}^{n} X^{-1}(X_k)\right)$$
$$= \sum_{k=1}^{n} P_X(B_k).$$

Actually, if $\{B_k\}_{k \in \omega}$ is a family of pairwise disjoint sets in $\mathcal{B}$,

$$X^{-1}\left(\bigcup_{k\in\omega} B_k\right) = \bigcup_{k\in\omega} X^{-1}(B_k),$$

and an analogous argument establishes that $P_X(\cup_{k \in \omega} B_k) = \sum_{k\in\omega} P_X(B_k)$. □

The probability measure P_X is called the *probability function of the r.v. X*. The *distribution function* of P_X is the application $F: \mathbb{R} \to \mathbb{R}$ defined by condition

$$F(x) = P_X\{X \leq x\} = P_X(\{\xi \in \mathbb{R} | \xi \leq x\}).$$

It is easy to see that F is non-decreasing continuous from the left. F is *discrete* if there is a set of distinct values x_i such that $p_i = P_X\{X = x_i\} > 0$ $(i = 1, 2, 3,\ldots)$ and $\sum_i p_i = 1$. If $P_X\{X = x\} = 0$ for every real number x, F is said to be *continuous*. If there is a nonnegative function $f(x)$ $(x \in \mathbb{R})$ such that

$$F(x) = \int_{-\infty}^{x} f(\xi)\, d\xi,$$

f is called the *probability density* of F. There are examples of r.v.s that are continuous but lack a probability density. Nevertheless, econometric theory considers only those that do have it.

12.6 Conditional probability as fundamental

The working econometrician takes the concept of a probability space as a formalization of the concept of a random experiment. This is fine if the adopted interpretation of probability is that of relative frequency. Nevertheless, it is more natural in economics to adopt the propensity interpretation, and so it should be adopted as basic the notion of (qualitative) conditional probability. I will introduce in what follows a rather natural axiomatization of this concept, due originally to Luce (1968).

The basic idea is that of the likelihood of an event A given an event B, denoted (as usual) by '$A|B$'. The elementary comparison is between the likelihood of certain events given other events, namely whether the occurrence of event A conditional on B having occurred is judged as qualitatively at least as probable as the occurrence of C conditional on D having occurred. This is expressed symbolically by means of notation:

$$A|B \succsim C|D.$$

Rather natural axioms over these notions entail the existence of a numerical conditional probability representation, which is a function P over an algebra $\mathcal{F}$ of events such that

$$A|B \succsim C|D \quad \text{iff} \quad P(A \cap B)/P(B) \geq P(C \cap D)/P(D).$$

for any $A, B, C, D \in \mathcal{F}$. Since the representation requires that $P(B)$, $P(D) > 0$, the conditional likelihood of an event cannot be taken relative to an impossible event. That is why it is necessary to collect the impossible events in a set $\mathcal{N}$; obviously all events in $\mathcal{N}$ are equivalent in likelihood to $\varnothing$.

These axioms are summarized in the following definition.

12.6.1 Definition

$\mathfrak{Q}$ is an *Archimedian structure of qualitative conditional probability* iff there exist S, $\mathcal{F}$, $\mathcal{N}$, and $\succsim$, such that, for every A, B, C, D, A', B' and C' in $\mathcal{F}$ (or $\mathcal{F}\backslash\mathcal{N}$ whenever the symbol appears to the right of |) the following axioms hold:

(0) $\mathfrak{Q} = \langle S, \mathcal{F}, \mathcal{N}, \succsim \rangle$.
(1) $\langle \mathcal{F} \times (\mathcal{F}\backslash\mathcal{N}), \succsim \rangle$ is a weak order.
(2) $S \in \mathcal{F}\backslash\mathcal{N}$; and $A \in \mathcal{N}$ iff $A|S \sim \varnothing|S$.
(3) $S|S \sim A|A$ and $S|S \succsim A|B$.
(4) $A|B \sim A \cap B|B$.
(5) Suppose that $A \cap B = A' \cap B' = \varnothing$. If $A|C \succsim A'|C'$ and $B|C \succsim B'|A$, then $A \cup B|C \succsim A' \cup B'|C'$; moreover, if either hypothesis is $\succ$, then the conclusion is $\succ$.
(6) Suppose that $C \subset B \subset A$ and $C' \subset B' \subset A'$. If $B|A \succsim C'|B'$ and $C|B \succsim B'|A'$, then $C|A \succsim C'|A'$; moreover, if either hypothesis is $\succ$, then the conclusion is $\succ$.
(7) Every standard sequence is finite, where $\{A_i\}$ is a standard sequence iff, for all i, $A_i \in \mathcal{F}\backslash\mathcal{N}$, $A_i \subset A_{i+1}$, and $S|S \succ A_i|A_{i+1} \sim A_1|A_2$.

Conditions (1)-(7) are necessary but not sufficient for the existence of a representation. KLST (1971) introduce an axiom that completes the axioms and yields the representation. The axiom is a sort of solvability axiom asserting that the structure is sufficiently rich so that, whenever $A|B \succ C|D$, it is possible to add enough to C in order to make $C'|D$ equivalent to $A|B$. In more precise terms,

(8) If $A|B \succsim C|D$, then there exists $C' \in \mathcal{F}$ such that $C \cap D \subseteq C'$ and $A|B \sim C'|D$.

An initial analysis of the DGP may reveal intuitively some of the dependences among the events, but, as it is usual in the application of any scientific theory, the methods of determination of the terms of a theory may be rather indirect (they are called, in econometrics, 'statistical inference'). Starting from structures of qualitative conditional probability, I will show how the apparatus of econometrics is built. Roughly, the steps are the following:

(1) A economic random system is identified as object of study, and converted in a target system by the scientist.
(2) The target system – also known as DGP – is described in a qualitative, not theoretical way, using ordinary language an the notion of qualitative conditional probability.
(3) Using the representation theorems, it is acknowledged that the target system can be represented by means of a standard probability space.
(4) Within the standard probability space, a random variable X is introduced, and the original probability space is replaced by the Borel space induced by X.
(5) The probability distributions of the random variables are assumed integrable out of a parametric family of density functions with unknown parameters $\boldsymbol{\theta} \in \boldsymbol{\Theta}$. The set of these functions is called the *probability model*; it is denoted as $\Phi = \{D(y; \boldsymbol{\theta}), \boldsymbol{\theta} \in \boldsymbol{\Theta}\}$.
(6) Assuming that the (probabilistic) laws of the theory are satisfied by the target system, it is taken for granted that the observed data (and potentially infinitely many more) are generated by the 'chance mechanism' represented by the 'true' density. The aim of the theory is to find the true parameter defining this density.
(7) Finally, a sampling model is introduced defining a sample from density $D(y; \boldsymbol{\theta}_0)$, for some 'true' parameter $\boldsymbol{\theta}_0 \in \boldsymbol{\Theta}$.

In order to find the true parameter, it is assumed that the observed data constitute a realization $\mathbf{Z} \equiv (\mathbf{Z}, \ldots, \mathbf{Z}_T)$ of a sequence of random vectors, or stochastic processes $\{\mathbf{Z}_t, t \in \mathbb{T}\}$. According to Spanos (1986: 665),

> This assumption provides the necessary link between the actual DGP and probability theory. It enables us to postulate a probabilistic structure for $\{\mathbf{Z}_t, t \in \mathbb{T}\}$ in the form of a joint distribution function $D(\mathbf{Z}; \psi)$. This will provide the basis for the statistical model specification.

12.7 From conditional to absolute probability

Even though conditional probabilities are more intuitive, it is necessary to transit from them to unconditional probabilities in order to get the relevant probability model, required to actually determine the values of the probability measures. The axioms that define 12.6.1, together with axiom (8), imply the following proposition.

12.7.1 Theorem

Suppose that $\mathfrak{Q} = \langle S, \mathcal{F}, \mathcal{N}, \succsim \rangle$ *is an Archimedean structure of qualitative conditional probability for which axiom 8 holds. Then there exists a unique real-valued function P on* $\mathcal{F}$ *such that for all* $A, C \in \mathcal{F}$ *and all* $B, D \in \mathcal{F} \backslash \mathcal{N}$:

(i) $\langle S, \mathcal{F}, P \rangle$ *is a finitely additive probability space*;
(ii) $A \in \mathcal{N}$ *iff* $P(A) = 0$;
(iii) $A|B \succsim C|D$ iff $P(A \cap B)/P(B) \geq P(C \cap D)/P(D)$.

Moreover, if $\mathfrak{Q}$ *satisfies condition*

(iv) *If* $B|S \succsim A_i|S$ then $B|S \succsim \bigcup_{i\in\omega} A|S$

for every $B \in \mathcal{F}$ *and any collection* $\{A_i\}_{i \in \omega}$ *of elements of* $\mathcal{F}$, *then* $\langle S, \mathcal{F}, P \rangle$ *is countably additive.*

PROOF: By the argument in section 5.7 of (KLST 1971: 228–232), there exists a function P satisfying conditions (i)-(iii) of Theorem 12.7.1. Define relation $\succsim'$ by condition

$$A \succsim' B \quad \text{iff} \quad A|S \succsim B|S.$$

By Theorem 9 on (KLST 1971: 232), $\mathfrak{Q}' = \langle S, \mathcal{F}, \succsim' \rangle$ is an Archimedean structure of qualitative probability. Hence, by Theorem 2 (KLST: 208), there exists a unique order-preserving function P' from $\mathcal{F}$ into [0, 1] such that $\langle S, \mathcal{F}, P' \rangle$ is a finitely additive probability space. Since P' is unique, $P' = P$.

Suppose now that $\mathfrak{Q}$ satisfies condition (iv), let $A_1, A_2, \ldots A_i, \ldots$ be any sequence in $\mathcal{F}$ and B any element of $\mathcal{F}$ such that $A_i \subset A_{i+1}$ and $B \succsim' A_i$ for all i. This is tantamount, by the definition of $\succsim'$, to $B|S \succsim A_i|S$ for each i and so, by (iv), $B|S \succsim \bigcup_{i\in\omega} A_i|S$; i.e. $B \succsim' \bigcup_{i\in\omega} A_i$. This is to say that $\succsim'$ is monotonically continuous (cf. Definition 6, KLST: 216) and therefore, by Theorem 4 on (KLST: 216), $\langle S, \mathcal{F}, P \rangle$ is countably additive. □

Theorem 12.7.1 provides the basis to represent any structure of qualitative conditional probability by means of a probability model, once the relevant random variables are specified.

12.8 Statistical inference

Once the probability model Φ has been defined, it is necessary, in order to determine numerical values for its parameters, to introduce a statistical model. This can be defined as follows (cf. Spanos 1986: 216–8).

12.8.1 Definition

A *statistical model* is a pair $\langle \Phi, \mathbf{X} \rangle$ such that

(1) Φ is a probability model; i.e. a family $\{D(\mathbf{x}; \boldsymbol{\theta}), \boldsymbol{\theta} \in \boldsymbol{\Theta}\}$ of density functions.
(2) $\mathbf{X}$ is a set of random variables $(X_1, \ldots, X_n)$ whose density functions coincide with the 'true' density function $f(\mathbf{x}; \boldsymbol{\theta}_0)$ as postulated by the probability model.
(3) The distribution of $\mathbf{X}$ is the joint distribution of the r.v.'s $X_1, \ldots, X_n$, denoted by

$$f(x_1, \cdots, x_n, \boldsymbol{\theta}) = f(\mathbf{x}; \boldsymbol{\theta}).$$

The observed data $(x_1 \ldots, x_n)$ are interpreted as a particular specification of the sampling model, i.e. $\mathbf{X} = \mathbf{x}$, and then processed computing $f(x_1, \ldots, x_n, \boldsymbol{\theta})$. The information obtained allows the consideration of the following questions, which delineate the main areas of statistical inference:

(1) Are the observed data consistent with the postulated statistical model? (*misspecification*)
(2) Assuming that the statistical model postulated is consistent with the observed data, what can we infer about the unknown parameters $\boldsymbol{\theta} \in \boldsymbol{\Theta}$?

(a) Can we decrease the uncertainty about $\boldsymbol{\theta}$ by reducing the parameter space from $\boldsymbol{\Theta}$ to $\boldsymbol{\Theta}_0$ where $\boldsymbol{\Theta}_0$ is a subset of $\boldsymbol{\Theta}$? (confidence estimation)
(b) Can we decrease the uncertainty about $\boldsymbol{\theta}$ by choosing a particular value in $\boldsymbol{\Theta}$, say $\hat{\boldsymbol{\theta}}$, as providing the most representative value of $\boldsymbol{\theta}$? (point estimation)
(c) Can we consider the question that $\boldsymbol{\theta}$ belongs to some subset $\boldsymbol{\Theta}_0$ of $\boldsymbol{\Theta}$? (hypothesis testing)

(3) Assuming that a particular representative value $\hat{\boldsymbol{\theta}}$ of $\boldsymbol{\theta}$ has been chosen what can we infer about further observations from the DGP as described by the postulated statistical model? (prediction) (Spanos 1986: 221)

It is particularly interesting to notice that answering the second question presupposes that the statistical model postulated (let alone the axioms of probability theory) is valid, "and considers various forms of inference relating to unknown parameters $\boldsymbol{\theta}$". This is typical of *T*-theoretical terms, indeed.

12.9 The logical structure of econometrics

What is, then, the logical structure of econometric theory (ET)? Which is its basic theory-element, specializations, domain of intended applications, *T*-theoretical terms?

The domain of intended applications of ET is vast, as many economic random phenomena have been successfully subjected to econometric analysis. I shall leave as an open problem the task of classifying these phenomena. My task in this final section is merely that of identifying the logical structure of the basic theory-element of ET. Nevertheless, we may say something relevant about the general nature of a non-ET-theoretic structure $\mathfrak{B}_\sigma$ describing a particular real-concrete DGP σ. Taking as a point of departure empirical data $\mathfrak{D} = (x_1 \ldots, x_n)$ about σ, the econometrician draws an histogram and a cumulative histogram which describe a particular effect of the random causal forces operating in σ. Out of the information provided by such histograms, it calculates numerical characteristics that describe the location, dispersion and shape of the histogram. These are the mean, the median, the mode, the variance, the standard deviation, higher central moments, and the skewness and kurtosis coefficients. Nevertheless, as Spanos (1986: 27) points out, "although the histogram can be a very useful way to summarise and study the observed data it is not a very convenient descriptor of data". Moreover,

> analytically the histogram is a cumbersome step function of the form
>
> $$h(z) = \sum_{i=1}^{m} \frac{\phi_i}{(z_{i+1} - z_i)} I([z_i, z_{i+1}]), \quad z \in \mathbb{R},$$
>
> where $[z_i, z_{i+1})$ represents the *i*th half-closed interval and $I(\cdot)$ is the indicator function
>
> $$I([z_i, z_{i+1})) = \begin{cases} 1 & \text{for} \quad z \in [z_i, z_{i+1}) \\ 0 & \text{for} \quad z \notin [z_i, z_{i+1}). \end{cases}$$
>
> Hence, the histogram is not an ideal descriptor especially in relation to the modeling facet of observed data (Ibid.).

Even though it is easy to obtain a continuous curve tracing the frequency polygon, the canonical way of representing the data is a Pearson frequency curve, which is a family based on the differential equation

$$\frac{d(\log \phi(z))}{dz} = \frac{z+a}{b_0 + b_1 z + b_2 z^2}$$

(for more details see Spanos 1986: 28). The non-ET-theoretic structure $\mathfrak{B}_\sigma \in M_{pp}$ describing the intended application in case is a Pearson curve that fits the data in a degree acceptable to the community of econometricians. Pearson curves are analogous, for instance, to the ellipses describing the planetary orbits as described by Johannes Kepler. Just as these orbits are described without presupposing dynamic notions, Pearson curves are introduced without presupposing in their determination any probability measure. A Pearson curve describes a particular factual behavior of a population S. Hence $\mathfrak{B}_\sigma$ seems to be of the form $\langle S, f^* \rangle$, where f^* is a frequency curve which is a non-stochastic function of the observed data, based entirely on the data at hand (in $\mathfrak{D}$).

The scientific aim of the econometrician is to 'explain' $\mathfrak{B}_\sigma = \langle S, f^* \rangle$ by means of probability theory, showing that $\mathfrak{B}_\sigma$ is but one possible realization of the random processes taking place in σ. The point is to find the probability space in which $\mathfrak{B}_\sigma$ belongs. This is done by postulating a probability model together with a sampling model, derived from a statistical model, describing the relationship between the probability model and the observable data. "The statistical model should represent a good approximation to the real phenomenon to be explained in a way that takes into account the nature of the available data" (Spanos 1986: 341). Using the data the parameters of the statistical model are determined and so are, in this way, the density functions of the probability model. Clearly, these functions allow, by integration, the determination of the probability measures of the underlying probability spaces as well. In particular, f^* must turn out to be a special case of the true density function in the probability space. Hence, it seems that we can synthesize the previous discussion by means of a compact definition.

12.9.1 Definition

$\mathfrak{A}$ is an *econometric structure* iff there exist S, f^*, Φ and $\mathbf{X}$ such that

(0) $\mathfrak{A} = \langle S, f^*, \Phi, \mathbf{X} \rangle$.
(1) S is a nonempty set.
(2) f^* is a Pearson curve over a set $\mathbf{X}$ of random variables defined on S.
(3) Φ is a probability model; i.e. a family $\{D(\mathbf{x}; \boldsymbol{\theta}), \boldsymbol{\theta} \in \boldsymbol{\Theta}\}$ of density functions.

(4) The Pearson curve over ($X_1,\ldots, X_n$) coincides with the 'true' density function $f(\mathbf{x};\boldsymbol{\theta}_0)$ as postulated by the probability model; i.e.

$$f^*(x_1,\cdots,x_n)=f(\mathbf{x};\boldsymbol{\theta}).$$

Axiom 12.9.1 (4) is the fundamental law of ET. The general form of its empirical claim is that the Pearson curves obtained out of a particular random phenomenon σ can be matched by a density function of a random variable defined over an appropriate probability space.

References

Ackerman, W. (1956). "Zur Axiomatik der Mengenlehre". *Mathematische Annalen* 131: 336–345.

Afriat, S. N. (1967). "The Construction of Utility Functions From Expenditure Data". *International Economic Review* 8(1): 67–77.

Althusser, L. (2005). *For Marx*. London: Verso.

Antonelli, G. B. (1971). "On the Mathematical Theory of Political Economy". In J. S. Chipman, L. Hurwicz, M. K. Richter and H. F. Sonnenschein (eds.) *Preferences, Utility, and Demand*. New York: Harcourt Brace Jovanovich, 333–364.

Arrow, K. J. (1951). "Alternative Proof of the Substitution Theorem for Leontief Models in the General Case". In T. C. Koopmans (ed.) *Activity Analysis of Production and Allocation*. New York: John Wiley & Sons, 155–164.

Arrow, K. J. and G. Debreu (1954). "Existence of an Equilibrium for a Competitive Economy". *Econometrica* 22: 265–290.

Aumann, R. (1964). "Mixed and Behavior Strategies in Infinite Extensive Games". In M. Dresher, L. S. Shapley and A. W. Tucker (eds.) *Advances in Game Theory*. Princeton: Princeton University Press, 627–650.

Ballesteros, A., P. Beato, M. Jerison and J. Oliu (1976). "The Mathematics of Sraffa's Model of Prices, Wage, and Rate of Profit". *Center for Economic Research Discussion Paper 76–77*. Minnessota: Department of Economics, University of Minnesota.

Balzer, W., C. U. Moulines and J. D. Sneed (1987). *An Architectonic for Science*. Dordrecht: D. Reidel.

Balzer, W. and G. Zoubek (1994). "Structuralist Aspects of Idealization". In M. Kuokkanen (ed.) *Idealization VII: Structuralism, Idealization and Approximation*. Amsterdam: Editions Rodopi, 57–79.

Barnes, J. (ed.) (1984). *The Complete Works of Aristotle*. Princeton: Princeton University Press.

Barten, A. B. and V. Bohm (1981). "Consumer Theory". In K. J. Arrow and M. D. Intriligator (eds.) *Handbook of Mathematical Economics*. Amsterdam: Elsevier, vol. 2, 381–429.

Bell, J. L. and A. B. Slomson (1969). *Models and Ultraproducts*. Amsterdam: North-Holland.

Blackwell, D. and M. A. Girshik (1954). *Theory of Games and Statistical Decisions*. New York: John Wiley & Sons.

Boolos, G. S., J. P. Burgess and R. Jeffrey (2002). *Computability and Logic*. Cambridge: Cambridge University Press.

Boumans, M. (2016). "Suppes's Outlines of an Empirical Measurement Theory". *Journal of Economic Methodology* 23(3): 305–315.
——— (2012). "Measurement in Economics". In U. Maki (ed.) *Handbook of the Philosophy of Science* (Volume 13. Philosophy of Economics). Amsterdam: North Holland/ Elsevier, 395–423.
——— (2008). "Measurement". In S. N. Durlauf and L. E. Blume (eds.) *The New Palgrave Dictionary of Economics*. New York: Palgrave MacMillan.
——— (ed.) (2007). *Measurement in Economics: A Handbook.* Amsterdam and New York: Elsevier.
Bourbaki, N. (1968). *Theory of Sets.* Redding: Addison-Wesley.
Bunge, M. (1978). *Filosofia de lafisica.* Barcelona: Ariel.
——— (1974a). *Treatise of Basic Philosophy I.* Dordrecht: D. Reidel.
——— (1974b). *Treatise of Basic Philosophy II.* Dordrecht: D. Reidel.
——— (1972). *Teoriay Realidad.* Barcelona: Ariel.
——— (1969). *La investigation cientifica.* Barcelona: Ariel.
Burns, A. F. and W. C. Mitchell (1946). *Measuring Business Cycles.* New York: National Bureau of Economic Research Studies in Business Cycles.
Caldwell, B. (ed.) (1984). *Appraisal and Criticism in Economics.* Boston: Allen & Unwin.
Chakrabarti, S. K. (1992). "Equilibrium in Behavior Strategies in Infinite Extensive Form Games With Imperfect Information". *Economic Theory* 2: 481–494.
Cohen, I. B. (1992). *The Birth of a New Physics.* London: Penguin Books.
Collins, H. and M. Kusch (1998). *The Shape of Actions: What Humans and Machines Can Do.* Cambridge, MA: MIT Press.
Corry, L. (1992). "Nicolas Bourbaki and the Concept of Mathematical Structure". *Synthese* 92: 315–348.
Crangle, C. E. (2015). "Representation, Isomorphism and Invariance in the Study of Language and the Brain". In C. E. Crangle, A. García de la Sienra and H. Longino (eds.) *Foundations and Methods From Mathematics to Neuroscience: Essays Inspired By Patrick Suppes.* Stanford: CSLI Publications, 205–218.
Da Costa, N. C. A. and R. Chuaqui (1988). "On Suppes' Set-Theoretical Predicates". *Erkenntnis* 29: 95–112.
Darnell, A. and J. Evans (1990). *The Limits of Econometrics.* Cheltenham: Edward Elgar Publishing.
Davis, G. C. (2000). "A Semantic Interpretation of Haavelmo's Structure of Econometrics". *Economics and Philosophy* 16: 205–228.
Debreu, G. (1983a). "Smooth Preferences". In G. Debreu (ed.) *Mathematical Economics: Twenty Papers By Gerard Debreu.* Cambridge: Cambridge University Press, 186–201.
——— (1983b). "Smooth Preferences: A Corrigendum". In G. Debreu (ed.) *Mathematical Economics: Twenty Papers by Gerard Debreu.* Cambridge: Cambridge University Press, 201–202.
——— (1981). "Existence of a Competitive Equilibrium". In K. J. Arrow and M. D. Intriligator (eds.) *Handbook of Mathematical Economics.* Amsterdam: Elsevier, vol. 2, 697–743.
——— (1959). *Theory of Value: An Axiomatic Analysis of Economic Equilibrium.* New Haven and London: Yale University Press.
De Donato, X. (2011). "Idealization Within a Structuralist Perspective". *Metatheoria* 1(2): 65–90.
Díez, J. A. (2000). "Structuralist Analysis of Theories of Fundamental Measurement". In W. Balzer, J. D. Sneed and C. U. Moulines (eds.) *Structuralist Knowledge*

Representation: Paradigmatic Examples (Poznan Studies in the Methodology of the Sciences and the Humanities, vol. 75). Amsterdam: Rodopi, 19–49.

Ellis, B. (1966). *Basic Concepts of Measurement*. Cambridge: Cambridge University Press.

Embree, J. (1939). *Suye Mura, a Japanese Village*. Chicago: University of Chicago Press.

Enderton, H. B. (2001). *A Mathematical Introduction to Logic*. Burlington: Hartcourt/ Academic Press.

Feferman, A. and S. Feferman (2004). *Alfred Tarski: Life and Logic*. Cambridge: Cambridge University Press.

Finkelstein, L. (1982). "Theory and Philosophy of Measurement". In P. H. Sydenham (ed.) *Handbook of Measurement Science. Volume 1 Theoretical Fundamentals*. Hoboken: John Wiley & Sons, 1–30.

Fleuriot, J. (2001). *A Combination of Geometry Theorem Proving and Nonstandard Analysis With Application to Newton's Principia*. London: Springer.

Frege, G. (1879). *Begriffsschrift. Eine derarithmetischen nachgebildete Formelsprache des reinen Denkens*. Halle: Verlag von Louis Nebert.

Frigg, R. (2010). "Models and Fiction". *Synthese* 72(2): 251–268.

Gale, D. (1960). *The Theory of Linear Economic Models*. Chicago and London: The University of Chicago Press.

García de la Sienra, A. (2015). "¿Es MCP-teorico el termino 'masa'?". *Revista de Filosofía* 140: 69–83.

——— (2011). "Suppes Methodology of Economics". *Theoria* 26(3): 347–366.

——— (2010). "The Economic Sphere". *Axiomathes* 20: 81–94.

——— (2009). "La aplicación a la Economía de la concepción estructuralista de las teorías". In J. C. García-Bermejo (ed.) *Sobre la Economía y sus métodos* (Enciclopedia Iberoamericana de Filosofía, vol. 30). Madrid: Editorial Trotta, 355–366.

——— (2008). "Teoría general de las clases". In A. García de la Sienra (ed.) *Reflexiones sobre la paradoja de Orayen*. Mexico: Universidad Nacional Autónoma de México/ Instituto de Investigaciones Filosóficas, 119–136.

——— (2007). "Idealization in the Labor Theory of Value". In J. Brzeziński, A. Klawiter, T. A. F. Kuipers, K. Lastowski, K. Paprzycka and P. Przybysz (eds.) *The Courage of Doing Philosophy: Essays Presented to Leszek Nowak*. Amsterdam and New York: Rodopi, 219–233.

——— (1996). "La medición del trabajo abstracto". *Economía Mexicana* 5(1): 63–75.

——— (1992). *The Logical Foundations of the Marxian Theory of Value*. Dordrecht: Kluwer Academic Publishers.

——— (1990). "Estructuras y representaciones". *Crítica* 22(64): 3–22.

——— (1988). "Review of W. Balzer, C. U. Moulines and J. D. Sneed *An Architectonic for Science*. Dordrecht: D. Reidel, 1987". *Theoria* 54: 73–78.

Georgescu-Roegen, N. (1967). "Some Properties of a Generalized Leontief Model". In N. Georgescu-Roegen (ed.) *Analytical Economics*. Cambridge, MA: Harvard University Press, 316–337.

Hamminga, B. (1990). "The Structure of Six Transformations in Marx's *Capital*". In J. Brzeziński, F. Coniglione, T. A. F. Kuipers and L. Nowak (eds.) *Idealization I: General Problems* (Poznań Studies in the Philosophy of the Sciences and the Humanities, vol. 16). Amsterdam: Rodopi, 89–111.

Hands, D. W. (1985). "The Structuralist View of Economic Theories: A Review Essay". *Economics and Philosophy* 1: 303–335.

Hausdorff, F. (1914). *Grundzüge der Mengenlehre*. Leipzig: Veit.

Heath, T. L. (ed.) (2010). *The Works of Archimedes*. Cambridge: Cambridge University Press.

——— (ed.) (1956). *The Thirteen Books of Euclid's Elements*. New York: Dover Publications.

Hegel, G. W. F. (1970). *Grundlinien der Philosophie des Rechts oder Naturrecht und Staatswissenschaft im Grundrisse*. Frankfurt am Main: Suhrkamp Verlag.

Hendry, D. (1995). *Dynamic Econometrics*. Oxford: Oxford University Press.

——— (1993). *Econometrics: Alchemy or Science*? Oxford: Blackwell Publishers.

Henkin, L., P. Suppes and A. Tarski (1959). *The Axiomatic Method With Special Reference to Geometry and Physics*. Amsterdam: North-Holland.

Hestenes, M. R. (1966). *Calculus of Variations and Optimal Control Theory*. New York: John Wiley & Sons.

Hicks, N. J. (1965). *Notes on Differential Geometry*. New York: Van Nostrand Reinhold.

Hilbert, D. (1950). *The Foundations of Geometry*. La Salle: The Open Court Publishing Company.

Hölder, O. (1997). "The Axioms of Quantity and the Theory of Measurement II". *Journal of Mathematical Psychology* 41: 345–356.

——— (1996). "The Axioms of Quantity and the Theory of Measurement I". *Journal of Mathematical Psychology* 40: 235–252.

——— (1901). "Die Axiome der Quantität und die Lehre vom Mass". *Berichte uber die Verhandlungen der Koniglich Sachsischen Gesellschaft der Wissenschaften zu Leipzig, Mathematisch-Physikalische Classe* 53: 1–64.

Holy Bible (1982). *The New King James Version*. New York: American Bible Society.

Houthakker, H. S. (1950). "Revealed Preference and the Utility Function". *Economica* 17 (66): 159–174.

Jammer, M. (1964). *Concepts of Mass in Classical and Modern Physics*. New York: Harper Torchbooks.

Kamke, E. (1950). *Theory of Sets*. New York: Dover Publications.

Katzner, D. W. (1970). *Static Demand Theory*. New York: The Macmillan Company.

Kemp, M. C. and Y. Kimura (1978). *Introduction to Mathematical Economics*. New York, Heidelberg and Berlin: Springer-Verlag.

Koopmans, T. C. (ed.) (1951). "Analysis of Production as an Efficient Combination of Activities". In T. C. Koopmans (ed.) *Activity Analysis of Production and Allocation*. New Haven and London: Yale University Press, 33–97.

——— (1947). "Measurement Without Theory". *The Review of Economic Statistics* 29(3): 161–172.

[KLST 1990] Suppes, P., D. H. Krantz, R. D. Luce and A. Tversky (1990). *Foundations of Measurement, Volume III: Representation, Axiomatization, and Invariance*. New York: Academic Press.

[KLST 1989] Luce, D. H., R. D. Krantz, P. Suppes and A. Tversky (1989). *Foundations of Measurement, Volume II: Geometrical, Threshold, and Probabilisic Representations*. New York: Academic Press.

[KLST 1971] Krantz, D. H., R. D. Luce, P. Suppes and A. Tversky (1971). *Foundations of Measurement, Volume I: Additive and Polynomial Representations*. New York: Academic Press.

Kreps, D. M. (1990). *Theory of Games and Economic Modelling*. Oxford: Clarendon Press.

Kuhn, H. W. (1953). "Extensive Games and the Problem of Information". In H. W. Kuhn and A. W. Tucker (eds.) *Contributions to the Theory of Games II*. Princeton: Princeton University Press, 193–216.

Kuhn, Th. S. (1970). *The Structure of Scientific Revolutions*. Chicago: University of Chicago Press.

Kurz, H. D. and N. Salvadori (2004). "'Man From the Moon': On Sraffa's Objectivism". *Economies et Societés* 35: 1545–1557.

Lakatos, I. (1973). "Falsification and the Methodology of Scientific Research Programmes". In I. Lakatos and A. Musgrave (eds.) *Criticism and the Growth of Knowledge*. Cambridge: Cambridge University Press, 91–196.

Levhari, D. (1965). "A Non-Substitution Theorem and Switching of Techniques". *Quarterly Journal of Economics* 79(1): 98–105.

Lorenzano, P. (2014). "What Is the Status of the Hardy-Weinberg Law Within Population Genetics?". In M. C. Galavotti, E. Nemeth and F. Stadler (eds.) *European Philosophy of Science – Philosophy of Science in Europe and the Viennese Heritage*. Dordrecht: Springer, 159–172.

Lowen, R. (1997). *Creating the Cold War University*. Berkeley: University of California Press.

Luce, R. D. (1968). "On the Numerical Representation of Qualitative Conditional Probability". *Annals of Mathematical Statistics* 39(2): 481–491.

Luce, R. D. and H. Raiffa (1957). *Games and Decisions*. New York: Wiley.

Luce, R. D. and P. Suppes (2002). "Representational Measurement Theory". In J. Wixted and H. Pashler (eds.) *Steven* s *Handbook of Experimental Psychology 4*. New York: Wiley, 1–41.

Mäki, U. (1994). "Isolation, Idealization and Truth in Economics". In B. Hamminga and N. B. De Marchi (eds.) *Idealization VI: Idealization in Economics* (Poznan Studies in the Philosophy of the Sciences and the Humanities, vol. 38). Amsterdam: Editions Rodopi, 147–168.

——— (1992). "On the Method of Idealization in Economics". In C. Dilworth (ed.) *Idealization IV: Intelligibility in Science* (Poznan Studies in the Philosophy of the Sciences and the Humanities, vol. 26). Amsterdam: Editions Rodopi, 317–351.

Mandel, E. (1968). *Marxist Economic Theory*. New York and London: MR Press.

Marx, K. (1983). *Okenomische Manuscripte 1857/1858* (Marx-Engels Werke 42). Berlin: Dietz Verlag.

——— (1976/1978/1981). *Capital*. Harmondsworth: Penguin.

——— (1973). *Grundrisse: Foundations of the Critique of Political Economy (Rough Draft)*. Harmondsworth: Penguin Books.

——— (1970). *Contribution to a Critique of Political Economy*. New York: International Publishers.

——— (1868). "Letter to Ludwig Kugelmann in Hannover, 11 July 1868". In *Marx-Engels Collected Works*, vol. 43, 67.

Mas-Colell, A. (1985). *The Theory of General Equilibrium: A Differentiable Approach*. Cambridge: Cambridge University Press.

Mas-Colell, A., M. D. Whinston and J. R. Green (1995). *Microeconomic Theory*. New York and Oxford: Oxford University Press.

McKinsey, J. C. C. (1952). *Introduction to the Theory of Games*. New York: McGraw-Hill.

McKinsey, J. C. C., A. C. Sugar and P. Suppes (1953). "Axiomatic Foundations of Classical Particle Mechanics". *Journal of Rational Mechanics and Analysis* 2(2): 253–272.

McKinsey, J. C. C. and P. Suppes (1955). "On the Notion of Invariance in Classical Mechanics". *British Journal for Philosophy of Science* 5(20): 290–302.

——— (1953). "Transformations of Systems of Classical Particle Mechanics". *Journal of Rational Mechanics and Analysis* 2(2): 273–289.

Michell, J. (2007). "Representational Theory of Measurement". In M. Boumans (ed.) *Measurement in Economics: A Handbook*. Amsterdam and London: Elsevier, 19–39.

Mirowski, P. (2002). *Machine Dreams: Economics Becomes a Cyborg Science*. Cambridge: Cambridge University Press.

Mirrles, J. A. (1969). "The Dynamic Non-Substitution Theorem". *Review of Economic Studies* 36: 67–76.

Morishima, M. and F. Seton (1961). "Aggregation in Leontief Matrices and the Labour Theory of Value". *Econometrica* 29(2): 203–220.

Moulines, C. U. (2007). "Model Construction, Idealization, and Scientific Ontology". In J. Brzeziński, J. A. Klawiter, Th. Kuipers, K. Łastowski, K. Paprzycka and P. Przybysz (eds.) *The Courage of Doing Philosophy: Essays Presented to Leszek Nowak*. Amsterdam: Rodopi, 257–271.

Muller, F. A. (2011). "Reflections on the Revolution at Stanford". *Synthese* 183: 87–114.

——— (2001). "Sets, Classes and Categories". *British Journal for the Philosophy of Science* 52: 539–573.

Nagel, E., P. Suppes and A. Tarski (1962). *Logic, Methodology and Philosophy of Science: Proceedings of the 1960 International Congress*. Stanford: Stanford University Press.

Nash, J. F. (1950). "Equilibrium Points in N-Person Games". *Proceedings of the National Academy of Sciences* 36(1): 48–49.

Newton, I. (1761). *Arithmetica universalis; sive de compositione et resolutio*. Amsterdam: Marcum Michaelem Rey.

Nicholas, H. (2011). *Marx's Theory of Price and Its Modern Rivals*. New York: Palgrave Macmillan.

Okishio, N. (1963). "A Mathematical Note on Marxian Theorems". *Weltwirtschaftliches Archiv* 91: 287–299.

Peano, G. (1889). *Arithmetices Principia Nova Methodo Exposita*. Roma and Florencia: Augustae Taurinorum.

Popper, K. (1968). *The Logic of Scientific Discovery*. London and New York: Hutchinson & Co.

Portides, D. (2013). "Idealization in Economics Modeling". In H. Andersen, D. Dieks, W. J. Gonzalez, Th. Uebel and G. Wheeler (eds.) *New Challenges to Philosophy of Science*. Dordrecht: Springer, 253–263.

Punzo, L. F. (1986). "La matematica di Sraffa". In R. Bellofiore (ed.) *Tra Teoria Economica e Grande Cultura Europea: Piero Sraffa*. Milan: Franco Angeli, 141–167.

Rao, M. M. (1981). *Foundations of Stochastic Analysis*. New York: Academic Press.

Richter, M. K. (1971). "Rational Choice". In J. S. Chipman, L. Hurwicz, M. K. Richter and H. F. Sonnenschein (eds.) *Preferences, Utility, and Demand*. New York: Harcourt Brace Jovanovich, 29–58.

Roemer, J. E. (1981). *Analytical Foundations of Marxian Economic Theory*. Cambridge: Cambridge University Press.

Rubin, H. and P. Suppes (1954). "Transformations of Systems of Relativistic Particle Mechanics". *Pacific Journal of Mathematics* 4: 563–601.

Samuelson, P. A. (1961). "A New Theorem on Non-substitution". In H. Hegeland (ed.) *Money, Growth and Methodology and Other Essays in Economics*. Lund: CWK Gleerup, 407–423.

——— (1951). "Abstract of a Theorem Concerning Substitutability in Open Leontief Models". In T. C. Koopmans (ed.) *Activity Analysis of Production and Allocation*. New York: John Wiley & Sons, 142–146.

——— (1948). "Consumption Theory in Terms of Revealed Preference". *Economica* 15: 243–253.

——— (1947). *Foundations of Economic Analysis*. Cambridge, MA: Harvard University Press.

——— (1938). "A Note on the Pure Theory of Consumer Behavior". *Economica* 5: 61–71.

Schefold, B. (2005). "Joint Production: Triumph of Economic Over Mathematical Logic?". *The European Journal of the History of Economic Thought* 12(3): 525–552.

Scott, D. and P. Suppes (1958). "Foundational Aspects of Theories of Measurement". *Journal of Symbolic Logic* 23: 113–128.

Skala, H. J. (1975). *Non-Archimedian Utility Theory.* Dordrecht: D. Reidel.

Slutsky, E. (1915/1952). "On the Theory of the Budget of the Consumer". In G. J. Stigler and K. E. Boulding (eds.) *Readings in Price Theory.* London: George Allen and Unwin, 27–56.

Sneed, J. D. (1971). *The Logical Structure of Mathematical Physics*. Dordrecht: D. Reidel.

Spanos, A. (1986). *Statistical Foundations of Econometric Modelling.* Cambridge: Cambridge University Press.

Spiegel, M. R. (1967). *Theoretical Mechanics*. New York: McGraw-Hill.

Sraffa, P. (1960). *Production of Commodities by Means of Commodities*. Cambridge: Cambridge University Press.

Stegmuller, W. (1976). *The Structure and Dynamics of Theories* New York: Springer-Verlag.

Stiglitz, J. E. (1970). "Non-Substitution Theorems With Durable Capital Goods". *Review of Economic Studies* 37(4): 543–552.

Stigum, B. (2003). *Econometrics and the Philosophy of Economics*. Princeton and Oxford: Princeton University Press.

Struik, D. J. (1954). *A Concise History of Mathematics*. London: G. Bell and Sons.

Suppe, F. (1989). *The Semantic Conception of Theories and Scientific Realism*. Urbana and Chicago: University of Illinois Press.

Suppes, P. (2011). "Future Development of Scientific Structures Closer to Experiments: Response to F. A. Muller". *Synthese* 183: 115–126.

——— (2002). *Representation and Invariance of Scientific Structures*. Stanford: CSLI Publications.

——— (1984). *Probabilistic Metaphysics*. Oxford: Basil Blackwell.

——— (1980). "Limitations of the Axiomatic Method in Ancient Greek Mathematical Sciences". In D. Gruender, J. Hintikka and E. Agazzi (eds.) *Theory Change, Ancient Axiomatics, and Galileo's Methodology: Proceedings of the 1978 Pisa Conference on the History and Philosophy of Science*. Dordrecht: D. Reidel, vol. I, 197–213.

——— (1979). "A Self Profile". In R. J. Bogdan (ed.) *Patrick Suppes*. Dordrecht: D. Reidel, 3–56.

——— (1976). "Testing Theories and the Foundations of Statistics". In Harper and Hooker (eds.) *Foundations of Probability Theory, Statistical Inference, and Statistical Theories of Science II*. Dordrecht: D. Reidel, 437–455.

——— (1971). "Archimedes's Anticipation of Conjoint Measurement". In *Proceedings of the 13th International Congress of the History of Science*. Moscow: Nauka Publishing House, 1–19.

——— (1968). "The Desirability of Formalization in Science". *Journal of Philosophy* 65: 651–664.

——— (1967). "What Is a Scientific Theory?". In S. Morgenbesser (ed.) *Philosophy of Science Today*. New York: Basic Book, 55–67.

——— (1960). "A Comparison of the Meaning and Uses of Models in Mathematics and the Empirical Sciences". *Synthese* 12: 287–301.

——— (1957). *Introduction to Logic*. New York: Van Nostrand Reinhold Company.

——— (1954). "Some Remarks on Problems and Methods in the Philosophy of Science". *Philosophy of Science* 21: 242–248.

Suppes, P. and R. C. Atkinson (1960). *Markov Learning Models for Multiperson Interactions*. Stanford: Stanford University Press.

Symon, K. R. (1953). *Mechanics*. Reading: Addison Wesley.

Takayama, A. (1985). *Mathematical Economics*. Cambridge: Cambridge University Press.

Tarski, A. (1956). "On Some Fundamental Concepts of Metamathematics". In A. Tarski (ed.) *Logic, Semantics, Metamathematics*. Oxford: Oxford at The Clarendon Press, 31–37.

——— (1930–1931). "O pojeciu prawdy w odnuesieniu do sformalizowanych nauk dedukcyjnych" ["On the Notion of Truth in Reference to Formalized Deductive Sciences"]. *Ruch Filozoficzny* 12: 210–211.

van der Waerden, B. L. (1949). *Modern Algebra*. New York: F. Ungar.

Van Heijenoort, J. (1967). *From Frege to Godel: A Source Book in Mathematical Logic, 1879–1931*. Cambridge, MA: Harvard University Press.

Varian, H. R. (2006). "Revealed Preference". In M. Szensberg, L. Ramrattan and A. A. Gottesman (eds.) *Samuelsonian Economics and the Twenty-First Century*. New York: Oxford University Press, 99–115.

——— (1983). "Non-Parametric Tests of Consumer Behaviour". *Review of Economic Studies* 50(1): 99–110.

——— (1982). "The Non-Parametric Approach to Demand Analysis". *Econometrica* 50: 945–973.

Vela Velupillai, K. (2008). "Sraffa's Mathematical Economics: *A Constructive* Interpretation". *Journal of Economic Methodology* 15(4): 325–342.

Walras, L. (1874). *Elements* d'economiepolitiquepure, L. Corbaz et Cie., Laus-sane. Traduccion al ingles: 1954, elements *of Pure Economics*. Londres: Allen and Unwin.

Author Index

Subject Index